DELIBERATE PRACTICE IN
BEHAVIORAL
PARENT TRAINING

Essentials of Deliberate Practice Series
Tony Rousmaniere and Alexandre Vaz, Series Editors

Deliberate Practice in Accelerated Experiential Dynamic Psychotherapy
Natasha C. N. Prenn, Hanna Levenson, Alexandre Vaz, and
Tony Rousmaniere

Deliberate Practice in Behavioral Parent Training
Mark D. Terjesen, Hilary B. Vidair, Phyllis S. Ohr, Olivia A. Walsh,
Tony Rousmaniere, and Alexandre Vaz

Deliberate Practice in Career Counseling
Jennifer M. Taylor, Alexandre Vaz, and Tony Rousmaniere

Deliberate Practice in Child and Adolescent Psychotherapy
Jordan Bate, Tracy A. Prout, Tony Rousmaniere, and Alexandre Vaz

Deliberate Practice in Cognitive Behavioral Therapy
James F. Boswell and Michael J. Constantino

Deliberate Practice in Dialectical Behavior Therapy
Tali Boritz, Shelley McMain, Alexandre Vaz, and Tony Rousmaniere

Deliberate Practice in Emotion-Focused Therapy
Rhonda N. Goldman, Alexandre Vaz, and Tony Rousmaniere

Deliberate Practice in Emotionally Focused Couple Therapy
Hanna Levenson, Sam Jinich, Alexandre Vaz, and Tony Rousmaniere

Deliberate Practice in Interpersonal Psychotherapy
Olga Belik, Scott Fairhurst, Jessica M. Schultz, Scott Stuart, Alexandre
Vaz, and Tony Rousmaniere

Deliberate Practice in Motivational Interviewing
Jennifer K. Manuel, Denise Ernst, Alexandre Vaz, and
Tony Rousmaniere

Deliberate Practice in Multicultural Therapy
Jordan Harris, Joel Jin, Sophia Hoffman, Selina Phan, Tracy A. Prout,
Tony Rousmaniere, and Alexandre Vaz

Deliberate Practice in Psychedelic-Assisted Therapy
Shannon Dames, Andrew Penn, Monnica Williams, Joseph A. Zamaria,
Tony Rousmaniere, and Alexandre Vaz

Deliberate Practice in Psychodynamic Psychotherapy
Hanna Levenson, Volney Gay, and Jeffrey L. Binder

Deliberate Practice in Rational Emotive Behavior Therapy
Mark D. Terjesen, Kristene A. Doyle, Raymond A. DiGiuseppe,
Alexandre Vaz, and Tony Rousmaniere

Deliberate Practice in Schema Therapy
Wendy T. Behary, Joan M. Farrell, Alexandre Vaz, and
Tony Rousmaniere

Deliberate Practice in Systemic Family Therapy
Adrian J. Blow, Ryan B. Seedall, Debra L. Miller, Tony Rousmaniere,
and Alexandre Vaz

ESSENTIALS OF DELIBERATE PRACTICE SERIES
TONY ROUSMANIERE AND ALEXANDRE VAZ, SERIES EDITORS

DELIBERATE PRACTICE IN
BEHAVIORAL PARENT TRAINING

MARK D. TERJESEN

HILARY B. VIDAIR

PHYLLIS S. OHR

OLIVIA A. WALSH

TONY ROUSMANIERE

ALEXANDRE VAZ

AMERICAN PSYCHOLOGICAL ASSOCIATION

Published by
American Psychological Association
750 First Street, NE
Washington, DC 20002
https://www.apa.org

Order Department
https://www.apa.org/pubs/books
order@apa.org

Typeset in Cera Pro by Circle Graphics, Inc., Reisterstown, MD

Printer: AGS, White Plains, MD
Cover Designer: Mark Karis

Library of Congress Cataloging-in-Publication Data

CIP data has been applied for.
Library of Congress Control Number: 2025947943

9781433840418 (paperback)
9781433840425 (epub)
9781433849893 (pdf)

https://doi.org/10.1037/0000484-000

Printed in the United States of America

10 9 8 7 6 5 4 3 2 1

Contents

Series Preface

Tony Rousmaniere and Alexandre Vaz

We are pleased to introduce the Essentials of Deliberate Practice series of training books. We are developing this book series to address a specific need that we see in many psychology training programs. The issue can be illustrated by the training experiences of Mary, a hypothetical second-year graduate school trainee. Mary has learned a lot about mental health theory, research, and psychotherapy techniques. Mary is a dedicated student; she has read dozens of textbooks, written excellent papers about psychotherapy, and receives near-perfect scores on her course exams. However, when Mary sits with her clients at her practicum site, she often has trouble performing the therapy skills that she can write and talk about so clearly. Furthermore, Mary has noticed herself getting anxious when her clients express strong reactions, such as hopelessness, skepticism about therapy, or becoming very emotional. Sometimes this anxiety is strong enough to make Mary freeze at key moments, limiting her ability to help those clients.

During her weekly individual and group supervision, Mary's supervisor gives her advice informed by empirically supported therapies and common factor methods. The supervisor often supplements that advice by leading Mary through role plays, recommending additional reading, or providing examples from her own work with clients. Mary, a dedicated supervisee who shares tapes of her sessions with her supervisor, is open about her challenges, carefully writes down her supervisor's advice, and reads the suggested readings. However, when Mary sits down with her clients, she often finds that her new knowledge seems to have flown out of her head, and she is unable to enact her supervisor's advice. Mary finds this problem to be particularly acute with the clients who are emotionally evocative.

Mary's supervisor, who has received formal training in supervision, employs supervisory best practices, including the use of video to review supervisees' work. She would rate Mary's overall competence level as consistent with expectations for a trainee at Mary's developmental level. But even though Mary's overall progress is positive, she experiences some recurring problems in her work. This is true even though the supervisor is confident that she and Mary have identified the changes that Mary should make in her work.

The problem with which Mary and her supervisor are wrestling—the disconnect between her knowledge about psychotherapy and her ability to reliably perform psychotherapy—is the focus of this book series. We started this series because most therapists experience this disconnect, to one degree or another, whether they are beginning trainees or highly experienced clinicians. In truth, we are all Mary.

To address this problem, we are focusing this series on the use of deliberate practice, a method of training specifically designed for improving reliable performance of complex skills in challenging work environments (Rousmaniere, 2016, 2019; Rousmaniere et al., 2017). Deliberate practice entails experiential, repeated training with a particular skill until it becomes automatic. In the context of psychotherapy, this involves two trainees role-playing as a client and a therapist, switching roles every so often, under the guidance of a supervisor. The trainee playing the therapist reacts to client statements, ranging in difficulty from beginner to intermediate to advanced, with improvised responses that reflect fundamental therapeutic skills.

To create these books, we approached leading trainers and researchers of major therapy models with these simple instructions: Identify essential skills for your therapy model where trainees often experience a disconnect between cognitive knowledge and performance ability—in other words, skills that trainees could write a good paper about but often have challenges performing, especially with challenging clients. We then collaborated with the authors to create deliberate practice exercises specifically designed to improve reliable performance of these skills and overall responsive treatment (Hatcher, 2015; Stiles et al., 1998; Stiles & Horvath, 2017). Finally, we rigorously tested these exercises with trainees and trainers at multiple sites around the world and refined them based on extensive feedback.

Each book in this series focuses on a specific therapy model, but readers will notice that most exercises in these books touch on common-factor variables and facilitative interpersonal skills that researchers have identified as having the most impact on client outcome, such as empathy, verbal fluency, emotional expression, persuasiveness, and problem focus (e.g., Anderson et al., 2009; Norcross et al., 2019). Thus, the exercises in every book should help with a broad range of clients. Despite the specific theoretical model(s) from which one may work, most therapists place a strong emphasis on pantheoretical elements of the therapeutic relationship, many of which have robust empirical support as correlates or mechanisms of client improvement (e.g., Norcross et al., 2019). We also recognize that therapy models have established training programs with rich histories, so we present deliberate practice not as a replacement but as an adaptable, transtheoretical training method that can be integrated into these existing programs to improve skill retention and help ensure basic competency.

About This Book

This book in the series is on behavioral parent training (BPT), an evidence-based approach that works on changing child externalizing (Daley et al., 2014; McCart et al., 2006; Michelson et al., 2013) and internalizing (Lebowitz et al., 2014; Sanders et al., 2014) behaviors by teaching and reinforcing specific adaptive parenting strategies to promote and maintain behavioral change. The targets of BPT are child symptom resolution, improved parent–child interpersonal functioning, and improved parent functioning (e.g., satisfaction, efficacy, stress). BPT is a unique therapeutic approach in that the parents are the agent of change, and many trainees find that to achieve competence in delivery of BPT, they have to consider child and parenting behavior and work on creating a new paradigm of learning. Competency in the clinical area requires mastery of knowledge, skills, and attitudes. Integrating readings on child behavior and BPT theory with practicing BPT skills and receiving constructive feedback facilitates learning. Lastly, understanding the mechanism of change within BPT and clinical moderators (e.g., stress) that may interfere with parents learning and competently applying these skills is essential. Practicing BPT skills with ongoing feedback will allow the clinician to calibrate their BPT practice and ultimately help them integrate their knowledge and skills into deeper BPT clinical practice.

In this book, we adopt deliberate practice methods to support experiential, "learning by doing" training opportunities. The described methods and stimuli facilitate practicing a range of important BPT skills that are present throughout many of the established BPT programs (e.g., the Helping the Noncompliant Child program, McMahon & Forehand, 2019; parent–child interaction therapy, McNeil & Hembree-Kigin, 2010; parent management training, Kazdin, 2005; positive parenting program, Sanders et al., 2007). In addition, by presenting diverse clinical scenarios that vary based on presenting problem, child age, parenting history, and parent emotional responsiveness, the exercises in this book support the fine-tuning of the "how" of intervention delivery. Importantly, this book is not intended to replace core coursework and exposure to foundational BPT theory and principles of practice. Rather, its purpose is to augment other common training components.

Thank you for including us in your journey toward psychotherapy expertise. Now let's get to practice!

Acknowledgments

We would like to acknowledge Rodney Goodyear for his significant contribution to starting and organizing this book series. We are grateful to Susan Reynolds, David Becker, Elizabeth Budd, Elizabeth Brace, and Emily Ekle at American Psychological Association (APA) Books for providing expert guidance and insightful editing that has significantly improved the quality and accessibility of this book. We would also like to acknowledge the International Deliberate Practice Society and its members for their many contributions and support for our work.

The exercises in this book series have undergone extensive testing at training programs around the world. More than 130 testers (trainees, therapists, and supervisors) from 16 countries contributed to testing the exercises. For everyone who volunteered to test run this work and provided critically important feedback throughout the method refinement and writing process, we cannot thank you enough.

Mark D. Terjesen: To my wife, Dr. Carolyn Waldecker, and my daughter Amelia. You both have helped me grow as a parent and provide an opportunity for application of the principles of behavioral parent training (BPT) in real time. I would also like to acknowledge the BPT community, and the terrific support of my coauthors. I am hopeful that this book may be an asset to clinicians, trainees, and researchers in helping the families with whom they work.

Hilary B. Vidair: To my husband, John Giuffo, and my children, Elliot and Leia, for encouraging my deliberate practice of BPT skills in a whole new way! Thank you and my whole family for bringing love and joy to my life in more ways than I had ever imagined. I am also incredibly thankful for my talented and creative coauthors who enlightened me with their innovative ideas for implementing BPT. In addition, I am grateful for my wonderful colleagues and trainees at Long Island University Post and Cognitive Behavioral Associates who continuously inspire me to develop and test novel methods for training clinicians to help families. I hope this book empowers clinicians and trainers to deliberately practice BPT skills together competently and confidently and encourages researchers to assess the impact of clinicians' deliberate practice of BPT on their skills performance as well as parent and child outcomes.

Phyllis S. Ohr: To my husband, Eric Ohr; my children, Nicole and Megan; and my son-in-law, Chretien. In so many ways, you have each helped me to attain a life–work balance so that I could experience both the immeasurable love of my family and the immense satisfaction of my professional pursuits. I can't imagine a life more fulfilling than mine. To my sister-friend Barbara, who has supported my dreams since we were teens talking and walking through the streets of Brooklyn together. I would be remiss not to mention Theo, the dog member of my family, who has become my sidekick and radiates genuine love and empathy toward everyone he meets, except for delivery workers and other dogs. I am grateful for my supportive colleagues at Hofstra who encouraged me to remain true to my passion for clinical mentoring. Finally, I am humbled to have mentored so many extraordinary students, most notably the very accomplished Mark and Hilary, whose lives touched mine and inspired me to become the best mentor I could be. I believe this book is one way I can continue shaping future generations.

Olivia A. Walsh: To my husband, Patrick, for his unwavering support and belief in me throughout this journey. To my parents, Dawn and Jimmy, who exemplified the very principles of BPT in ways that continue to inspire me as I think about the parent I hope to become one day. As a recent graduate and an advocate for high-quality training, I am passionate about ensuring that trainees receive the best preparation in BPT. My research on deliberate practice in BPT has reinforced my belief in the importance of skill development, and I hope this book serves as a valuable resource for clinicians, trainees, and researchers alike. I am deeply grateful to my brilliant coauthors and the BPT community for their collaboration, insights, and dedication to helping families thrive.

Mark D. Terjesen, Hilary B. Vidair, Phyllis S. Ohr, and Olivia A. Walsh: Our joint gratitude to all the prior faculty mentors, supervisors, trainees, and clients who have shaped us as professionals and allowed us to become the clinicians, trainers, and researchers that we are today. We are so very grateful for the opportunity to work together with our editors, Alexandre Vaz and Tony Rousmaniere. We thank you for your continued patience, editorial support, and guidance! They provided terrific and specific labeled praise (see Exercise 4).

Overview and Instructions

In Part I, we provide an overview of deliberate practice, including how it can be integrated into clinical training programs for deliberate practice in behavioral parent training (BPT) and instructions for performing the deliberate practice exercises in Part II. **We encourage both trainers and trainees to read both Chapters 1 and 2 before performing the deliberate practice exercises for the first time.**

Chapter 1 provides a foundation for the rest of the book by introducing important concepts related to deliberate practice and its role in psychotherapy training more broadly and training in BPT more specifically. We also individually review the 12 skills from these exercises.

Chapter 2 lays out the basic, most essential instructions for performing the BPT deliberate practice exercises in Part II. These instructions are designed to be quick and simple and provide you with just enough information to get started without being overwhelmed by too much information. Chapter 3 in Part III provides more in-depth guidance, which we encourage you to read once you are comfortable with the basic instructions in Chapter 2.

Introduction and Overview of Deliberate Practice and Behavioral Parent Training

Behavioral parent training (BPT) is a well-researched (McCart et al., 2006) and effective (Daley et al., 2014) clinical approach designed to treat and prevent problem behaviors among youth. There are many models of BPT, such as helping the noncompliant child (McMahon & Forehand, 2019), parent–child interaction therapy (PCIT; McNeil & Hembree-Kigin, 2010), and the Positive Parenting Program, or Triple P (Sanders et al., 2007), that, although distinct in their training and clinical application, share many common components. Clinical decision making regarding what components to focus on within BPT may vary as a function of the presenting problem(s) as well as the family system. Some parents have limited time to engage in BPT, and parents will differ in terms of the types of skills that they may need to work on. As an example, some parents may benefit from clinical focus on providing positive reinforcement, while for others, targeting parent emotion regulation may be key to allowing them to make better parenting decisions and apply skills learned in BPT. A strength of BPT is that these skills can be delivered to parents in different orders that target their greatest needs. This book provides 12 of the most common skills seen within the BPT literature, defines each skill, and demonstrates how to deliver these skills effectively and competently within the structure of deliberate practice.

While the name implies that the focus of BPT will be on clinical work with the parents, a common question from parents often relates to the fact that since the child is the problem, why are we not working directly with the child? Another typical response from new trainees upon initial exposures to BPT is that it is a simple, almost mechanistic approach to clinical work. Many of the procedures used within BPT are rooted in learning theory, which is often viewed in simplistic terms (i.e., reward the positive and punish the negative). However, the application of these learning principles within BPT for children and adolescents with a range of behavioral, clinical, and emotional difficulties is anything but easy. Although there are many "how to" books when it comes to parenting and myriad podcasts and videos, these can be very misleading. As an example, research has shown that 25% of parents continue to believe that sugar "causes" attention-deficit/hyperactivity disorder (Bussing et al., 2012).

https://doi.org/10.1037/0000484-001

Deliberate Practice in Behavioral Parent Training, by M. D. Terjesen, H. B. Vidair, P. S. Ohr, O. A. Walsh, T. Rousmaniere, and A. Vaz

A good BPT clinician will have a strong knowledge of learning theory, as well as the core skills of BPT and be able to apply the skills within a therapeutic context. Upon review of the lead authors' collective school and clinical-based training in BPT, it was apparent that there is a gap between skill knowledge and skill application. We have found that in training clinicians in clinical work with parents, it is important to model the skill, have the trainee demonstrate the skill, receive feedback on the skill and then have them continue to demonstrate the skill and receive specific feedback until competency is demonstrated.

Two well-known BPT programs, PCIT (McNeil & Hembree-Kigin, 2010) and Helping the Noncompliant Child (HNC; McMahon & Forehand, 2019), both have a mastery component to the training of their parents, and the extension to working toward developing competency among clinicians is logical. In considering the training of clinicians, it became apparent to us that there were elements of deliberate practice embedded in the provision of training, albeit not as structured or explicit.

Beginning clinicians often want to be told a BPT technique, and although they communicate an understanding of that skill, they often struggle in its application or demonstration, either in supervision or in clinical work with parents. When providing training in BPT, we often ask beginning clinicians about specific BPT skills in which they believe they are not as competent and find difficult to do within clinical practice, then we work on developing that skill. This is consistent with a deliberate practice approach toward skill development. Group settings for skills training are often quite helpful, as peers get to observe the skill development in their colleagues, role-play a number of clinical problems, and demonstrate many skills within BPT. Deliberate practice as it is presented in this series, and specifically in this book on BPT, is a natural and more structured approach to building high-quality training in BPT. The addition of continuing to work on one or several of the specific skills addressed in this book until trainees gain a sense of mastery serves to promote further professional development. The exercises provided for each of the skills included here contain different clinical presentations of parents' descriptions of emotional and behavioral problems seen with their children and offer trainees opportunities to enhance their BPT skills and develop their own unique style of delivering BPT.

Overview of the Deliberate Practice Exercises

The main focus of the book is a series of 14 exercises that have been thoroughly tested and modified based on feedback from BPT trainers and trainees. The first 12 exercises each represent an essential BPT skill. The last two exercises are more comprehensive, consisting of an annotated BPT transcript and improvised mock therapy sessions that teach practitioners how to integrate all these skills into more expansive clinical scenarios. Table 1.1 presents the 12 exercises.

Throughout all the exercises, trainees work in pairs under the guidance of a supervisor and role-play as a parent and a therapist, switching back and forth between the two roles. Each of the 12 skill-focused exercises consists of multiple scripted parent statements grouped by difficulty—beginner, intermediate, and advanced—that calls for a specific skill. For each skill, trainees are asked to read through and absorb the description of the skill, its criteria, and some examples of it. The trainee playing the parent then reads the statements. The trainee playing the therapist then responds in a way that demonstrates the appropriate skill. Trainee therapists will have the option of practicing a

TABLE 1.1. The 12 Behavioral Parent Training Skills Presented in the Deliberate Practice Exercises

Beginner Skills	Intermediate Skills	Advanced Skills
1. Psychoeducation about behavioral parent training	5. Teaching parents to provide positive attention	9. Teaching parents about consequence interventions
2. Psychoeducation about the functions of child behaviors	6. Teaching planned ignoring with positive attention	10. Providing strategies for parent affect management
3. Identifying and validating parent affect	7. Teaching parents about effective communication	11. Teaching parents about managing behavior in public settings
4. Teaching parents how to provide praise	8. Teaching parents how to implement positive incentives to bring about behavioral change	12. Development of homework assignments

response using one of the examples supplied in the exercise or immediately improvising and supplying their own.

After each parent statement and therapist response couplet is practiced several times, the trainees will stop to receive feedback from the supervisor. Guided by the supervisor, the trainees will be instructed to try statement–response couplets several times, working their way down the list. In consultation with the supervisor, trainees will go through the exercises, starting with the least challenging and moving through to more advanced levels. The triad (supervisor–parent–therapist) will have the opportunity to discuss whether exercises present too much or too little challenge and adjust up or down depending on the assessment.

Trainees, in consultation with supervisors, can decide which skills they wish to practice and for how long. Based on our testing experience, we have found practice sessions last about 1 to 1.25 hours to receive maximum benefit. After this, trainees become saturated and need a break.

Ideally, BPT learners will both gain confidence and achieve competence through practicing these exercises. Competence is defined here as the ability to perform a BPT skill in a manner that is flexible and responsive to the parent and their needs and concerns about their child. Skills have been chosen that are considered essential to BPT and that practitioners often find challenging to implement.

The skills identified in this book are not comprehensive in the sense of representing all one needs to learn to become a competent BPT clinician. Some skills will present particular challenges for trainees. A short overview of BPT and a brief description of the deliberate practice methodology is provided to explain how we have arrived at the union between them.

The Goals of This Book

The primary goal of this book is to help trainees achieve competence in core BPT skills. Therefore, the expression of that skill or competency may look somewhat different across clients or even within a session with the same client.

The BPT deliberate practice exercises are designed to achieve the following:

1. Help BPT therapists develop the ability to apply the skills in a range of clinical situations and across child ages.

2. Move the skills into procedural memory (Squire, 2004) so that BPT therapists can access them even when they are tired, stressed, overwhelmed, or discouraged.

3. Provide BPT therapists in training with an opportunity to exercise a particular skill using a style and language that is congruent with who they are.

4. Provide the opportunity to use the BPT skills in response to varying parent statements and affect that represent a range of clinical problems seen among children. This is designed to build confidence to adopt skills in a broad range of circumstances within different parent–child contexts.

5. Provide BPT therapists in training with many opportunities to fail and then correct their failed response on the basis of feedback. This helps build confidence and persistence.

Finally, this book aims to help trainees discover their own personal learning style so that they can continue their professional development long after their formal training is concluded.

Who Can Benefit From This Book?

This book is designed to be used in multiple contexts, including in graduate-level courses, supervision, postgraduate training, and continuing education programs. It assumes the following:

1. The trainer is knowledgeable about and competent in BPT.

2. The trainer can provide good demonstrations of how to use BPT skills across a range of therapeutic situations, via role-play and/or video. Or the trainer has access to examples of BPT being demonstrated through the many psychotherapy video examples available.

3. The trainer can provide feedback to students regarding how to craft/improve their application of BPT skills.

4. Trainees will have accompanying reading, such as books and articles, that explain the theory, research, and rationale of BPT and each particular skill. Recommended reading for each skill is provided in the sample syllabus (Appendix C).

The deliberate practice exercise formats covered in this book series were piloted in training sites from 16 countries across four continents (North America, South America, Europe, and Asia). This book is designed for trainers and trainees from different cultural backgrounds worldwide.

This book is also designed for those who are training at all career stages, from beginning trainees, including those who have never worked with real clients, to seasoned therapists. All exercises feature guidance for assessing the adjusting of the difficulty to precisely target the needs of each individual learner. The term *trainee* in this book is used broadly, referring to anyone in the field of professional mental health who endeavors to acquire BPT skills. For further guidance on how to improve multicultural deliberate practice skills, see the book *Deliberate Practice in Multicultural Therapy* (Harris et al., 2024).

Deliberate Practice in Psychotherapy Training

How does one become an expert in their professional field? What is trainable, and what is simply beyond our reach, due to innate or uncontrollable factors? Questions such as these touch on our fascination with expert performers and their development. A mixture of awe, admiration, and even confusion surround people such as the artists Mozart, Mary Cassatt, and Leonardo da Vinci, or more contemporary top performers such as the painter Frida Kahlo, basketball legend Michael Jordan, and chess virtuoso Garry Kasparov. What accounts for their consistently superior professional results? Evidence suggests that the amount of time spent on a particular type of training is a key factor in developing expertise in virtually all domains (Ericsson & Pool, 2016). "Deliberate practice" is an evidence-based method that can improve performance in an effective and reliable manner.

The concept of deliberate practice has its origins in a classic study by K. Anders Ericsson and colleagues (1993). They found that the amount of time practicing a skill and the quality of the time spent doing so were key factors predicting mastery and acquisition. They identified five key activities in learning and mastering skills: (a) observing one's own work, (b) getting expert feedback, (c) setting small incremental learning goals just beyond the performer's ability, (d) engaging in repetitive behavioral rehearsal of specific skills, and (e) continuously assessing performance. Ericsson and his colleagues termed this process deliberate practice, a cyclical process that is illustrated in Figure 1.1.

Research has shown that lengthy engagement in deliberate practice is associated with expert performance across a variety of professional fields, such as medicine, sports, music, chess, computer programming, and mathematics (Ericsson et al., 2018). People may associate deliberate practice with the widely known "10,000-hour rule" popularized by Malcolm Gladwell in his 2008 book *Outliers*, although the actual number of hours required for expertise varies by field and by individual (Ericsson & Pool, 2016). This idea, though, perpetuates two misunderstandings—first, that this is the number

FIGURE 1.1. Cycle of Deliberate Practice

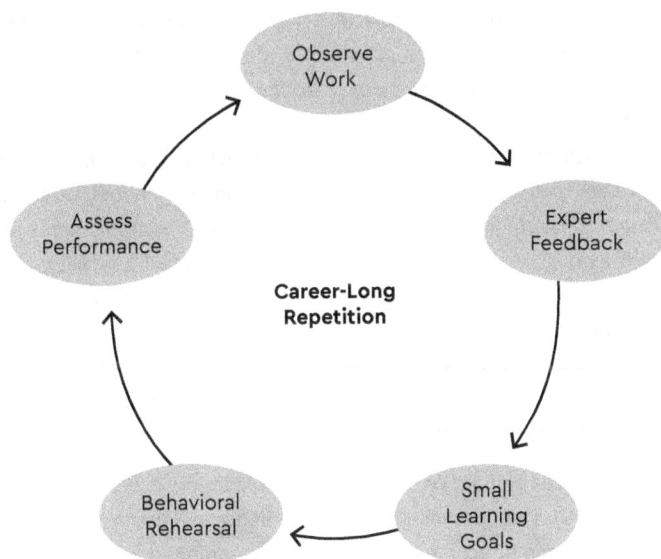

Note. From *Deliberate Practice in Emotion-Focused Therapy* (p. 7), by R. N. Goldman, A. Vaz, and T. Rousmaniere, 2021, American Psychological Association (https://doi.org/10.1037/0000227-000). Copyright 2021 by the American Psychological Association.

of deliberate practice hours that everyone needs to attain expertise, no matter the domain. In fact, there can be considerable variability in how many hours are required.

The second misunderstanding is that engagement in 10,000 hours of work performance will lead one to become an expert in that domain. This misunderstanding holds considerable significance for the field of psychotherapy, where hours of work experience with clients has traditionally been used as a measure of proficiency (Rousmaniere, 2016). Research suggests that the amount of experience alone does not predict therapist effectiveness (Goldberg et al., 2016). It may be that the quality of deliberate practice is a key factor.

Psychotherapy scholars, recognizing the value of deliberate practice in other fields, have called for deliberate practice to be incorporated into training for mental health professionals (e.g., Bailey & Ogles, 2019; Hill et al., 2020; Rousmaniere et al., 2017; Taylor & Neimeyer, 2017; Tracey et al., 2015). There are, however, good reasons to question analogies made between psychotherapy and other professional fields, like sports or music, because by comparison psychotherapy is so complex and free form. Sports have clearly defined goals, and classical music follows a written score. In contrast, the goals of psychotherapy shift with the unique presentation of each client at each session. Therapists do not have the luxury of following a score.

Instead, good psychotherapy is more like improvisational jazz (Noa Kageyama, cited in Rousmaniere, 2016). In jazz improvisations, a complex mixture of group collaboration, creativity, and interaction are coconstructed among band members. Like psychotherapy, no two jazz improvisations are identical. However, improvisations are not a random collection of notes. They are grounded in a comprehensive theoretical understanding and technical proficiency that is only developed through continuous deliberate practice. For example, prominent jazz instructor Jerry Coker (1990) lists 18 different skill areas that students must master, each of which has multiple discrete skills including tone quality, intervals, chord arpeggios, scales, patterns, and licks. In this sense, more creative and artful improvisations are actually a reflection of a previous commitment to repetitive skill practice and acquisition. As legendary jazz musician Miles Davis put it, "You have to play a long time to be able to play like yourself" (Cook, 2005, p. 112).

The main idea that we would like to stress here is that we want deliberate practice to help BPT therapists become themselves. The idea is to learn the skills so that you have them on hand when you want them. Practice the skills to make them your own. Incorporate those aspects that feel right for you. Ongoing and effortful deliberate practice should not be an impediment to flexibility and creativity. Ideally, it should enhance it. We recognize and celebrate that psychotherapy is an ever-shifting encounter and by no means want it to become or feel formulaic. Strong BPT therapists mix an eloquent integration of previously acquired skills with properly attuned flexibility. The core BPT responses provided are meant as templates or possibilities, rather than "answers." Please interpret and apply them as you see fit, in a way that makes sense to you. We encourage flexible and improvisational play!

Simulation-Based Mastery Learning

Deliberate practice uses simulation-based mastery learning exercises (Ericsson, 2004; McGaghie et al., 2014). That is, the stimulus material for training consists of "contrived social situations that mimic problems, events, or conditions that arise in professional encounters" (McGaghie et al., 2014, p. 375). A key component of this approach is that the stimuli being used in training are sufficiently similar to the real-world experiences so that what they mimic provokes similar reactions. This facilitates *state-dependent learning*, where professionals acquire skills in the same psychological environment where they will have to perform the skills (Fisher & Craik, 1977). For example, pilots train with flight simulators that present mechanical failures and dangerous weather conditions, and surgeons practice with surgical simulators that present medical complications. Training in simulations with challenging stimuli increases professionals' capacity to perform effectively under stress. For the psychotherapy training exercises in this book, the "simulators" are typical parent statements that might actually be presented in the course of therapy sessions and call upon the use of the particular skill.

Declarative Versus Procedural Knowledge

Declarative knowledge is what a person can understand, write, or speak about. It often refers to factual information that can be consciously recalled through memory and often can be acquired relatively quickly. In contrast, procedural learning is implicit in memory, and "usually requires repetition of an activity, and associated learning is demonstrated through improved task performance" (Koziol & Budding, 2012, p. 2694). Procedural knowledge is what a person can perform, especially under stress (Squire, 2004). People can display a wide difference between their declarative and procedural knowledge. For example, an "armchair quarterback" is a person who understands and talks about athletics well but would have trouble performing it at a professional ability. Likewise, most dance, music, or theater critics have a very high ability to write about their subjects but would be flummoxed if asked to perform them.

The sweet spot for deliberate practice is the gap between declarative and procedural knowledge. In other words, effortful practice should target those skills that the trainee could write a good paper about but would have trouble actually performing with a real client. We start with declarative knowledge, learning skills theoretically and observing others perform them. Once learned, with the help of deliberate practice, we work toward the development of procedural learning, with the aim of therapists having "automatic" access to each of the skills that they can pull on when necessary.

Let us turn to a little theoretical background on BPT. This will help contextualize the skills of the book and how they fit into the greater training model.

Behavioral Parent Training: Theoretical Overview

Research indicates behavioral or conduct problems are the most common disorders children and adolescents face, with more than half of these children undergoing mental health treatment (Ghandour et al., 2019). BPT is an evidence-based treatment designed to reduce child misbehavior, increase desired/adaptive behaviors, and improve parent–child interactions. A substantial body of research has demonstrated the efficacy of BPT, which is a well-established intervention for treating childhood externalizing behavior disorders, such as oppositional defiant disorder, conduct disorder, and attention-deficit/hyperactivity disorder (Evans et al., 2014; Eyberg et al., 2008; Kaminski & Claussen, 2017). Treatment gains from several BPT programs have demonstrated maintained gains over time (Eyberg et al., 2008; Kaminski & Claussen, 2017). BPT prevention programs have also demonstrated the ability to improve child behavioral and emotional outcomes (e.g., Lebowitz et al., 2014; Sanders et al., 2014; Webster-Stratton, 1998). BPT has also been shown to increase parent functioning, such as improvements in parental efficacy and competence and reductions in parenting stress (Colalillo & Johnston, 2016; Gardner et al. 2006; Graf et al., 2014).

There are a variety of BPT programs that are evidence-based with considerable content overlap, including praise, positive attention and planned ignoring, positive incentives/token economies, and consequences (e.g., time out, response cost); however, various programs have slightly different structures. For example, the Parent Management Training (Kazdin, 2005) program focuses on meeting with a parent individually, although parents may occasionally be asked to bring their children into sessions. In some BPT programs such as parent–child interaction therapy (McNeil & Hembree-Kigin, 2010) and HNC (McMahon & Forehand, 2005), parents practice BPT skills directly with their child while the therapist observes and provides feedback in the form of live coaching. This live, in-the-moment coaching and feedback to build parental skill competency is very similar to the deliberate practice approach to building clinician competency in BPT that is demonstrated within this book. The Incredible Years program (Webster-Stratton, 2012) includes parent groups with video vignettes demonstrating parenting skills, while the Defiant Children program (Barkley, 2013) can be used with individual parents or in a group setting. Some programs for older children, like Defiant Teens (Barkley & Robin, 2014), include parent sessions alone as well as some joint parent–child sessions. Regardless of structure, across BPT programs, clinicians typically teach a parent the rationale behind a skill, explain how to implement it with their child, model the skill, and then have the parent practice it, often in the form of a role play, where they provide immediate feedback. Parents are then assigned homework to practice skills learned in session with their child. The demonstration, feedback, and practice often seen in BPT is why deliberate practice lends itself nicely to teaching this approach.

Much of BPT is based on reducing what is referred to as the coercive cycle that can develop between parents and children (Patterson, 1982). This cycle is rooted in social learning theory and suggests that children have their noncompliant behavior reinforced through maladaptive interactions with their parents (Wierson & Forehand, 1994). Similarly, parents' negative behaviors are reinforced through their child's responses, leading to a coercive cycle in which both parent and child reinforce each others' negative behaviors. For example, a parent might ask a child to turn off the television. If the child says no, the parent is likely to raise their voice and demand the television be turned off. This can lead to the child tantruming, the parent frustratingly leaving the room, and the child getting to continue to watch TV. Unfortunately, this has taught the child that escalating their negative behavior gets their parent to leave them alone and they get what they want (i.e., continue to watch TV). At the same time, the parent learns that backing off leads to the child's tantruming stopping in the short term. Over time, this coercive cycle becomes faster, more frequent, and more intense, leading to a variety of negative parent–child interactions.

BPT programs typically start by providing parents with psychoeducation about child misbehavior, as well as relevant treatment strategies. They then focus on improving parent–child interactions via a variety of positive parenting skills. For example, it is common for parents of children with behavioral problems to focus selectively on their child's negative behaviors. BPT focuses on shifting parents' attention from negative to positive behaviors using strategies such as "catch your child being good" because a child is more likely to comply with a parent when they feel good about the parent–child relationship (Barkley, 2013). Many BPT programs have parents purposefully implement a short, daily "special playtime" with their child, teaching the parent strategies to focus only on positive comments and actions during this time, such as providing specific praise, describing what the child is doing, and conveying enthusiasm for it (e.g., Barkley, 2013; McNeil & Hembree Kigin, 2010). Additional goals of special playtime include improving the parent–child relationship and improving a child's self-esteem (McNeil & Hembree Kigin, 2010).

BPT programs also focus on having parents strategically positively reinforce desired child behaviors because this makes it more likely that the child will perform these behaviors again. Parents can be taught various methods for positively reinforcing their child's behavior, including providing specific praise, tangible rewards, and privileges. Parents are taught how to communicate praise effectively, such as by providing labeled praise immediately after a behavior they wish to see more of, every time they see it (McNeil & Hembree-Kigin, 2010). They can also learn to develop contingencies, which involves identifying specific child behaviors they would like to see and incentivizing their performance by pairing them with specific rewards or privileges their child would like to earn. Children can earn a small reward or privilege immediately, or they can be awarded points, chips, or checks for each behavior that can be saved and exchanged later for a larger reward or privilege as part of a token economy (e.g., Barkley, 2013). An effective incentive involves choosing items or activities that the child likes and will be motivated to earn. It can be useful to involve the child in developing a contingency plan to ensure the child is excited about the rewards or privileges being offered. A parent and child can be encouraged to sign a contract to ensure each family member is clear on what is expected of them (e.g., Barkley & Robin, 2014).

Although BPT programs often first teach parents positive parenting skills designed to increase wanted child behaviors, they also involve teaching parents strategies for reducing negative child behaviors. For example, they are typically taught the concept of differential reinforcement, or focusing on their child's desired behaviors while ignoring mildly aversive behaviors (e.g., McNeil & Hembree-Kigin, 2010). When a child aims to obtain parental attention through negative behavior, actively ignoring them will eventually lead to a decrease in the behavior. Parents are also taught strategies for how to tell their child exactly what is expected of them through a direct command, rather than ask or tell them indirectly (e.g., Barkley, 2013). In addition, parents are taught how to provide consequences for negative behavior, such as time-out, removal of a desired item or privilege, or logical consequences (e.g., losing cell phone privileges if not getting homework done due to phone use; Kazdin, 2005; Webster-Stratton, 2012). Once parents have a good deal of practice using BPT skills in session and at home, clinicians typically work with parents to generalize their skill use to managing challenging behaviors in public settings, such as stores, restaurants, and playgrounds (Barkley, 2013). Parents of older children can be taught problem solving and communication strategies (Barkley & Robin, 2014).

Although many variables can interfere with application of skills learned within BPT to real-world situations (e.g., Kazdin et al., 1997), we have also chosen to focus on skills that address parent affect and emotions. A considerable body of research links parents' maladaptive emotional responses and child behavior problems (Johnson et al., 2017). Further, negative parent emotions are linked to ineffective parenting behaviors (Lunkenheimer et al., 2023; Rueger et al., 2011; Zitzmann et al., 2024). Given calls for incorporating emotion regulation strategies into parent interventions (e.g., Hajal & Paley, 2020; Zalewski et al., 2018), we thought it important to introduce these types of skills for BPT clinicians to develop.

Finally, to provide BPT clinicians with an opportunity to learn about applications of BPT for different age groups, the parent statements within each difficulty level in every exercise reflect concerns with children and adolescents across various development stages.

Overall, the exercises included in this book are designed to develop BPT skills across all the aforementioned concepts. We accomplish this through deliberate practice.

The Role of Deliberate Practice in Teaching Behavioral Parent Training

Returning to the discussion earlier in this chapter, training in BPT has always focused on skill knowledge and development through a variety of approaches to develop competencies in BPT skills among parents. Training clinicians in BPT draws the distinction between declarative and procedural knowledge, which is similar to deliberate practice. Knowing the learning theory principles that BPT is based on and the skills that are among the core components of BPT is one thing, but then carrying this knowledge into clinical work with parents can often be challenging for clinicians at varied levels of experience. Practicing skills in BPT is crucial.

Three of the authors (M.T., H.V., and P.O.) have been training clinicians in BPT for many years and using training activities similar to, but not using the term, deliberate practice are often part of this training. While working in separate institutions, the clinical training and supervision that they have provided generally involved three types of activities. First, they learn declarative knowledge about the theory and activities of BPT from readings and lectures. Second, the core skills of BPT are modeled for the learners. Finally, we have learners identify specific BPT skills that they want to work on that would be beneficial for their clinical work with parents, and they role-play this with either a peer or their supervisor. They then receive feedback on their performance of the skill. This approach is consistent with that of deliberate practice skill training in therapist training, just not as explicitly as we now do in this book.

We also have used therapy recordings as an opportunity to provide supervision and offer clinical feedback, but without direct practicing of the skill and receipt of immediate feedback, this approach is limited. Although recordings remain part of the supervisory experience, they do not provide an opportunity for immediate feedback after live practice sessions. Offering immediate feedback of a specific skill, even during a simulated setting (i.e., role-play), we have found is an approach that helps move skill development from conceptual to procedural, helps build competence, and is consistent with the deliberate practice approach to developing clinical skills.

We also thought it important to point out that although we focus on BPT skills in this book, we cannot ignore that such skills have the common factors in psychotherapy (Wampold, 2015) as cornerstones of good clinical practice. The common factors such as therapeutic alliance, empathy, goal consensus, and positive regard are not directly taught within this book nor are they evaluated as skill criterion; nonetheless, it is important for BPT clinicians to consider these factors in their work with parents.

With the focus of BPT being to teach parents skills to have an impact on their child's behavior, we thought it important to stress the role of data collection throughout BPT. While we do offer a number of examples of how and where data collection could occur throughout the exercises, we do not have this as a discrete skill. We believe that it is important for clinicians to gather data at the outset of treatment as to how problematic the parent views the child behavior with specific data as to frequency, intensity, and duration of the behavior to allow for progress monitoring, the context of these misbehaviors from a functional analytic perspective (see Exercise 2), and how their own behavior and affective responses may need to change. From the onset, we suggest BPT clinicians make data collection a weekly expectation for between-session work. We also like to have parents engage in self-reflection as to their competency in delivering the BPT techniques applied and will often have them demonstrate these skills in session and provide feedback in a manner that is consistent with a competency/mastery-based approach of PCIT (Thomas et al., 2017) and HNC (McMahon & Forehand, 2005).

Further, behavioral problems experienced by parents are often reported by professionals within the schools as well. Given that students spend a significant portion of their day in school, there obviously may be school- and peer-based factors that influence their behavior. Within the structure of this book, we could not adequately address how to engage effectively with the school to develop a comprehensive plan, but we do strongly believe that BPT clinicians will better serve the parents with whom they work if they promote effective parent–school communication as well as gather data from school-based professionals as to child behavior within the school.

The deliberate practice exercises in this book are not sufficient by themselves to obtain competence in BPT and are intended to supplement other training and education protocols. The skills included here are suited to a first course in BPT and are presented in a sample syllabus (see Appendix C). Trainees should have more extensive exposure to BPT theory and application in subsequent coursework and readings and supervisory experiences.

Behavioral Parent Training Skills in Deliberate Practice

Next, we outline each of the core skills that are the focus of Exercises 1 through 12, including how they fit into BPT's general goals and processes.

The Behavioral Parent Training Skills Presented in Exercises 1 Through 12

When parents initiate BPT, they often begin by describing their concerns about the behavior of their child, their past efforts to address this behavior and, at times, some of their own thoughts and emotional responses to their child's behavior. Unlike with traditional self-referred clients for psychotherapy who want to change how they feel and behave, here in BPT, they often want to change how someone else (their child) feels and behaves. The exercises presented in this book follow the format that represents how a BPT clinician would progress through helping a parent understand their role as an agent of change for their child and then progress through the steps of doing BPT. The exercises are presented in the sequence that therapists usually follow in applying BPT for a clinical problem. The order of exercise presentation was an area that we discussed considerably and were informed by our own clinical experience, as well as the sequence structure of many of the evidence-based approaches of BPT. These 12 exercises represent skills from a beginning level early in the BPT sequence, to later skills that are of more moderate difficulty, to the late-stage skills that are more advanced and more difficult. The order of the exercises is provided in Table 1.1.

Although not specific skills taught here, as described earlier, many of the common factor skills of psychotherapy (Wampold, 2015) are integrated throughout the core BPT skills. That is, as an example, through discussion about child behavior and clinical steps, the BPT clinician is achieving agreement on the goals and tasks of therapy, which form two steps in the formation of the therapeutic alliance. The alliance is considered pantheoretical and a component of the common factors of psychotherapy, not a formal skill we teach within this book; we still believe it is an essential skill for BPT clinicians.

The beginning steps include teaching the parent about child behavior and about BPT (Exercise 1), an analysis of the context of the child's behavior to help understand why the behavior has developed and persisted (Exercise 2), recognition and validation of parents' own emotional responses as they relate to their child's behavior (Exercise 3), and then introducing the concept of praise as a beginning step toward building change in their child's behavior (Exercise 4). We think educating parents about BPT and child behavior (Exercise 1) is an important beginning skill and allows the BPT clinician to correct any misperceptions about clinical work and also orient parents to specific goals and their role (i.e., tasks) in actively working toward addressing the problem. The second skill (Exercise 2) involves a functional analysis of the child's behavior to help address the "why" of their behavior but also to set the stage for subsequent interventions. As we begin to move toward teaching specific interventions, we thought it important to recognize and validate early on parental emotional responses within the context of their child's behavior and their role as parents. Strong emotions may interfere with effective parenting as well as skill acquisition. This leads to the next skill, which is validating and discussing their emotional responses (Exercise 3). The final beginning skill (Exercise 4) involves teaching parents the concept of praise and how to use it effectively to bring about behavior change. Praise can, and very often will, be integrated within many of the subsequent skills.

The intermediate skills involve many core aspects seen across BPT models and are skills that help facilitate change by parents changing how they respond to their child's behavior. Exercise 5 builds on praise and teaches parents how to pay attention to the behaviors that they want to see. This may also help address the function (i.e., attention) of many children's behaviors, which links back to Exercise 2. Often, parents will report that it is difficult to provide positive attention when their child is misbehaving. Further, if negative behavior has a history of being reinforced by parental attention, this becomes even more challenging to change. This leads to Exercise 6, where the BPT clinician teaches the parent how to ignore misbehavior. Although we think that teaching parents how to offer praise (Exercise 4), provide attention (Exercise 5), and ignore misbehavior (Exercise 6) are the building blocks toward change, it still may not provide the kind of specific behavior change toward adaptive behaviors that parents want to see. Communication (Exercise 7) teaches parents how to use effective commands to increase compliance and problem-solving in situations where the parent is open to negotiation. This skill may also serve to enhance the parent–child relationship within the context of the therapeutic alliance. That is, they may now be working toward what they want to see behaviorally in their child (e.g., compliance) rather than what they do not want to see (e.g., oppositionality). We then build on these skills by teaching parents about the use of incentives to change behavior (Exercise 8). The placement of this skill toward the end of the intermediate level was intentional in that we believe that the preceding skills are important and more natural skills to learn before having parents use incentives to change behavior.

The advanced-level skills in Exercises 9 and 11 involve two more clinical interventions for parents to change child behavior. There was a degree of intentionality on our part in having consequential interventions (Exercise 9) later in the process and being part of an advanced skill. We have found that many parents want to know how to best punish their child to stop the negative behaviors and want to know this early on in the BPT process. In the earlier exercises, we discussed ways to promote the behaviors that we want to see, and we believe it is important to instill in parents that before specifically teaching consequential interventions to change negative behaviors, we want to have a system in place that promotes desired or adaptive behaviors that will also compete with these negative behaviors. Exercise 10 describes a skill in which the BPT clinician discusses strategies to help parents manage their own emotional responses. As discussed in Exercise 3, parents often have strong thoughts and emotional reactions to their child's behavior, and these reactions often interfere with their parenting responses and ability to apply the skills taught. These responses may also lead to parents discontinuing treatment earlier. We recognize that typically parents do not come to BPT to work on their own thoughts and feelings, but we do believe that the ability to understand and communicate about how their emotional responses affect their parenting can be an important part of effective BPT and is seen in Exercise 10. Exercise 11 moves clinical work beyond the home environment and focuses on helping parents apply the earlier skill in public settings, which parents often find more challenging—and hence why we view this as an advanced skill. The final skill in Exercise 12 involves assignment of between-session work to build on skills taught and begin the process of applying parent training skills taught earlier in the process. Ultimately, it's what happens between the sessions that will begin the process of change beyond the clinical office and provide the best reflection as to BPT skills competence and the effectiveness of BPT. In the last skill (Exercise 12), clinicians will work with parents on collaboratively developing homework activities for them to do between sessions. Although assigning homework is presented as a separate exercise, we believe it is an essential addendum to each skill from the preceding exercises—that is, after parents have learned a skill in session, the clinician can ask them to practice it as homework. In the next session, the clinician should evaluate whether the homework was attempted, the process of attempting it, and the outcome. In addition, based on parental response, the clinician is encouraged to address any barriers encountered or help modify the homework so the skill is more feasible or effective going forward.

Effectively teaching the previously described skills to parents is often the initial step in BPT, but it is the application of the taught skill that may often be a challenge for many parents. The difficulties in transition between knowledge and application/practice are important for the clinician to consider. To that end, for many of the skills in this book, we have examples of questions that reflect any barriers to BPT skill application. These barriers may involve understanding of the skill; assessing parent belief that they can complete the skill effectively (i.e., self-efficacy); and clarifying if they think that this intervention would be effective, if they are willing to try this intervention, and whether they foresee any barriers (practical or emotional) that would interfere with the application of this intervention. These concepts may be broadly understood under the umbrella of treatment acceptability (Kazdin, 2000). Many of the concepts of treatment acceptability described earlier could in fact be their own skill that would be helpful for clinicians to develop, but that is beyond the scope of this book. As such, in many of the skills, we have set forth a criterion in which the clinician is asked to demonstrate competency for not just communicating about the skill itself but also in checking about treatment acceptability. This can, and very often will, involve many of the aforementioned areas, and in our examples of clinical responses, we provide multiple demonstrations of each of these areas.

Overview of the Book's Structure

This book is organized into three parts. Part I contains this chapter and Chapter 2, which provides basic instructions on how to perform these exercises. We found through testing that providing too many instructions up front overwhelmed trainers and trainees, and they skipped past them as a result. Therefore, we kept these instructions as brief and simple as possible to focus only on the most essential information that trainers and trainees will need to get started with the exercises. Further guidelines for getting the most from deliberate practice are provided in Chapter 3, and additional instructions for monitoring and adjusting the difficulty of the exercises are provided in Appendix A. **Do not skip the instructions in Chapter 2, and be sure to read the additional guidelines and instructions in Chapter 3 and Appendix A once you are comfortable with the basic instructions.**

Part II contains the 12 skill-focused exercises, which are ordered based on the order that they would be used in an actual therapy situation. This order corresponds to the difficulty levels of the skills: beginner, intermediate, and advanced (Table 1.1). The discussion of each of the 12 skills contains a brief overview of the exercise, example client–therapist interactions to help guide trainees, a list of criteria for mastering the relevant skill, and step-by-step instructions for conducting that exercise. The client statements and sample therapist responses are then presented, also organized by difficulty (beginner, intermediate, and advanced). The statements and responses are separated so that the trainee playing the therapist has more freedom to improvise responses without being influenced by the sample responses, which should only be turned to if the trainee has difficulty improvising their own responses.

The last two exercises in Part II provide opportunities to practice the 12 skills within simulated psychotherapy sessions. Exercise 13 provides a sample psychotherapy session transcript in which the BPT skills are used and clearly labeled, thereby demonstrating how they might flow together in an actual therapy session. BPT trainees are invited to run through the sample transcript with one playing the therapist and the other playing the client to get a feel for how a session might unfold. Exercise 14 provides suggestions for undertaking mock sessions, as well as client profiles ordered by difficulty (beginner, intermediate, and advanced) that trainees can use for improvised role plays.

Part III contains Chapter 3, which provides additional guidance for trainers and trainees. While Chapter 2 is more procedural, Chapter 3 covers big-picture issues. It highlights six key points for getting the most out of deliberate practice and describes the importance of appropriate responsiveness, attending to trainee well-being and respecting their privacy, and trainer self-evaluation, among other topics.

Three appendixes conclude this book. Appendix A provides instructions for monitoring and adjusting the difficulty of each exercise as needed. It provides a Deliberate Practice Reaction Form for the trainee playing the therapist to complete to indicate whether the exercise is too easy or too difficult. Appendix B includes a Deliberate Practice Diary Form that can be used during a training session's final evaluation to process the trainees' experiences, but its primary purpose is to provide trainees a format to explore and record their experiences while engaging in additional, between-session deliberate practice activities without the supervisor. Appendix C presents a sample syllabus demonstrating how the 12 deliberate practice exercises and other support material can be integrated into a wider BPT training course. Instructors can choose to modify the syllabus or pick elements of it to integrate into their own courses.

Downloadable versions of this book's appendixes, including a color version of the Deliberate Practice Reaction Form, can be found in the "Resources" tab at https://www.apa.org/pubs/books/deliberate-practice-behavioral-parent-training.

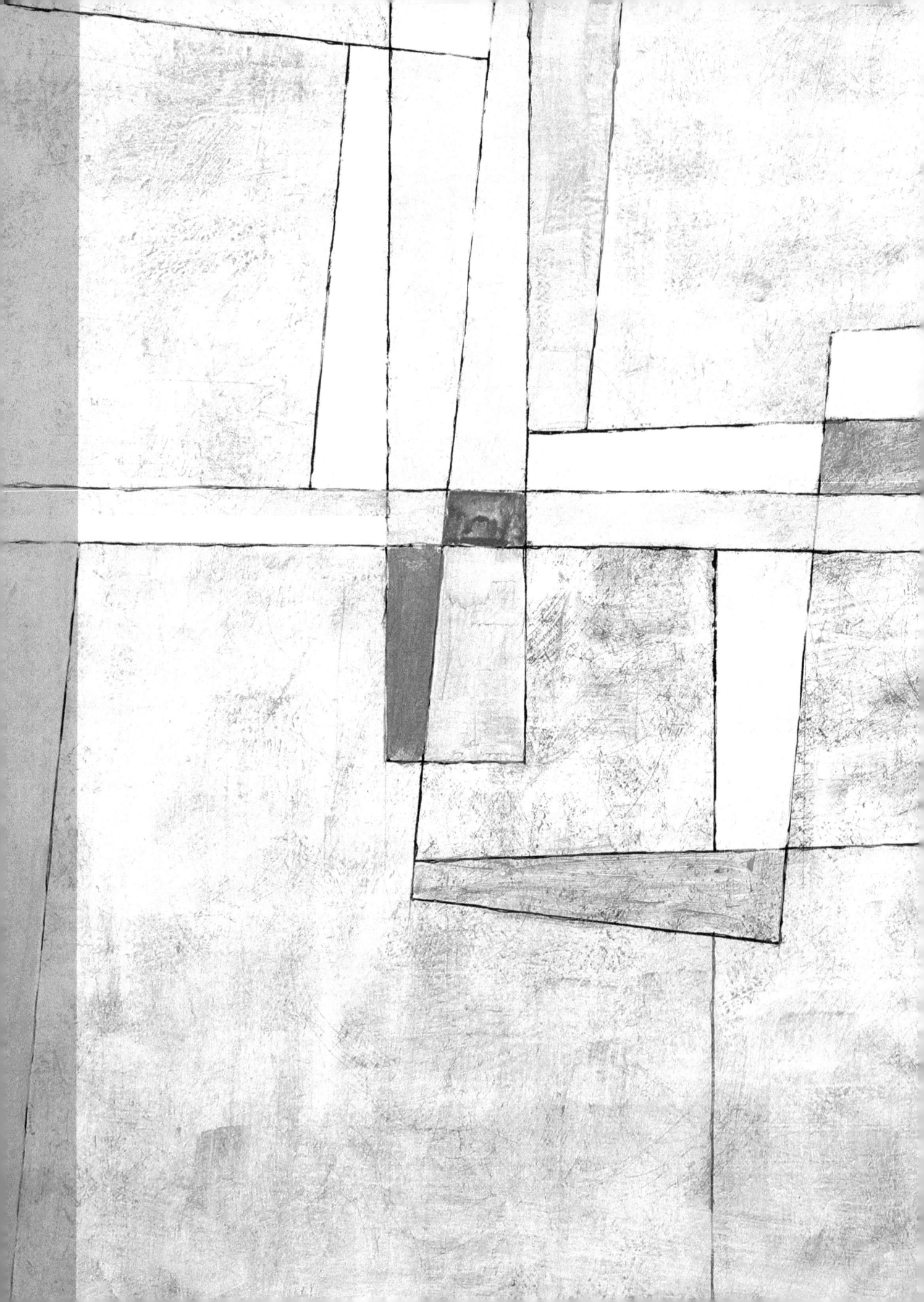

Instructions for the Behavioral Parent Training Deliberate Practice Exercises

This chapter provides basic instructions that are common to all the exercises in this book. More specific instructions are provided in each exercise. Chapter 3 also provides important guidance for trainees and trainers that will help them get the most out of deliberate practice. Appendix A offers additional instructions for monitoring and adjusting the difficulty of the exercises as needed after getting through all the parent statements in a single difficulty level, including a Deliberate Practice Reaction Form the trainee playing the therapist can complete to indicate whether they found the statements too easy or too difficult. **Difficulty assessment is an important part of the deliberate practice process and should not be skipped.**

Overview

The deliberate practice exercises in this book involve role plays of hypothetical situations in therapy. The role-play involves three people: one trainee role-plays the therapist, another trainee role-plays the parent, and a trainer (professor/supervisor) observes and provides feedback. Alternately, a peer can observe and provide feedback.

This book provides a script for each role play, each with a parent statement and also with an example therapist response. The parent statements are graded in difficulty from beginning to advanced, although these difficulty grades are only estimates. The actual perceived difficulty of parent statements is subjective and varies widely by trainee. For example, some trainees may experience a stimulus of a parent being angry to be easy to respond to, whereas another trainee may experience it as very difficult. Thus, it is important for trainees to provide difficulty assessments and adjustments to ensure that they are practicing at the right difficulty level: neither too easy nor too hard.

https://doi.org/10.1037/0000484-002

Deliberate Practice in Behavioral Parent Training, by M. D. Terjesen, H. B. Vidair, P. S. Ohr, O. A. Walsh, T. Rousmaniere, and A. Vaz

Time Frame

We recommend a 90-minute time block for every exercise, structured roughly as follows:

- First 20 minutes: Orientation. The trainer explains the behavioral parent training (BPT) skill and demonstrates the exercise procedure with a volunteer trainee.

- Middle 50 minutes: Trainees perform the exercise in pairs. The trainer or a peer provides feedback throughout this process and monitors/adjusts the exercise's difficulty as needed after each set of statements (see Appendix A for more information about difficulty assessment).

- Final 20 minutes: Review, feedback, and discussion

Preparation

1. Every trainee will need their own copy of this book.

2. Each exercise requires the trainer to fill out a Deliberate Practice Reaction Form after completing all the statements from a single difficulty level. This form is available in the "Resources" tab at https://www.apa.org/pubs/books/deliberate-practice-behavioral-parent-training and in Appendix A.

3. Trainees are grouped into pairs. One volunteers to role-play the therapist and one to role-play the parent (they will switch roles after 15 minutes of practice). As noted previously, an observer who might be either the trainer or a fellow trainee will work with each pair.

The Role of the Trainer

The primary responsibilities of the trainer are as follows:

1. Provide corrective feedback, which includes both information about how well the trainees' response met expected criteria and any necessary guidance about how to improve the response.

2. Remind trainees to do difficulty assessments and adjustments after each level of parent statements is completed (beginning, intermediate, and advanced).

How to Practice

Each exercise includes its own step-by-step instructions. Trainees should follow these instructions carefully, as every step is important.

Skill Criteria

Each of the first 12 exercises focuses on one essential BPT skill with skill criteria that describe the important components or principles for that skill.

The goal of the role play is for trainees to practice improvising responses to the parent statement in a manner that (a) is attuned to the parent, (b) meets skill criteria as much

as possible, and (c) feels authentic for the trainee. Trainees are provided scripts with example therapist responses to give them a sense of how to incorporate the skill criteria into a response. **It is important, however, that trainees do not read the example responses verbatim in the role plays!** Therapy is highly personal and improvisational; the goal of deliberate practice is to develop trainees' ability to improvise within a consistent framework. Memorizing scripted responses would be counterproductive for helping trainees learn to perform therapy that is responsive, authentic, and attuned to each individual parent.

The book's authors wrote the scripted example responses. However, trainees' personal style of therapy may differ slightly or greatly from that in the example scripts. It is essential that, over time, trainees develop their own style and voice, while simultaneously being able to intervene according to the model's principles and strategies. To facilitate this, the exercises in this book were designed to maximize opportunities for improvisational responses informed by the skill criteria and ongoing feedback.

Review, Feedback, and Discussion

The review and feedback sequence after each role play has these two elements:

- First, the trainee who played the parent **briefly** shares how it felt to be on the receiving end of the therapist response. This can help assess how well trainees are attuning with the parent.

- Second, the trainer provides **brief** feedback (less than 1 minute) based on the skill criteria for each exercise. Keep feedback specific, behavioral, and brief to preserve time for skill rehearsal. If one trainer is teaching multiple pairs of trainees, the trainer walks around room, observing the pairs and offering brief feedback. When the trainer is not available, the trainee playing the parent gives peer feedback to the therapist, based on the skill criteria and how it felt to be on the receiving end of the intervention. Alternately, a third trainee can observe and provide feedback.

Trainers (or peers) should remember to keep all feedback specific and brief and not to veer into discussions of theory. There are many other settings for extended discussion of BPT theory and research. In deliberate practice, it is of utmost importance to maximize time for continuous behavioral rehearsal via role plays.

Final Evaluation

After both trainees have role-played the parent and the therapist, the trainer provides an evaluation. Participants should engage in a short group discussion based on this evaluation. This discussion can provide ideas for where to focus homework and future deliberate practice sessions. To this end, Appendix B presents a Deliberate Practice Therapist Diary Form, which can also be downloaded from the "Resources" tab at https://www.apa.org/pubs/books/deliberate-practice-behavioral-parent-training. This form can be used by trainees as a template as part of the final feedback to help trainees process their experiences from that session with the supervisor. However, it is designed primarily to be used as a template for exploring and recording their thoughts and experiences between sessions, particularly when pursuing additional deliberate practice activities without the supervisor, such as rehearsing responses alone or if two trainees want practice the exercises together—perhaps with a third trainee filling the supervisor's role. Then, if they want, the trainees can discuss these experiences with the supervisor at the beginning of the next training session.

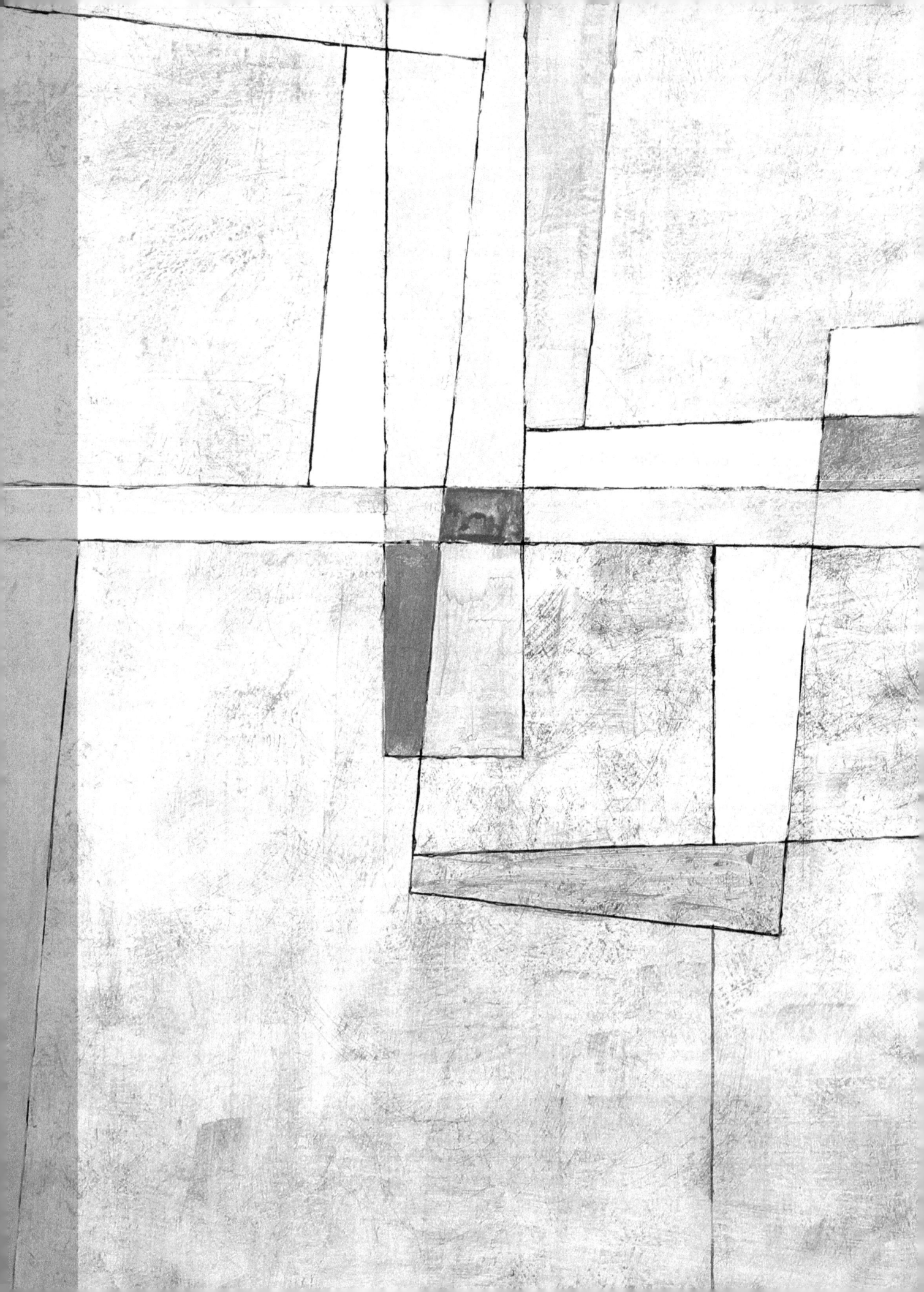

Deliberate Practice Exercises for Behavioral Parent Training Skills

This section of the book provides 12 deliberate practice exercises for essential behavioral parent training (BPT) skills. These exercises are organized in a developmental sequence, from those that are appropriate for someone just beginning BPT training to exercises for those who have progressed to a more advanced level. Although we anticipate that most trainers will use these exercises in the order we have suggested, some trainers may find it more appropriate for their training circumstances to use a different order. We also provide two comprehensive exercises that bring together the BPT skills using an annotated BPT session transcript and mock sessions.

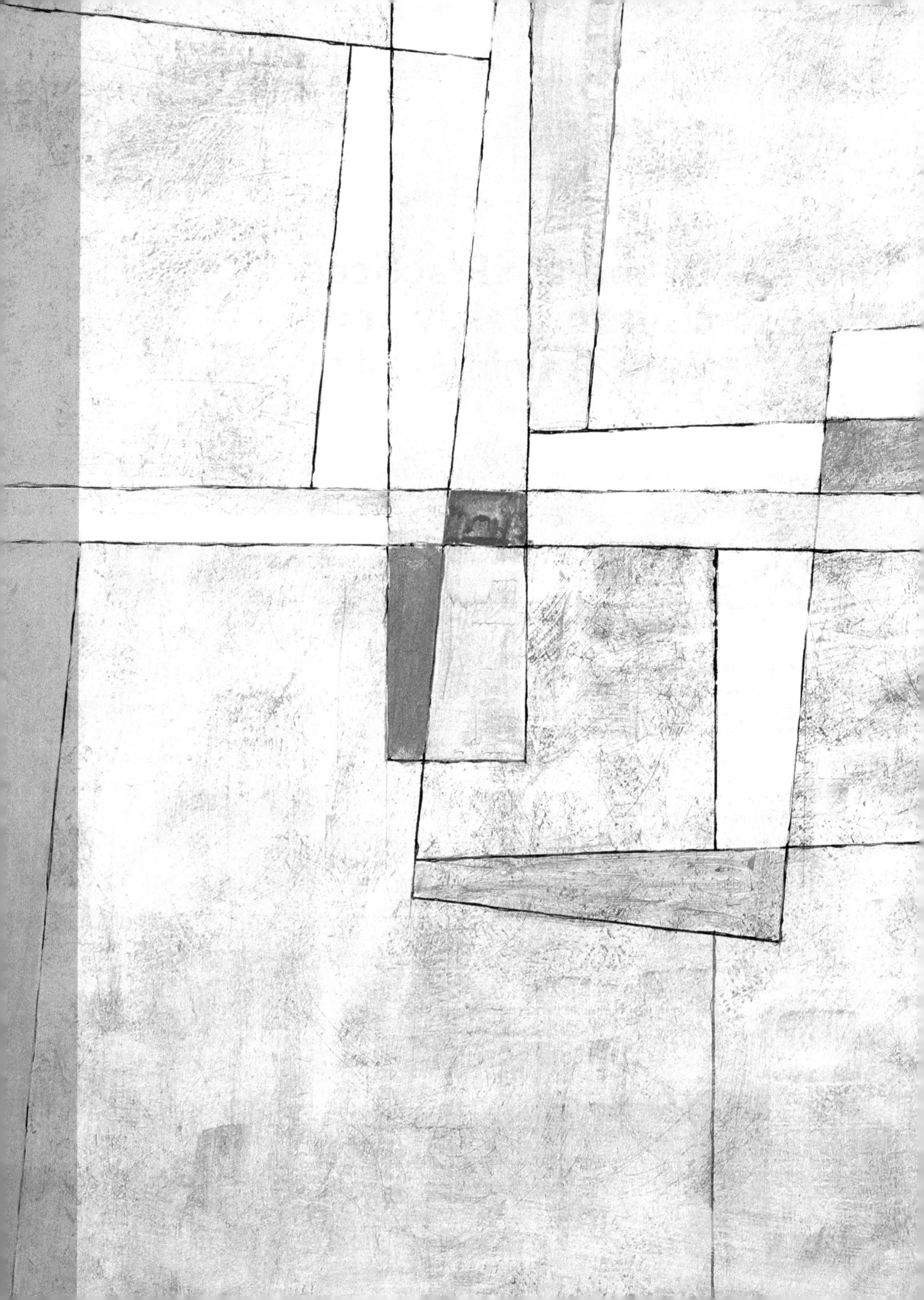

Psychoeducation About Behavioral Parent Training

Preparations for Exercise 1

1. Read the instructions in Chapter 2.

2. Download the Deliberate Practice Reaction Form and the Deliberate Practice Diary Form at https://www.apa.org/pubs/books/deliberate-practice-behavioral-parent-training (see the "Resources" tab; also available in Appendixes A and B, respectively).

Skill Description

Skill Difficulty Level: Beginner

It is important to do psychoeducation about how behavioral parent training (BPT) works before starting direct clinical work to change parenting behavior to improve child outcomes. The psychoeducational component of BPT assists parents in understanding more about the child's behavior and their current role in responding to and possibly maintaining the behavior; it also sets the stage for the work that they will be encouraged to do within BPT. Psychoeducation will be didactic in nature as well as collaborative and utilizes both psychotherapeutic and educational interventions to inform parents about the behavior and the treatment approach proposed (Montoya et al., 2011).

While psychoeducation will tend to target specific child and parenting behaviors, a number of core behaviors of effective parenting have been identified (Kaminski et al., 2008). Psychoeducation about BPT may include communicating that the focus will be on strategies to improve parenting skills as well as the competence and confidence to deliver them. Psychoeducation may also involve discussing BPT as both a prevention strategy and as one that they will work on implementing in response to problematic behavior. Finally, psychoeducation about BPT stresses a balanced focus on both the behavior of the child and those of the parents.

https://doi.org/10.1037/0000484-003

Deliberate Practice in Behavioral Parent Training, by M. D. Terjesen, H. B. Vidair, P. S. Ohr, O. A. Walsh, T. Rousmaniere, and A. Vaz

As we discussed in Chapter 1, the third criterion of some of the BPT skills involves having the clinician ask a treatment acceptability question (ask the parent if they believe that this approach will be helpful to address their child's problem and their willingness to try BPT). This skill is more informational and general than the other skills, and therefore we focus on asking parents about (a) their belief that this would be helpful for their child, (b) their willingness to focus on their parenting behavior as an agent of change, and (c) any potential barriers they see toward doing this. We recommend that trainees ask more acceptability questions at each level of difficulty to help them become more comfortable with this criterion—that is, ask one acceptability question at the beginner level, ask two questions at the intermediate level, and ask three questions at the advanced level. The clinician can also ask an open-ended question such as, "What are your thoughts?" as a summary of or transition into the other questions, but it shouldn't count toward the total number of questions per difficulty level.

The client prompts provided offer a range of difficulties as they relate to psychoeducation, so clinicians can practice using them in situations with various presenting problems and different levels of difficulty. All prompts are at the beginning or early period of treatment, when the parent describes their concerns about their child's behavior. The prompts at the beginner difficulty level have parents present specific behavior problems and, in the context of doing so, present some behaviors of theirs that may be targets for change within BPT. The prompts at the intermediate difficulty level involve times when the parent focuses on situations where they have difficulty recognizing their role in the process. Finally, prompts at the advanced difficulty level present situations where the parent has already presented potential barriers to treatment.

SKILL CRITERIA FOR EXERCISE 1

1. Summarize what the parent stated about the child's behavior and their affective and/or behavioral response.
2. Provide information about how behavioral parent training will be used.
3. Ask the parent if they believe that this approach will be helpful to address their child's problem and about their willingness to try BPT. The three questions relate to (a) whether this would be helpful for their child, (b) parents' willingness to focus on their parenting behavior as an agent of change, and (c) any potential barriers they see toward doing this.
   - Beginner level: Ask one question.
   - Intermediate level: Ask two questions.
   - Advanced level: Ask three questions.

Examples of Therapists Demonstrating Psychoeducation About Behavioral Parent Training

Example 1

CLIENT: [*frustrated*] Honestly, no matter how hard I try or how loud I yell, I just cannot get Frank to do what I want. I try to help him plan and give him reminders about expectations, and regardless, he doesn't comply. At 10 years old, he really should be more responsible at this point. On the weekend, I got so upset, I took away his screens for a month. I know I can't stick to that, but I also can't keep having him behave this way.

THERAPIST: I hear some frustration in your voice when you describe the situation with Frank. In this example, you describe his noncompliant behavior and both preventative and reactive strategies that regrettably don't seem to be changing his behavior and also lead to your frustration and making parenting decisions that maybe are not your best choices. (Criterion 1) The approach that I think would be most beneficial is referred to as behavioral parent training, and here we try to understand the child's behavior as well as your responses to the behavior. We then review the strategies you are using and see if we can work together to develop more effective, consistent parenting behaviors that will hopefully increase Frank's compliance. (Criterion 2) What are your thoughts? Do you think initially reviewing current parenting practices and then discussing different parenting approaches toward changing Frank's behavior would be a strategy you would be willing to try? (Criterion 3)

Example 2

CLIENT: [*exasperated*] Caroline will do pretty much anything . . . except her school-work. This is her junior year, and her grades are so important to get into college. I remind her all day, provide her with tutors, offer her rewards to complete it, yet she just doesn't do it until the last possible minute. It usually ends up in a shouting match around 9 p.m., and then she stays up late, finishes it, and I have to stay up and make sure she completes it. We both are exhausted the next day, and it really has a negative impact on our relationship.

THERAPIST: It sounds like you get very frustrated with the fact that you try to provide her with as much support as you can, yet she still does not prioritize this; gets it done at the last minute; and as a result there is conflict between you two. (Criterion 1) I think it would be helpful for us to look at both your and her behaviors and try to understand how we can break this cycle not only to increase her completing her schoolwork earlier but also to help your relationship. The approach that I believe would be most helpful is referred to as behavioral parent training and does the majority of the work with the parents at the onset. (Criterion 2) Would you want to address your parenting using this approach because it would be effective in addressing your concerns about her schoolwork completion but also organically help change those behaviors, like screaming, that impact your relationship? Are you willing to try this? (Criterion 3)

Example 3

CLIENT: [*hopeless*] I am not the best parent when it comes to sticking to a plan. I have stopped and started maybe a half dozen of those sticker charts, but the moment that Kim argues about the points received or lost or how it is so unfair and tells me I am the worst parent ever, I just give in. This happened last week when I tried to delete all of her social media accounts from her phone. She became so difficult to deal with, I put them back on the phone. She clearly runs the home.

THERAPIST: It sounds like you are caught in a pattern where you have started to try and address the behaviors, and then when she pushes back, that plan goes out the window and she gets what she wants—in this case, the phone. (Criterion 1) Parenting can be tough, and I admire your past efforts to try and change her behavior. In listening to you, I think we could start doing work on you and your behavior to try and change her behaviors. The approach of behavioral parent training has good research behind it, and the initial work is primarily with the parents to promote helpful skills that can be used consistently to address the challenging behaviors of their child. I also hear some frustration in response to her behavior and that sounds like it may impact how you parent. (Criterion 2) Do you agree that the initial goal will be to work on changing Kim's behavior, but the approach to get there will involve working on your parenting behavior and maybe your parenting emotions? Do you think this would be helpful for Kim, are you willing to try this, and is there anything that could interfere with working on this? (Criterion 3)

INSTRUCTIONS FOR EXERCISE 1
Step 1: Role-Play and Feedback
• The client says the first beginner client statement. The therapist **improvises** a response based on the skill criteria. • The trainer (or, if not available, the client) provides **brief** feedback based on the skill criteria. • The client then repeats the same statement, and the therapist again improvises a response. The trainer (or client) again provides brief feedback.
Step 2: Repeat
• Repeat Step 1 for all the statements **in the current difficulty level** (beginner, intermediate, or advanced).
Step 3: Assess and Adjust Difficulty
• The therapist completes the Deliberate Practice Reaction Form (see Appendix A) and decides whether to make the exercise easier or harder or to repeat the same difficulty level.
Step 4: Repeat for Approximately 15 Minutes
• Repeat Steps 1 to 3 for at least 15 minutes. • The trainees then switch therapist and client roles and start over.

> **Now it's your turn! Follow the exercise instructions.**

Remember: The goal of the role play is for trainees to practice improvising responses to the client statements in a manner that (a) uses the skill criteria and (b) feels authentic for the trainee. **Example therapist responses for each client statement are provided at the end of this exercise. Trainees should attempt to improvise their own responses before reading the examples.**

BEGINNER-LEVEL CLIENT STATEMENTS FOR EXERCISE 1
Beginner Client Statement 1
[Annoyed] Rebecca is the "avoidant queen" and always puts things off until the last minute, then she's stressed, I'm stressed, and the house becomes chaotic. She could pull this off in middle school, but in high school, this strategy won't work. We both were up until 2 a.m. on Tuesday. I'm at a loss as to how get her to change.

BEGINNER-LEVEL CLIENT STATEMENTS FOR EXERCISE 1

Beginner Client Statement 2

[Annoyed] Ray's use of technology is ridiculous. We have taken to calling him iRay. I get that technology is how students communicate now, but we can't get him to turn off his devices and do what he is supposed to. We have rules about technology that he violates often and he fights with us when we try to enforce them. It's really out of hand. I just want him to follow the rules and not have these blow-up fights.

Beginner Client Statement 3

[Sad] Every house sets rules, and we have ours, but no matter what, Maddy and Olivia just cannot seem to follow them without fighting. We see these problems in many areas, but the bedtime routine is the worst. They know what they are supposed to do and no matter what, I have to remind them. To be honest, it's annoying and sometimes I punish them by not reading them a story, which is something I know they love. I then go to bed more nights than I care to thinking I'm a bad parent.

Beginner Client Statement 4

[Frustrated] George's lying is just out of control. It's like it comes so easy to him and he never owns up to his behavior and attributes any problems to someone else—often us. On one level, it's smart for him to lie, because he probably has gotten away with it more times than I care to think. He knows when I catch him in a lie that the punishment can be pretty severe, and so he keeps lying. I just want him to follow the house rules and then, when he violates them, not to lie about it.

Beginner Client Statement 5

[Irritated] Given her busy schedule, and these are things she has chosen to do, it is even more important that Grace follow the schedule we set up. I let her help set it up, yet now it's a fight pretty much every day. It's rare that we have a positive interaction with one another because it is always me telling her to do something and, usually, her not doing it. These arguments set a bad example for her sisters, and sometimes I end up doing some of the work for her anyway to avoid the fight. It's crazy for a 42-year-old to be doing third-grade math assignments.

✋ **Assess and adjust the difficulty before moving to the next difficulty level (see Step 3 in the exercise instructions).**

INTERMEDIATE-LEVEL CLIENT STATEMENTS FOR EXERCISE 1

Intermediate Client Statement 1

[Annoyed] Honestly, I'm a little confused. Michael is the one with the anger issues, and he is so incredibly disrespectful. I get that you need some background information from us, but why are we here and not him? He is the one that keeps lying, breaking curfew, and stealing our money to buy Lord knows what.

Intermediate Client Statement 2

[Exasperated] I know people use the term sibling rivalry loosely, but it really describes my kids. They fight over everything and everyone. I try to be fair and balanced with my attention and use of praise. Even for something as silly as the number of french fries they each get, I try and make sure it is equal. It doesn't work. They have no patience for one another, and I really want to have someone teach them skills to get along. Wouldn't your time be better spent teaching them the skills than wasting it with me?

INTERMEDIATE-LEVEL CLIENT STATEMENTS FOR EXERCISE 1

Intermediate Client Statement 3

[Hopeless] Bryan's arguing got so bad that the neighbors called the police on us and did a safety check. It was mortifying. Nothing came of it, but he now threatens that if we don't give him what we want, he will call the police on us. I'm at a loss and walk on eggshells around him. Meeting with me won't change him. I think he needs to see you.

Intermediate Client Statement 4

[Resignation] Sebastian's behavior during unstructured activities is, to put it mildly, awful. Waiting his turn has never been a strength of his, but he gets aggressive and impulsive and demands attention from everyone. We have his classmate's birthday party next weekend, and I just want him to listen and behave. He doesn't listen to me anymore and never really has. I really thought you would be working with him to have him learn how to manage his behavior.

Intermediate Client Statement 5

[Stressed] Tahira's ability to try something new, especially in front of others, is quite bad. She has always been this way, but it seems like it is getting worse. As an example, she loves basketball and is really quite good for a first grader—she's the only one who can reach the hoop. But when I took her to tryouts last week for a team where she would not have known anyone, we sat in the parking lot for 25 minutes with her screaming and crying and she even hit me a few times. I just took her home. It's clear she has some anxiety, but it's not clear to me why you want to work with me.

✋ **Assess and adjust the difficulty before moving to the next difficulty level (see Step 3 in the exercise instructions).**

ADVANCED-LEVEL CLIENT STATEMENTS FOR EXERCISE 1

Advanced Client Statement 1

[Angry] Allegra's behavior has become too much to deal with. I am this close to being done with her. I try to take her perspective and try to support her, but she just curses at me and calls me horrible names. She's 10 now, can you imagine what she'll be like at 15? I must be doing something wrong, since she doesn't listen or respect her mother. Not sure if you are going to tell me anything I have not tried.

Advanced Client Statement 2

[Exasperated] I know that you have not met him, but Jordan is pretty tough to deal with. There is a purposeful aggression in his behavior toward others, especially when he is not getting attention. He's just 8, but has three younger siblings, and logically they need more attention than him, but he wants my attention 24/7. When he believes he's not getting it, he acts out. His teachers say he doesn't act like this in school, but I just don't know what to do. I punish him, I offer rewards, I yell, and I ignore . . . and nothing works. I can't stop everything I am doing to deal with Jordan.

Advanced Client Statement 3

[Embarrassed] Camila has moved from being nasty and rude to me to being nasty and rude to her friends, teammates, and, lately, other parents. She has been asked to leave the team carpool because of how she talks to other parents. This is so embarrassing—these are friends of mine and her behavior makes me look bad as a parent. I have begged, bribed, yelled, and nothing works. I just want to crawl into a hole at points and I am thinking about not signing her up for camp this summer just to avoid situations where she will most likely be rude. Unless you have a miracle in your notebook, I am giving up trying to change her.

ADVANCED-LEVEL CLIENT STATEMENTS FOR EXERCISE 1
Advanced Client Statement 4
[Frustrated] Izabela doesn't handle being told "no." Her mother sets no limits, and then when she comes to my house on the weekend and I try to set limits, it doesn't work. As an example, 2 weeks ago, she would not get off her phone, so I shut down all her apps. She screamed at me, cried, called me names, and then called her mother who then took off the blocker I put on the apps. Her mother does this all the time and refuses to try and change. How is anything you and I do going to be effective?
Advanced Client Statement 5
[Angry] Whoever invented the smartphone must not have had teenagers because the problems it has created in Devin are really sad and challenging to deal with. Eighty percent of our fights are about his use of his phone and the bad choices he makes. Two weeks ago, I got called into his school because he was posting pictures and making nasty comments about his peers on his social media account. I took his phone away—you know, a natural consequence—and he found a way to use my phone to post things. We had a major blowup. I see his phone use as an addiction and am not sure anything can be done to help him without fixing this addiction.

> **Assess and adjust the difficulty here (see Step 3 in the exercise instructions). If appropriate, follow the instructions to make the exercise even more challenging (see Appendix A).**

Example Therapist Responses: Psychoeducation About Behavioral Parent Training

Remember: Trainees should attempt to improvise their own responses before reading the example responses. **Do not read the following responses verbatim unless you are having trouble coming up with your own!**

EXAMPLE RESPONSES TO BEGINNER-LEVEL CLIENT STATEMENTS FOR EXERCISE 1
Example Response to Beginner Client Statement 1
It sounds like when Rebecca avoids doing her work, everyone gets stressed and then everyone stays up late to make sure the work gets done. (Criterion 1) One approach that I think may be helpful is that of behavioral parent training, or BPT. Within BPT, you and I would work together to try and change her behavior by changing your behavior. Ideally, we could use BPT to develop systems in advance to prevent these behaviors as well as strategies to respond to her when she doesn't get her work done. (Criterion 2) We can discuss this approach more, but do you think this is something that would be helpful to address Rebecca's problems? (Criterion 3)
Example Response to Beginner Client Statement 2
It sounds like many of your challenges with Ray focus on technology and his difficulty in following rules and expectations and that there are considerable arguments about this. (Criterion 1) While I am sure you have done many things to try and address this, in listening to you, I think that an approach we may wish to consider is referred to as behavioral parent training, or BPT. BPT has many core strategies that involve changing his behavior by changing the expectations and consequences. That is, we discuss his behavior and see what strategies we can implement to help bring about change and hopefully improve your relationship. (Criterion 2) What are your thoughts? Would starting with an approach like this be helpful for Ray's behavior? (Criterion 3)

EXAMPLE RESPONSES TO BEGINNER-LEVEL CLIENT STATEMENTS FOR EXERCISE 1

Example Response to Beginner Client Statement 3

Using the bedtime routine as an example, it sounds like your girls struggle with following it and you experience some frustration to the point where you described punishing them by withholding something valued. And as a result, you also engage in some thoughts that we could describe as self-doubt. (Criterion 1) To try and change their behavior, both the noncompliance with rules and the arguing, we could consider trying an approach referred to as behavioral parent training or BPT. With BPT, we try to look at how to have children learn and follow expectations by adapting some of the ways that you plan for and respond to their behavior. (Criterion 2) What are your thoughts? Is there anything that you think would pose a challenge to implementing BPT? Do you think it would be helpful to address their behavior? (Criterion 3)

Example Response to Beginner Client Statement 4

I appreciate your understanding as to why he lies as well as your awareness as to how you respond as well as what your goals are for George and your home. (Criterion 1) Changing his behavior is the priority, but how we do this will involve more work with you. An approach that is centered around this is called behavioral parent training, or BPT. For example, as part of the approach, we work to set clear expectations and then establish rewards and consequences when they are met. (Criterion 2) With the goal of changing his behavior being primary, what are your thoughts about me starting BPT with you to help begin the change process with George? Do you think this would be helpful? (Criterion 3)

Example Response to Beginner Client Statement 5

From what I hear, this daily struggle about getting her work done and sticking to a schedule leads to many arguments and some considerable frustration on your part to the point where you end up doing her work for her. (Criterion 1) This can't continue, and we want to work on changing Grace's behavior. An approach that would be good to consider is called behavioral parent training, or BPT. In BPT, we work directly with you to look at the antecedents and consequences of Grace's behavior and see which approaches we would want to target to change from a parenting perspective. Grace changing is the main goal, but in BPT, at the beginning we work on changing parent behavior to address her difficulties. (Criterion 2) What are your thoughts? Based on my brief discussion, is there anything about BPT that would be tough for you to implement? (Criterion 3)

EXAMPLE RESPONSES TO INTERMEDIATE-LEVEL CLIENT STATEMENTS FOR EXERCISE 1

Example Response to Intermediate Client Statement 1

From what you said, I hear that Michael engages in some pretty disrespectful behavior toward you, in the forms of both lying and stealing. I also appreciate the question as to why you are here and not Michael. (Criterion 1) As I listened to you, I thought of an approach that is referred to as behavioral parent training, or BPT. This approach looks at his behaviors in a context to understand the "why" of his behavior. This would involve looking at what comes before and after these behaviors and then changing your responses to his behavior. Yes, we want him to *want* to follow the rules, but he is not motivated to do so. Changing the context by changing your behavior can help bring out a change in his behavior. (Criterion 2) Do you think something like this would be helpful to start in your situation, and are you willing to try BPT? (Criterion 3)

EXAMPLE RESPONSES TO INTERMEDIATE-LEVEL CLIENT STATEMENTS FOR EXERCISE 1

Example Response to Intermediate Client Statement 2

I hear how frustrating their continual fighting must be and appreciate your efforts to try and anticipate and manage their behaviors. In listening to you, I don't think that our time together is wasted. In fact, I think quite the opposite. (Criterion 1) We can work on changing their behavior through an approach called BPT, or behavioral parent training. Here, I work with the parents to better understand their children's behavior and then review what events come before and after that behavior. These events set the stage for and maintain the rivalry and fighting. Then, we work on changing those events. By changing the conditions of the behavior, we change the behavior. (Criterion 2) Do you think it would be helpful to use this approach to help you manage their behavior? Anything you can think of that would stop you from trying this approach? (Criterion 3)

Example Response to Intermediate Client Statement 3

I have to imagine that going through that was very difficult and that the ongoing threats from Bryan have to be hard to deal with. I do think we want him to change, but right now, he may not be motivated to do so. (Criterion 1) In trying to change his behavior, maybe we can have a discussion about why you think he does things and examine what strategies you have used to try and change his behavior. Different children respond to different approaches. We just want to find the one that works best for you and Bryan. This is consistent with an approach called behavioral parent training, or BPT. (Criterion 2) At least initially, do you think it would be helpful to try BPT to understand and intervene in Bryan's behavior? Is there anything that you think would stop you from doing this? (Criterion 3)

Example Response to Intermediate Client Statement 4

From what you reported, it sounds like Sebastian really struggles to behave in public, but more specifically while doing nonstructured activities. I liked how you stated what your goals are, and I think your comment about having me work directly with him is understandable. (Criterion 1) A research-based approach to managing children's behavior is referred to as behavioral parent training, or BPT. Here we work with parents to set up systems of communication, praise, and rewards and consequences to help manage these behaviors. This approach operates under the premise that there is a history of environmental factors that surround this behavior that have led to its occurrence or recurrence of the behavior. We would work together to understand these factors and then change them to change Sebastian. (Criterion 2) Do you think an approach like this would be helpful in addressing his behaviors, and are you willing to try it? (Criterion 3)

Example Response to Intermediate Client Statement 5

What you describe does in fact sound like some anxiety, and it does sound like Tahira may not like doing things in front of others. In listening to you speak, your question about why I am meeting with you and not her is a sensical one—that is, she has anxiety so we should work with her. (Criterion 1) What we know about anxiety is that sometimes the experience of anxiety gets reinforced. In the example you provided, Tahira may have experienced anxiety, started tantruming because she was uncomfortable, and then she was taken home. By going home, I imagine her distress dissipated, and as a result, her tantruming behavior got reinforced because her anxiety went away. One of the approaches that I think may be helpful to change her behavior is referred to as behavioral parent training, or BPT. Although typically used with aggressive and noncompliant children, there is research showing that with children who have anxiety, teaching parents skills such as understanding what comes before and after the behavior and setting up expectations and rewards for desired behavior may be effective in changing her anxiety. (Criterion 2) Are you open to trying this? Do you think an approach like this may be helpful in changing her behavior? (Criterion 3)

EXAMPLE RESPONSES TO ADVANCED-LEVEL CLIENT STATEMENTS FOR EXERCISE 1

Example Response to Advanced Client Statement 1

When Allegra treats you that way, yelling and cursing at you, it has to be very frustrating for you. I also hear you questioning your own skills as a parent. (Criterion 1) I think when you question yourself, it may lead you to give up trying. I thought we could discuss an approach called behavioral parent training, or BPT. I would want us to look at the skills that you have used in the past and consider whether they address the "why" of her behavior and help develop new skills that could change it. (Criterion 2) Are you open to trying this approach and do you think an approach like this would be helpful to address Allegra's behavior? Is there anything from a practical level that would interfere with this? (Criterion 3)

Example Response to Advanced Client Statement 2

When you describe some of Jordan's behaviors—more specifically, his aggression and constant need for attention—it sounds quite frustrating. Further, with four children under 8 in your home, I can imagine how difficult it may be to find the time to address his behaviors. It also sounds like your responses have not brought about the change you wanted. (Criterion 1) Initially, I think we have to carefully choose a strategy that is not only effective but practical for you to do. This is what we do within behavioral parent training: We work together to better understand Jordan's behavior, and then we work together to set up a practical system that integrates effective communication, praise, attention, and rewards to help him learn to do what he is expected to do. (Criterion 2) Do you think the behavioral parent training approach would be helpful initially, and would you want to try it? Can you think of anything that may make this tough to do? (Criterion 3)

Example Response to Advanced Client Statement 3

It makes sense that when Camila acts that way, it is upsetting and I hear your concern that some of her disrespectful behavior has now carried over to how she interacts with others, especially other parents. It also sounds like although you have tried to change her behavior, it hasn't worked. I also hear an emotional reaction to her behavior, which can impact your current and future efforts to change her. (Criterion 1) In listening to you, I think an approach called behavioral parent training may be helpful. Here, we would work together to understand her behavior and consider strategies such as planned ignoring, rewards, and consequences to change her behavior. We will also want to try and plan for any emotional response on your part, especially if it would impact how you would implement these strategies. (Criterion 2) What are your thoughts? Would you want to start with this approach to try and work on getting Camila to change her behavior? Do you think it would work? We should also discuss if there are any barriers you can identify that may make it tough to do. (Criterion 3)

Example Response to Advanced Client Statement 4

It does sound like Izabela's behavior is challenging, and managing it becomes more challenging when there is a lack of consistency across homes. (Criterion 1) While that consistency would be ideal, it's not happening right now, but that doesn't mean we don't try to change her behavior. I would recommend that we try something that is referred to as behavioral parent training, or BPT. Here, we would work mostly independent of Izabela on trying to understand what motivates her to engage in these behaviors. From what you described, it sounds like she has learned that when she acts a certain way, she gets what she wants. We would work together to have her learn new ways of responding, and we do so by changing the contingencies of her behavior. That is, we reward the behavior that we want to see. Rewards are just part of BPT. (Criterion 2) Do you think that you—and by extension, Izabela—would benefit from an approach like this to reduce these behaviors? Are you willing to try this, and is there anything that would have an impact on how you carry out the plans associated with BPT? (Criterion 3)

EXAMPLE RESPONSES TO ADVANCED-LEVEL CLIENT STATEMENTS FOR EXERCISE 1

Example Response to Advanced Client Statement 5

It sounds like Devin's phone use and the fights you have had with him about his bad decisions really are difficult for you to deal with. (Criterion 1) While Devin may benefit from his own support to learn better decision-making strategies, let's not sell short the role that you can have as a parent. Perhaps before any direct work with Devin, we could try an approach called behavioral parent training, or BPT, where we learn how to change his behavior by setting expectations, communicating more effectively, and rewarding the behaviors we want to see and implementing consequences for when these expectations are not met. (Criterion 2) Are you open to looking at your parenting strategies, and do you think that BPT would work to bring about change for Devin? It's early, but based on what we discussed, is there anything you think would interfere with you applying what we discuss? (Criterion 3)

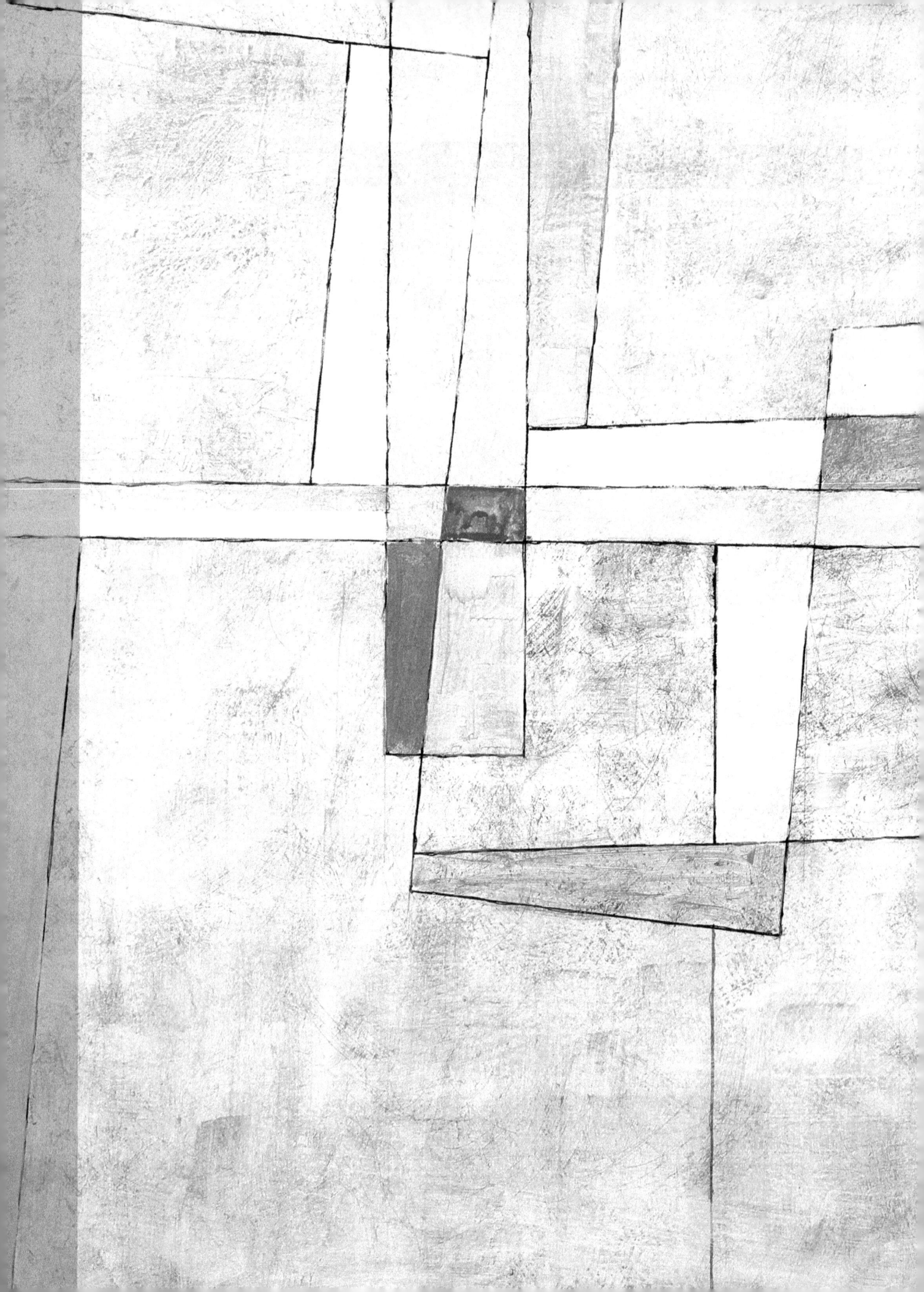

Psychoeducation About the Functions of Child Behaviors

Preparations for Exercise 2

1. Read the instructions in Chapter 2.

2. Download the Deliberate Practice Reaction Form and the Deliberate Practice Diary Form at https://www.apa.org/pubs/books/deliberate-practice-behavioral-parent-training (see the "Resources" tab; also available in Appendixes A and B, respectively).

Skill Description

Skill Difficulty Level: Beginner

As discussed in Chapter 1 and Exercise 1, the presence of disruptive behavior problems are apparent in many children and adolescents and are often the highest rates of referral for mental health services (Ghandour et al., 2019). These behaviors may have a significant impact on children's functioning and on the home environment (Johnston & Chronis-Tuscano, 2015; Mackler et al., 2015). Disruptive behaviors among children have been associated with negative outcomes, such as social (Brennan et al., 2015) and academic (Arnold et al., 2020; Liu et al., 2017) problems, increased risk of psychopathology (Hawes et al., 2020), substance use and dependence problems (Howard et al., 2020), juvenile delinquency (Retz et al., 2021), and conviction for violent crimes (Baggio et al., 2018; Wojciechowski, 2021).

These behaviors may also have an impact on family functioning and parent emotional responses. They may also lead to parental stress (Mackler et al., 2015) and frustration due to the frequent negative interactions between parents and their children related to disruptive behaviors (Burke et al., 2008). Behavioral parent training (BPT) aims to address these behaviors and improve child functioning and the parent–child relationship, but before teaching BPT skills and implementing a plan, it is important for the BPT clinician and the parent to understand the "why" or the function of the child's behavior.

https://doi.org/10.1037/0000484-004

Deliberate Practice in Behavioral Parent Training, by M. D. Terjesen, H. B. Vidair, P. S. Ohr, O. A. Walsh, T. Rousmaniere, and A. Vaz

Functional behavioral assessments (FBAs) have long been used in schools to develop behavior intervention plans (BIPs) for children and have demonstrated positive results in decreasing behavior problems (Miller & Lee, 2013). An approach to help gather data as to the context of the behavior is often referred to as an *ABC approach*, referring to the *antecedent* (what precedes or may set the stage for the behavior), the *behavior*, and the *consequence* (what follows the behavior that may maintain it going forward). By helping parents conceptualize the behavior this way, patterns may emerge that help them understand the "why" or the function of the behavior. Increasing parents' knowledge as to why their child behaves the way they do is an important first step within BPT. There is evidence to support a functional-based approach to interventions with parents (Fettig & Barton, 2014), and it is recommended as an early clinical intervention (Chronis et al., 2004). A functional-based approach assists parents in understanding the rationale for their child's behavior, and then, as a result, the clinical skills taught within BPT may make more sense to the parent, which may improve parental efficacy in the application of these skills and ultimately improve child behavior and the parent–child relationship.

BPT clinicians will engage with the parent in a problem-solving and data collection process (e.g., ABC data collection sheet) to develop a hypothesis about the variables in the environment that are associated with the negative behaviors. Although we do want a description of the behavior, we want to understand why the child engages in the behavior and under what conditions these behaviors are most likely to occur. Using the ABC model, these conditions may be what precedes the behavior (e.g., the parent requests that the child put their tablet down and begin homework) and what follows the behavior (e.g., the parent gives in to the tantrum and offers 10 more minutes of tablet access).

Barnhill (2005) described the four categories of functions that exist and serve to maintain the behavior: (a) attention, (b) tangible reward, (c) escape, and (d) sensory stimulation. BPT clinicians have parents gather data to better understand a hypothesized function of the behavior and then develop interventions based on the data provided and the functional hypothesis. For a good review of functional analysis of problem behavior, we refer you to Martin and Pear (2019).

By working with parents to examine the function or purpose of a child's behavior—basically the "why" of the behavior—the BPT clinician and the parent can then develop strategies to address this. The goal here is to implement strategies that make problem behaviors inefficient, irrelevant, and ineffective in that they do not get what they want compared with the replacement behavior. When strategies do not consider the "why" of the behavior or incorrectly assume the function, the intervention may be limited in its effectiveness. As an example, if a child is engaging in disruptive behavior and we think that the function of this behavior is to get attention and thus we withhold attention, yet they continue to engage in that behavior, perhaps we incorrectly identified the function. In looking at the context of the behavior and the parental responses, we see that the child does these behaviors when requested to do nonpreferred tasks (e.g., bedtime) and here the function of these disruptive behaviors may be to escape something they see as aversive.

We have found that parents who have an understanding of the function of their child's behavior are better able to address challenging behavior through the strategies used within BPT. We have structured the skills in this exercise to add a degree of complexity to the problems described. In the beginner-level statements, we have parents describe behaviors that have relatively clear functions. The clinician will define a functional analysis and frame it within the context of BPT. In the intermediate-level statements, the parent describes behaviors that may serve multiple functions. Here, the clinician is asked to summarize the behavior and discuss both possible functions while suggesting that the next step be a functional analysis. In the advanced-level statements, parent descriptions of behavior may have a function, but the clinician response is complicated by the fact that parents indicate a preference for the clinician to work with the child rather than engaging in BPT. Here, BPT clinicians are to address the parents' motivation and explain the role of a functional analysis as part of an initial approach toward clinical change.

SKILL CRITERIA FOR EXERCISE 2

1. Summarize what the parent stated about the child's behavior.
2. Provide information about a functional analysis of behavior and how this will be used within behavioral parent training.
   - **Beginner level: Define a functional analysis of child behavior.**
   - **Intermediate level: Define a functional analysis of behavior, propose more than one specific function of the behavior, and suggest conducting a functional analysis.**
   - **Advanced level: Define a functional analysis of child behavior and address the rationale for behavioral parent training when the parents mention barriers (e.g., they prefer the clinician works with their child directly).**
3. Ask the parent if they agree with beginning to address the child's behavior through a functional approach.

Examples of Therapists Demonstrating Psychoeducation About the Functions of Child Behaviors

Example 1

CLIENT: [*exasperated*] You could set your clock to when Anton is going to have his meltdowns. Basically, every time we try to get him to start his homework—and more specifically his math homework. We give him warnings, try and make it fun, and offer rewards, but he still loses it, ripping up the homework sheets. Some nights we give up trying and just ask his teacher if he can do it during the resource room. If he hates homework this much at 7, what will he be like when doing algebra?

THERAPIST: Despite all your best efforts, it sounds like when Anton has his predictable homework meltdown, he on occasion gets out of doing it. (Criterion 1) In listening to you describe this sequence, an approach that I think may be helpful is that of behavioral parent training, or BPT. Within BPT, we work together to understand the "why" behind his meltdowns and see if we can develop preventative as well as reactive strategies to help improve his homework completion. It sounds like escape or avoidance may be motivating his behavior. (Criterion 2) Is BPT and understanding the "why" of his behavior something that you would like to explore as an approach to help address this? (Criterion 3)

Example 2

CLIENT: [*stressed*] Natalia has been doing some behaviors that I think are concerning, especially for a 9-year-old. Maybe four or five times over the last two weekends, she was using a sharp pencil to try and draw on herself while doing homework. At first I was treating this as harmless but kept asking her what she was doing and why. Her simple answer was because "she wanted to and it felt good." Then last weekend she drew blood, and I freaked out and yelled at her. I then made this a "no homework day," and I took her to the trampoline amusement park. I asked her mother if she does this at home, and she said no. I am at a loss.

THERAPIST: Thanks for sharing. I have to imagine this is stressful for you. From what you described, when Natalia does her homework, she begins to draw on herself, and sometimes it gets so bad that she draws blood. When she does this, she reports that it feels good, gets your attention, and she also sometimes gets out of doing the homework. (Criterion 1) These behaviors and your response make me think of an approach that is called behavioral parent training, or BPT. The theory behind this approach is that most behaviors can be changed when we better understand the "why" of their behavior. That is, what does Natalia gain by behaving like this? This would involve looking at what comes before and after these disrespectful behaviors. (Criterion 2) Do you think BPT and understanding the why of her behavior would be helpful to consider as we begin to try and help Natalia? (Criterion 3)

Example 3

CLIENT: [*angry*] Last week, I was in the kitchen when I noticed water dripping from the ceiling. I ran upstairs and saw that Yasmine had tried to flush some of my things down the toilet and now it got backed up. I flipped out and asked her why she was doing this, and she said because she was mad at me, and I was always too busy to help her. Well, a $1,200 plumber bill later, I have come to learn that there were many personal things of mine she had flushed over the past few months. Yes, I am busy, but she gets plenty of attention. I don't know what to do about it. She clearly has issues with me, and I think the sessions would be more productive if you spoke with her and got her to stop doing this.

THERAPIST: Thanks for sharing and that sounds like an expensive lesson to learn. It sounds like Yasmine is doing these behaviors to get your attention, even though you do offer it to her at times. (Criterion 1) It may make sense at some point to address these issues directly with Yasmine, but to begin, I would like to discuss an approach called behavioral parent training, or BPT. Put simply, Yasmine's behavior doesn't exist in isolation, as there are things that occur before the behavior and things that occur after that may serve to influence her behavior. Here, she complains that she doesn't get your attention and then does these behaviors, which certainly does get your attention. In BPT, we would work together to better understand why she does this and then modify some of these setting issues or consequences that influence the behavior. (Criterion 2) Do you think an approach like this would be helpful for addressing Yasmine's behavior? (Criterion 3)

INSTRUCTIONS FOR EXERCISE 2
Step 1: Role-Play and Feedback
• The client says the first beginner client statement. The therapist **improvises** a response based on the skill criteria.
• The trainer (or, if not available, the client) provides **brief** feedback based on the skill criteria.
• The client then repeats the same statement, and the therapist again improvises a response. The trainer (or client) again provides brief feedback.

INSTRUCTIONS FOR EXERCISE 2
Step 2: Repeat
• Repeat Step 1 for all the statements **in the current difficulty level** (beginner, intermediate, or advanced).
Step 3: Assess and Adjust Difficulty
• The therapist completes the Deliberate Practice Reaction Form (see Appendix A) and decides whether to make the exercise easier or harder or to repeat the same difficulty level.
Step 4: Repeat for Approximately 15 Minutes
• Repeat Steps 1 to 3 for at least 15 minutes.   • The trainees then switch therapist and client roles and start over.

Now it's your turn! Follow the exercise instructions.

Remember: The goal of the role play is for trainees to practice improvising responses to the client statements in a manner that (a) uses the skill criteria and (b) feels authentic for the trainee. **Example therapist responses for each client statement are provided at the end of this exercise. Trainees should attempt to improvise their own responses before reading the examples.**

BEGINNER-LEVEL CLIENT STATEMENTS FOR EXERCISE 2
Beginner Client Statement 1
[Frustration] Michelle has found ways to avoid doing her homework, and we just end up in a screaming match at the end of the day. She eventually gets it done, but only after we have fought about it. It impacts my mood all afternoon, and I struggle to have positive interactions with her because I know the "homework storm" is coming.
Beginner Client Statement 2
[Annoyed] Tom's use of technology is beyond any acceptable level. He often has three devices going at once, and my efforts to manage his usage, which typically are threats or shutting down all access and having an actual conversation with him are obviously not working. I speak with other parents and while I know tech is a problem for many, this seems to be really too much. I just want to set limits for his access and not have a fight about it.
Beginner Client Statement 3
[Resignation] We have rules in our home, and I don't think my expectations for their chores are too much. As an example, each night one of the girls is supposed to set the table for dinner and the other one is supposed to clear the table after dinner. They know the rules, but no matter how often they are told them, we have to remind them pretty much daily. Something that should take 5 minutes ends up leading to 20 minutes of arguing to get it done. Sometimes we don't even bother to ask. It leads us to wonder if we are just bad parents.

BEGINNER-LEVEL CLIENT STATEMENTS FOR EXERCISE 2

Beginner Client Statement 4

[Irritated] Jaden blames everyone but himself and never takes personal responsibility. He will stick to his story even in the presence of conflicting evidence. He just lies and lies some more. I know he doesn't want to get in trouble, and that makes sense, but the complete disrespect for me as a parent at this stage drives me nuts. The biggest issue for me is that I punish the behavior, but then punish the lying even more. Often at a level that some would say is too much.

Beginner Client Statement 5

[Exasperated] The after-school schedule is pretty clear each day: 30 minutes of snack and Maya time, followed by 75 minutes of homework, a 15-minute break, a homework review with whoever is home for 30 minutes, dinner, and then a fun activity, which could be alone or with family. Yet each day is a struggle to get her to follow these directions and involves many arguments and some bribery on my part. The homework completion keeps getting pushed off every night to later and later.

🕐 **Assess and adjust the difficulty before moving to the next difficulty level (see Step 3 in the exercise instructions).**

INTERMEDIATE-LEVEL CLIENT STATEMENTS FOR EXERCISE 2

Intermediate Client Statement 1

[Hopeless] It seems like I am a trigger and no matter what I do, I set him off. I would think that a mother should be able to have a conversation with her teenage son about colleges without being told to "shut up" and that I am "so annoying" and "don't interrupt me when I am gaming." This happens all the time, and now I just avoid speaking with him at all, which is quite sad.

Intermediate Client Statement 2

[Stressed] They are close in age at 7 and 9, but they just cannot seem to stop fighting over almost everything and, quite frankly, some of the silliest things, like the toys received in their Happy Meals from McDonalds. This really is quite infuriating. If my 7-year-old has something new, my 9-year-old wants it. If my 9-year-old has something, my 7-year-old wants it. The fighting is incessant, and I am constantly yelling at them. I have taken to just splitting them up. I even signed them up for different summer camps, which is a pain for me but maybe can help manage this.

Intermediate Client Statement 3

[Resignation] Sophia spent the better part of an hour in the back of a police car because she was arrested for shoplifting. We saw this coming, and it seems no matter what we have tried to do to teach her right from wrong, we have failed. Oddly, she was kind of happy that both me and my ex-husband showed up at the police station. Given that she is 16, is it too late for us?

Intermediate Client Statement 4

[Embarrassed] Antonio is a terror when we go out to the mall. I expect an 8-year-old not to find shopping for clothes or gifts for his cousin's birthday to be fun, but there is no reason he should act that way. The constant yelling, complaining, and whining is pretty ridiculous. Either I buy him something there to shut him up, or I have to bother my in-laws or neighbors to watch him so I can go out.

INTERMEDIATE-LEVEL CLIENT STATEMENTS FOR EXERCISE 2

Intermediate Client Statement 5

[Worried] Amani's ability to separate from me really is quite bad. It started in preschool, and here we are in third grade and she cannot be away from me or not have contact with me for too long a period of time. She won't go to a birthday party unless I go with her. She has to know my routine at all points, basically when I am coming and going, and will text me repeatedly to check on me. She has even figured out a way to instant message me from her school's computer maybe eight to 10 times/day. My husband says I shouldn't respond, and I tried that one day, and her anxiety just got worse. Now I just respond but keep it simple. I am hopeful that with age, she will just grow out of this.

🛑 **Assess and adjust the difficulty before moving to the next difficulty level (see Step 3 in the exercise instructions).**

ADVANCED-LEVEL CLIENT STATEMENTS FOR EXERCISE 2

Advanced Client Statement 1

[Annoyed] It doesn't matter what I say or do, Jasmine just flips out on me. When I try to correct her mistakes on her schoolwork in a supportive manner, she says that she is dumb and yells "you hate me" and "no one likes me." It breaks my heart, and I back off on pushing the homework and give her the space she needs, but as a result, the work doesn't get done. And for a third grader, we are only talking about 30 or 40 minutes of work. So it's not a lot. I think she has a self-esteem issue, and it may be better if you speak with her.

Advanced Client Statement 2

[Frustrated] I don't mean to label my 8-year-old as evil, but Jeremiah is evil. He cannot let things go and holds grudges. We saw him do this with his cousins, and now the school has reported that he "exacted revenge" for a perceived slight from 2 months ago by stabbing a girl with a pencil. He ended up getting a 2-day suspension. We yelled at him when he got home and took away his screen access. He doesn't seem to care. I know in our initial call you wanted to meet with me, but I am not sure why. I didn't stab the girl with a pencil.

Advanced Client Statement 3

[Angry] Malik is frankly inconsiderate. He thinks that the world revolves around him and doesn't seem to care how his behavior impacts others. As an example, we probably have been late for his sister's games 80% of the time, because he cannot be rushed in the morning and does things at his own pace. He will be on his tablet usually, and we have put together a visual schedule, have tried rewards, and even threatened punishment, but he doesn't seem to care. Does your approach work to get 9-year-olds motivated to do what's right?

Advanced Client Statement 4

[Stressed] If there is any change in routine or plans, Julianna cannot handle it. In fact, she freaks out—and more than any other 10-year-old. She is a planner of the worst sort. As an example, if we have plans for Friday, she will start checking the weather 4 days out and maybe six to eight times a day and will constantly ask, "What will we do if it rains?" She needs to know who will be there and I probably answer the same questions at least half a dozen times. If I don't answer, she freaks out. This really is anxiety, right? I can give you information about her behavior, but shouldn't the work you do be with her?

ADVANCED-LEVEL CLIENT STATEMENTS FOR EXERCISE 2

Advanced Client Statement 5

[Exasperated] The arguments we have about technology and bedtime are pretty much a daily occurrence. Javier tells me that he is the only sophomore who has a screen limit and doesn't understand why I care what he watches and what time he goes to bed since he gets good grades. It is a daily fight, and we have replaced one phone, one keyboard, and two doors and have a hole in the wall that needs patching, all from these blowups. I know he continues to find ways to use screens after the limits and have more or less given up. If you can teach him anger management skills and get him to follow the house rules, I would be thrilled.

> Assess and adjust the difficulty here (see Step 3 in the exercise instructions). If appropriate, follow the instructions to make the exercise even more challenging (see Appendix A).

Example Therapist Responses: Psychoeducation About the Functions of Child Behaviors

Remember: Trainees should attempt to improvise their own responses before reading the examples. **Do not read the following responses verbatim unless you are having trouble coming up with your own!**

EXAMPLE RESPONSES TO BEGINNER-LEVEL CLIENT STATEMENTS FOR EXERCISE 2

Example Response to Beginner Client Statement 1

It sounds like when Michelle avoids doing her homework, you get frustrated, and then eventually you argue with her, which has a negative impact on your relationship. (Criterion 1) One approach that I think may be helpful is that of behavioral parent training, or BPT. Within BPT, you and I would work together to try and understand the "why" behind her behaviors and see if we can develop preventative as well as reactive strategies to help improve her completion of her homework as well as your relationship with her. (Criterion 2) Is that something that you would like to explore as an approach to help address this? (Criterion 3)

Example Response to Beginner Client Statement 2

If I am hearing you correctly, it sounds like the majority of the challenges you are experiencing with Tom relate to his use of technology, and your strategy of shutting off all of his devices doesn't change his subsequent behavior. (Criterion 1) An approach that can be helpful for a variety of behaviors that I think we can implement here is referred to as behavioral parent training, or BPT. BPT involves a number of approaches, but at its core, we would try to look at Tom's behavior—and what precedes and what follows this behavior—to understand *why* he engages in these behaviors. We then would work to have you change the precipitates of the behavior as well as what follows to help bring about change. (Criterion 2) What are your thoughts? Would starting with an approach like this be helpful for Tom's behavior? (Criterion 3)

EXAMPLE RESPONSES TO BEGINNER-LEVEL CLIENT STATEMENTS FOR EXERCISE 2

Example Response to Beginner Client Statement 3

Based on what you have described, it sounds as if, even though there are clear rules, it is a struggle to get the girls to comply with them. And as a result, you will engage in arguments as well as some self-doubt. (Criterion 1) If our goal is to change their behavior, as well as reduce the arguing and self-doubt, an approach that I have found helpful with other families is referred to as behavioral parent training, or BPT. With BPT, we try to look at the behavior more objectively and understand factors that occur both before and after the behavior that may maintain it. In doing so, we understand better the "why" of their behavior. (Criterion 2) Do you think an approach like this would be helpful to address their behavior? (Criterion 3)

Example Response to Beginner Client Statement 4

I appreciate the frustration that you described in relation to Jaden's behavior and your awareness as to your own responses, both emotionally as well as behaviorally, with possible excessive punishment when he does not accept responsibility. (Criterion 1) Although we want to change his behavior, and this will be a main goal, we may want to start by looking at what surrounds this behavior. That is, we can look at things that come before and after his behavior to help understand *why* he continues to do this. This approach is consistent with a model of intervention called behavioral parent training, or BPT, where we look to understand the "why" or function of behavior. (Criterion 2) With the goal of changing his behavior being primary, what are your thoughts about starting to try and understand the "why" of his behavior to help begin the change process with Jaden? (Criterion 3)

Example Response to Beginner Client Statement 5

Yes, that sounds like a pretty straightforward after-school schedule. From what I hear, she doesn't stick to it, and it is almost a daily struggle, which leads to arguments and other behaviors such as bribery to get her to stick to the schedule. (Criterion 1) As we try and work on understanding how to bring about change, an approach that I think would be good for us to consider is called behavioral parent training, or BPT. In BPT, we work directly with the parents to look at the antecedents and consequences of Maya's behavior and see which ones may make sense for us to change from a parenting perspective. Yes, we want Maya to change, but in this approach at the beginning we work on changing parent behavior to address the "why" of her difficulties following the schedule. (Criterion 2) Might this approach be something you think would be helpful to address Maya's behaviors as well as your responses to these behaviors? (Criterion 3)

EXAMPLE RESPONSES TO INTERMEDIATE-LEVEL CLIENT STATEMENTS FOR EXERCISE 2

Example Response to Intermediate Client Statement 1

Thanks for sharing. From what I hear, your son engages in some fairly dismissive or even disrespectful behavior toward you, and as a result, you disengage from him, and that you consider your interaction to be quite sad. (Criterion 1) As I listened to you, I thought of an approach that is referred to as behavioral parent training, or BPT. The theory behind this approach is that most behaviors of children can be understood by discerning the "why" of their behavior—that is, what do they gain by behaving like this? This would involve looking at what comes before and after these disrespectful behaviors. He somewhat gets to escape a conversation that he does not want and also gets to keep doing what he wants. Those may be his "whys." (Criterion 2) Do you think addressing the "why" of his behavior would be helpful to consider in your situation? (Criterion 3)

EXAMPLE RESPONSES TO INTERMEDIATE-LEVEL
CLIENT STATEMENTS FOR EXERCISE 2

Example Response to Intermediate Client Statement 2

If I understand what you described, it sounds like your 7- and 9-year-old fight often, and you get pretty frustrated about it, and one of the strategies you use to manage it is to yell, and going forward you will split them up despite it being a challenge for you. (Criterion 1) Although the arguing and fighting may in fact be silly, for them, there is a reason behind it. Actually, there may be two reasons: They fight over a desired object, but maybe they also fight to get your attention, whether good or bad. We can explore these reasons and hopefully change your and their behavior through something referred to as BPT, or behavioral parent training. Here, we would look to explore the "why" of their behavior by seeing what events come before and after their behavior that set the stage for and maintain it. Then, we would work on changing those events. (Criterion 2) What are your thoughts about trying to use this approach to help you manage their behavior? (Criterion 3)

Example Response to Intermediate Client Statement 3

I have to imagine that even though you saw this coming, this must have been difficult to deal with. In addition to your description of her behavior, I also hear some self-doubt, blame, and questioning if it is too late. (Criterion 1) Obviously, you have tried and want to change her behavior. Without knowing all the circumstances, I imagine she stole something she wanted, but also based on her "happy" response you described, that she may have done this, or other behaviors, to get attention. Maybe we can have a discussion as to *why* you think she does things and look at what comes before these behaviors that may set the stage for them as well as what follows that may influence if she will do this again going forward. This is consistent with an approach called behavioral parent training and more specifically a functional, "why" analysis of behavior. (Criterion 2) Do you think it would be helpful to explore this approach to understand and intervene in Sophia's behavior? (Criterion 3)

Example Response to Intermediate Client Statement 4

Listening to you, I hear that managing Antonio's behavior in public, but more specifically while shopping for nonpreferred items, is quite challenging. (Criterion 1) I would think that if we could develop strategies to help manage these public behaviors, that would be better all around. One approach that we may wish to consider is referred to as behavioral parent training, or BPT. BPT operates under the premise that there are environmental factors surrounding this behavior that historically have led to its occurrence or recurrence. We would work together to figure out the reason for Antonio's behavior and then change these environmental factors. In the example provided, you have found these behaviors to be so difficult that you avoid taking him with you, which for him is a form of escape, or when you take him, you buy him something to manage his behavior, which for him is a reward for his difficult behavior. (Criterion 2) Do you think an approach like this would be helpful in addressing these public behaviors? (Criterion 3)

Example Response to Intermediate Client Statement 5

What you describe sounds like Amani really has difficulty separating from you and that she has certain expectations or rules about your behavior. (Criterion 1) One of the approaches that I think may be helpful is referred to as behavioral parent training. Here, we try to understand Amani's behavior by looking at the context of the event—put simply, what comes before and after the event that may in fact be accommodating her anxiety and maintaining it. She ends up avoiding doing things if you can't go and tries to get—and quite often gets—your attention when she is uncomfortable. It also sounds like you have tried not to respond and give that attention, but that made it worse. This avoidance and attention may be the reason for these behaviors. We then would work on trying to change the context and your responses. (Criterion 2) I know you have tried not responding before, but do you think us working to gather data to understand the "why" of her behavior may be helpful in changing it? (Criterion 3)

EXAMPLE RESPONSES TO ADVANCED-LEVEL CLIENT STATEMENTS FOR EXERCISE 2

Example Response to Advanced Client Statement 1

From what I hear, when you approach Jasmine to get work done, she makes a number of comments that concern you and lead you to back off, and as a result the work doesn't get done. (Criterion 1) You may be right that there may be some issues that are best addressed directly with Jasmine, but to begin, I thought we could discuss an approach called behavioral parent training, or BPT. Simply put, Jasmine's behavior doesn't exist in a vacuum. That is, there are things that occur before the behavior and things that occur after it that can influence her behavior. Here she complains and makes negative comments and then gets to escape doing the work. In BPT, we work with the parents to understand *why* she does this and then modify some of these setting issues or consequences of the behavior. (Criterion 2) While I hear your view that you think it would be better to work with her, do you think an approach like this would be helpful for addressing Jasmine's behavior initially? (Criterion 3)

Example Response to Advanced Client Statement 2

This does sound challenging when I hear you describe some of Jeremiah's behaviors and difficulty in letting things go both at home and at school. It also sounds like your responses have not brought about the change you wanted. (Criterion 1) Your comment about why to meet with you is a fair one. Initially, I think it may be helpful to try and understand *why* Jeremiah does these things by reviewing together what happens before and then after he does these behaviors. Here, based on what was described, he got "revenge" but now also gets to avoid school. The understanding of the "why" and making changes to the factors that influence his behaviors is at the core of a clinical approach known as behavioral parent training. (Criterion 2) While we may eventually work with Jeremiah to promote some flexibility in how he thinks, do you think the behavioral parent training approach, and trying to understand the events that surround his misbehavior, would be helpful initially? (Criterion 3)

Example Response to Advanced Client Statement 3

It makes sense that you want to get Malik to do what is right and, in the example you provided, to be more considerate of others, especially family members. It also sounds like you have tried a few approaches, and they have not really changed his behavior. (Criterion 1) What may be helpful initially is that we use an approach called behavioral parent training. Here, we would work together to try and examine the context where his behavior occurs. That is, what comes before and what comes after that impacts the behavior. This helps us understand the function or the "why" of his behavior. We then work to address this function by changing the context. In the example provided, he gets to spend more time on his tablet. That may somewhat be *why* he does these behaviors. (Criterion 2) I know that you want him to be motivated to change his behaviors, but what are your thoughts—would you want to start with this approach of working with you to try to get Malik to change his behavior? (Criterion 3)

Example Response to Advanced Client Statement 4

Based on what you describe, yes, it sounds like this is anxiety and like Julianna does a number of behaviors such as checking the weather and seeking reassurance that, at least in the short term, reduce her anxiety. But in the long run, those reassurance-type behaviors actually strengthen these anxious thoughts and behaviors. (Criterion 1) An approach that I would recommend is referred to as behavioral parent training. Here, initially we would work mostly independent of Julianna on understanding what motivates her to engage in these behaviors. Basically the "why." Often the "why" comes from factors that precede and follow her anxious behaviors. Then, we would work together on changing these factors. Here, her "why" may be the attention and reassurance that she gets. (Criterion 2) Wanting me to work with her makes sense, and we may get there eventually, but do you think an approach like this where we work together to reduce the strength of her worries would be helpful for Julianna and your family? (Criterion 3)

**EXAMPLE RESPONSES TO ADVANCED-LEVEL
CLIENT STATEMENTS FOR EXERCISE 2**

Example Response to Advanced Client Statement 5

It sounds like these daily arguments about technology and bedtime have gotten pretty explosive and have led to some destruction of property in the home and also to some degree have led to you give up trying to change his behaviors. (Criterion 1) I do think it would be helpful for Javier to learn some anger management strategies, and we can introduce that. I imagine he may not be so motivated at this point to change. Perhaps before any direct work with Javier, we could try and understand the "why" of his behavior and what factors may in fact influence those behaviors. This is consistent with an approach called behavioral parent training, where we learn how to change his behavior by changing your behavioral responses to his anger. Based on what you described, he finds ways to get the screen time anyway, and his anger has, at points, led you to give up. These may be the "whys" of his behavior. (Criterion 2) I know you want him to learn anger management skills and follow rules, but do you think if we are able to understand *why* he does these behaviors and then change your behaviors we might start to bring about change for Javier? (Criterion 3)

Identifying and Validating Parent Affect

Preparations for Exercise 3

1. Read the instructions in Chapter 2.

2. Download the Deliberate Practice Reaction Form and the Deliberate Practice Diary Form at https://www.apa.org/pubs/books/deliberate-practice-behavioral-parent-training (see the "Resources" tab; also available in Appendixes A and B, respectively).

Skill Description

Skill Difficulty Level: Beginner

The main purpose of this skill is for clinicians to learn how to recognize and validate emotions that parents may be experiencing and provide psychoeducation on how parents' emotions can influence their response to their child. Many of the principles of behavioral parent training (BPT) are fairly straightforward, as they aim to teach parents how to use positive reinforcement (e.g., praise, privileges, or tokens that may be exchanged for a reward) more effectively to promote behavioral change (Eyberg et al., 2008). However, dissemination of information to parents and then having this knowledge lead to effective application may be influenced by a number of variables, including parent emotion or affective responses to their child's behavior. Parents will often report considerable emotional experiences within their role as parents (Rueger et al., 2011). Positive feelings have been found to be more strongly related to supportive parenting, whereas negative feelings have been found to be more strongly related to hostile parenting (Rueger et al., 2011). As you work with parents, it is critical to not just teach them the principles of behavior management but to also recognize when they themselves are experiencing strong emotions and validate what they are experiencing and help them consider the impact of that emotion on their behavior as parents.

https://doi.org/10.1037/0000484-005

Deliberate Practice in Behavioral Parent Training, by M. D. Terjesen, H. B. Vidair, P. S. Ohr, O. A. Walsh, T. Rousmaniere, and A. Vaz

Clarifying the emotion identified and its role in parenting is often not the reason that parents engage in BPT. That is, they come to learn techniques or approaches to change their child's behavior rather than their own emotions. As such, it is important to help parents understand why it is important to be aware of their emotions. Clinicians should acknowledge parents' emotions. Validation lowers emotional intensity and increases the likelihood the person will remain engaged in the conversation (Rathus & Miller, 2015). In addition, validating parent emotions helps strengthen the relationship between you, as the clinician, and the parent (Rathus & Miller, 2015). By validating a parent's emotional experience, you can help foster a strong therapeutic alliance between you and the parent (Rathus & Miller, 2015). It is also important to provide psychoeducation on how our emotions affect our responses. When validating an emotion, it can also be beneficial to identify a healthier emotion for the parent (Collard & O'Kelly, 2011). For instance, if a parent is discussing how angry they are, validating frustration as the emotion to work toward may be helpful for the parent in assisting with their coping and management of that emotional state (Collard & O'Kelly, 2011).

Examples of this skill range in difficulty so that clinicians can practice initial mastery of it, as well as its use in more challenging interactions with parents. In the beginner difficulty level, the parent's emotion is stated in the client prompt. In the intermediate level, parents do not explicitly state their emotional state but describe emotional behaviors for the clinician to identify their emotion. Finally, in the advanced difficulty level, parents identify more than one emotion they are experiencing in relation to a challenging situation with their children.

SKILL CRITERIA FOR EXERCISE 3

1. **Identify and validate the feeling or feelings the parent is expressing in the moment.**
2. Provide psychoeducation on how their feelings can influence their response to their child's behaviors.
3. Invite the client to examine emotions related to their parenting skills.
   - **Beginner level: The emotion is stated in the prompt.**
   - **Intermediate level: The emotional state is described.**
   - **Advanced level: More than one emotion is experienced by the parent.**

Examples of Therapists Identifying and Validating Parent Affect

Example 1

CLIENT: [*regretful*] I missed her first day of preschool when I probably could have rescheduled that meeting. What kind of father am I? I felt so guilty and ended up trying to make up for it by giving her everything she wanted all weekend. That was also a big mistake.

THERAPIST: I hear you are feeling guilty about missing Sam's first day of school. I can understand feeling some regret over that. (Criterion 1) I think it's great that you noticed how it changed your parenting behaviors because you were feeling guilty. This is common for many parents as parenting does not operate in an emotional vacuum and emotions can impact parenting and vice versa. (Criterion 2) I am wondering if you have noticed your guilt impacting your parenting in another situation and if you would want to explore this. (Criterion 3)

Example 2

CLIENT: [*exasperated*] If there is a "how to push your parents' buttons" book, then my 9-year-old, Yoel, is one of the authors. I get so upset at him that even after the argument has ended, it takes me a long time to calm down.

THERAPIST: I hear you describe getting really upset at Yoel and I am wondering if during the arguments that upset experience is anger more than any other emotion. Some level of anger or frustration makes sense when you think that someone is pushing your buttons constantly. (Criterion 1) When we are in a heightened emotional state, it can affect how we respond to different situations, like engaging in an argument. (Criterion 2) I imagine that you respond to him differently when you are this angry compared to when you are calm. Do you think that to start, it would be beneficial for us to consider your emotional responses so that we do not let your buttons get pushed? (Criterion 3)

Example 3

CLIENT: [*distressed*] I try and I try and no matter what, I cannot get Jamie, my 14-year-old son, to listen to me. He treats me so disrespectfully and yells at me in front of my in-laws. I know they are all judging me, and I just want to cry. I try to avoid family events now, which is so sad. When it comes to parenting, I'm a failure.

THERAPIST: This sounds really challenging, and I am hearing a few different emotions you are having, which makes complete sense. It sounds like you believe that you are being judged by others when Jamie is disrespectful and feel embarrassed by this and like you also feel sad you are missing family events. (Criterion 1) When our emotions become so strong, they can affect the decisions we make with our children, like deciding to skip a family event. (Criterion 2) Are these feelings happening often or are there other situations that you are avoiding, and do you think it would be helpful for us to discuss the role of emotions in this? (Criterion 3)

INSTRUCTIONS FOR EXERCISE 3
Step 1: Role-Play and Feedback
• The client says the first beginner client statement. The therapist **improvises** a response based on the skill criteria. • The trainer (or, if not available, the client) provides **brief** feedback based on the skill criteria. • The client then repeats the same statement, and the therapist again improvises a response. The trainer (or client) again provides brief feedback.
Step 2: Repeat
• Repeat Step 1 for all the statements **in the current difficulty level** (beginner, intermediate, or advanced).
Step 3: Assess and Adjust Difficulty
• The therapist completes the Deliberate Practice Reaction Form (see Appendix A) and decides whether to make the exercise easier or harder or to repeat the same difficulty level.
Step 4: Repeat for Approximately 15 Minutes
• Repeat Steps 1 to 3 for at least 15 minutes. • The trainees then switch therapist and client roles and start over.

➡️ **Now it's your turn! Follow the exercise instructions.**

Remember: The goal of the role play is for trainees to practice improvising responses to the client statements in a manner that (a) uses the skill criteria and (b) feels authentic for the trainee. **Example therapist responses for each client statement are provided at the end of this exercise. Trainees should attempt to improvise their own responses before reading the examples.**

BEGINNER-LEVEL CLIENT STATEMENTS FOR EXERCISE 3
Beginner Client Statement 1
[Hopeless] I was at the supermarket yesterday, and Jason, who is 5 years old, just threw a temper tantrum in the middle of the store. I know I'm supposed to ignore him, but everyone was staring at me, and it was really so embarrassing. They were definitely judging me. I couldn't do it. I bought him the candy he so desperately had to have.
Beginner Client Statement 2
[Exasperated] I asked Seamus to put his laundry away on Sunday before the school week started. I even folded it for him. All he had to do was open his drawers and put the clothes in it. It's nothing crazy. He's 10 now. Monday morning, I go into his room and what's there? His clothes. I just got so angry at him that I started screaming at the top of my lungs for him to come to the room. It was not the best start of the week for either of us and set us both up for a rough day at school and work.
Beginner Client Statement 3
[Stressed] Penny is in the third grade, and she has her first field trip tomorrow. I am just so nervous about her going without me. I have gone on every trip. I am thinking about following the bus. My partner said I am crazy.
Beginner Client Statement 4
[Resignation] I know I keep saying this, but I am a single parent to a highly hormonal 15-year-old girl. Every second Lucy is pushing my buttons and at this point I give up. I just feel depressed and helpless about what to try next with her. I just don't even set boundaries anymore. I cannot deal with the fight it becomes.
Beginner Client Statement 5
[Defeated] My husband and I got into a huge argument about how to deal with Noah skipping school. This may sound silly, but I'm just feeling incredibly sad about Noah's behaviors and blame myself for not being a good enough parent to get him to school. This is my job, and I am a failure. It was dinnertime, and we were supposed to talk about the plan for school this week. I just couldn't go. Instead, I got into bed and just laid under the covers.

🛑 **Assess and adjust the difficulty before moving to the next difficulty level (see Step 3 in the exercise instructions).**

INTERMEDIATE-LEVEL CLIENT STATEMENTS FOR EXERCISE 3
Intermediate Client Statement 1
[Exasperated] My kids will not leave me alone while I am trying to make dinner. They say, "Mommy, I need this" or "I need help with my homework" and are constantly interrupting me. I just find myself getting so upset with them. They are all older than 7 and can handle things themselves now. I have yelled at them more times than I care to mention about things that really don't warrant that kind of response.

INTERMEDIATE-LEVEL CLIENT STATEMENTS FOR EXERCISE 3

Intermediate Client Statement 2

[Stressed] I let Cody carpool for soccer practice for the first time this past Tuesday, since that is something he has always wanted to do and he completed all his chores this week. He is 12 now too. I am so proud of him. He really likes this friend and the mother seems responsible, but I just kept thinking about everything that could go wrong. I was a wreck the whole time—couldn't get anything done on my list. I just kept checking his location and I almost called him.

Intermediate Client Statement 3

[Hopeless] I walk in from a long day of work and Audrey and Maddie immediately start fighting. They are so young, only 7 and 9, and already hate each other. I just keep thinking to myself, what did I do wrong? I must have done something wrong. I started sobbing immediately in the middle of the living room in front of the babysitter. I just had to leave them with her and lock myself in my room. I wish that didn't happen.

Intermediate Client Statement 4

[Anxious] My 14-year-old, Yianna, asked me if she could go to the movies alone with her friends. I know she is getting older, but I still don't know if she can handle it. I just keep thinking, what if she chokes on popcorn and no one can help her? I know it sounds silly, but I can't stop these thoughts from racing through my mind. I told her no, but now I am thinking maybe that wasn't fair and I just acted on my impulses.

Intermediate Client Statement 5

[Upset] Wilma got invited to the senior prom and is so excited. Before you know it, I am going to be all alone. You know, she leaves for college in only 8 weeks. It will just be me. I know I should have been happy when she told me, but I wasn't. I gave her a hard time about going and almost told her she couldn't. I don't even know why I would think to not let my daughter go to her prom.

🖐 **Assess and adjust the difficulty before moving to the next difficulty level (see Step 3 in the exercise instructions).**

ADVANCED-LEVEL CLIENT STATEMENTS FOR EXERCISE 3

Advanced Client Statement 1

[Stressed] Jordan starts preschool in a few weeks. I know this could be a good opportunity for him, but I still don't know if I made the right decision to let him go. If something happens, how do I know the teachers are going to call me? And I am just so upset that I am even letting myself think about these horrible situations. Jordan has repeatedly asked me if his friend Calla would be in his class, and I got so upset I flipped out and did not answer in the nicest way. He started crying and saying that he doesn't want to go to school now.

Advanced Client Statement 2

[Overwhelmed] Until yesterday, Jessica, my 4-year-old, had been doing so well in not having any tantrums this week. I was just so happy. I brought her to the playground, and we had such a nice time. Then, on the way home, she wanted ice cream, but we hadn't had dinner yet. She had one of her worst meltdowns when I told her no. I was so taken aback and angry. I screamed at her so loud. I think the people at the park could hear us from the car. Now, of course, I feel terrible. How can I have so many feelings in such a short period of time?

ADVANCED-LEVEL CLIENT STATEMENTS FOR EXERCISE 3
Advanced Client Statement 3
[Frustrated] So I was on the phone with my friend who I haven't talked to in forever, and Jackson literally would not stop interrupting me. He is old enough to leave me alone for 5 minutes. I couldn't help myself, I screamed at him to leave my room. Then I felt so bad that I had to hang up with my friend anyway because I couldn't even focus on what they were saying. I feel so embarrassed because I can only imagine what they think of me as a parent.
Advanced Client Statement 4
[Anxious] Based on the reward system we built, Mickey earned getting to go away to camp for a full week. Honestly, when we made it, I only agreed to that being a reward because I never thought he could do it. I am feeling so guilty that I had that little faith in my son. And now he is going to camp alone. What happens if he reverts to his old behaviors? I just keep having nightmare after nightmare. I think I may still tell him he can't go.
Advanced Client Statement 5
[Ashamed] I am so embarrassed to even be telling you this. Andreas came to me to tell me he broke up with his partner and the first thing I said was "Well you haven't been together that long anyway and you're only 16." The second I said it, I completely regretted it. They weren't good together, but why did I say that? He definitely didn't appreciate that response and now may not confide in me. You must think I am a terrible parent. I certainly do. I cried for close to an hour that night.

> 🕐 **Assess and adjust the difficulty here (see Step 3 in the exercise instructions). If appropriate, follow the instructions to make the exercise even more challenging (see Appendix A).**

Example Therapist Responses: Identifying and Validating Parent Affect

Remember: Trainees should attempt to improvise their own responses before reading the examples. **Do not read the following responses verbatim unless you are having trouble coming up with your own!**

EXAMPLE RESPONSES TO BEGINNER-LEVEL CLIENT STATEMENTS FOR EXERCISE 3
Example Response to Beginner Client Statement 1
I can completely understand believing that you are being judged and feeling embarrassment over Jason's temper tantrum at the store. (Criterion 1) Great job in trying to ignore him. I am wondering if the intensity of your embarrassment led to you buying him the candy. We know that our own emotions as parents play a role in how we parent. (Criterion 2) When you think back, has your embarrassment changed your parenting before, and do you think it's something you want to explore more? (Criterion 3)

EXAMPLE RESPONSES TO BEGINNER-LEVEL CLIENT STATEMENTS FOR EXERCISE 3

Example Response to Beginner Client Statement 2

It sounds like you are really angry with Seamus for not following directions and not putting his laundry away. Getting frustrated, especially after you tried to make it easier by folding it for him, makes sense. (Criterion 1) When our emotions become heightened, it can impact how we react to our kids, like screaming at the top of our lungs. (Criterion 2) I am wondering if it would make sense to discuss other settings in which you become so angry that screaming seems to be the only option and see if we can work on having you feel a healthier emotion, like frustration. (Criterion 3)

Example Response to Beginner Client Statement 3

Oh wow, Penny's first field trip! I hear you describe that you are feeling nervous about this milestone, and I think logically some discomfort or concern makes sense. (Criterion 1) I am wondering if your intense worries are affecting your decision to follow the bus. We know that our feelings, like nervousness, can alter how we respond to situations our children are going through. (Criterion 2) Can you think of any other time your nervousness impacted how you responded to a situation with Penny? Is this something you think may be worth exploring? (Criterion 3)

Example Response to Beginner Client Statement 4

That sounds really challenging. I hear that you are feeling depressed right now in trying to figure out how to best parent Lucy. (Criterion 1) Parenting is really hard, and then when we throw our own emotions into the mix, it becomes even more challenging. Our emotions can play a big role in our decisions on how to parent. (Criterion 2) I am wondering if your feelings of depression may be related to your behavior of not setting boundaries anymore. Is this something you think is worth us discussing? (Criterion 3)

Example Response to Beginner Client Statement 5

That does not sound silly at all. I think it is completely understandable to have some level of sadness regarding this situation with Noah. (Criterion 1) When feeling sad, sometimes we want to withdraw from situations. I am curious if you think your feelings of sadness prevented you from going to dinner to talk about the plan for school this week. Evidence shows that our own feelings can affect our parental decision making. (Criterion 2) Have you ever noticed your emotions like sadness before in a tough parenting situation and how they may impact your decision making, and do you think it could be worth discussing in more detail? (Criterion 3)

EXAMPLE RESPONSES TO INTERMEDIATE-LEVEL CLIENT STATEMENTS FOR EXERCISE 3

Example Response to Intermediate Client Statement 1

While you called it upset, what I hear is that it sounds like you were becoming really angry and frustrated. I can completely understand feeling some frustration, and it has to be really hard to get things done. (Criterion 1) I imagine that if you are getting angry it may also impact you in other ways. Evidence suggests that our own emotions also play a big role in how we parent. (Criterion 2) I am wondering if, to start, maybe it would be worth talking about your own emotional responses to when your kids are interrupting you? (Criterion 3)

EXAMPLE RESPONSES TO INTERMEDIATE-LEVEL CLIENT STATEMENTS FOR EXERCISE 3

Example Response to Intermediate Client Statement 2

Thank you for sharing this. From what you described, I hear some considerable anxiety that you were experiencing when you let him carpool to practice on Tuesday. Given that this was the first time that you have done this, some discomfort makes sense. (Criterion 1) It seems like your anxiety led you to checking his location. We know that our feelings impact our behaviors, and this happens with parenting behaviors too. (Criterion 2) Considering how high your anxiety was, do you think it would be helpful for us to explore your emotions as they relate to parenting? (Criterion 3)

Example Response to Intermediate Client Statement 3

It sounds like you are having a lot of self-blaming thoughts, and while you didn't specifically say your emotion, it sounds like you are experiencing intense sadness about the girls' relationship. That makes a lot of sense. (Criterion 1) It sounds like the emotions were so strong, you just started crying. Our own emotions can affect how we handle challenging situations with our kids and sometimes react in ways we do not want to. (Criterion 2) I am curious if you can think of other times when your emotions impacted your parenting and if it would be worth diving into more? (Criterion 3)

Example Response to Intermediate Client Statement 4

Concern here doesn't sound silly. It sounds like you were experiencing some anxiety around Yianna going to the movies alone. This makes sense, since she is now hitting that age where she wants to be more independent from you. (Criterion 1) Great job in noticing that your emotions affected the first decision you made. Evidence shows that parents' emotions impact our parenting decisions. (Criterion 2) I am wondering if you have ever noticed your anxiety impacting your parenting before and if it is worth us exploring. (Criterion 3)

Example Response to Intermediate Client Statement 5

It sounds like when you think about being alone—not just on the night of the prom, but when Wilma leaves for college in a few weeks—that you feel very sad. I can completely understand some sadness—being an empty-nester is a big transition. First, I just want to tell you I can understand feeling that way. (Criterion 1) Second, great job in recognizing that you had the reaction not to let her go to prom. Our emotions, including those feelings of loneliness in the future, can affect how we make parental decisions, like letting your daughter go to prom. (Criterion 2) I think it may be helpful to recognize if these emotions have affected your parenting in any other ways. What do you think? (Criterion 3)

EXAMPLE RESPONSES TO ADVANCED-LEVEL CLIENT STATEMENTS FOR EXERCISE 3

Example Response to Advanced Client Statement 1

It sounds like you are anxious about Jordan starting preschool and then get very frustrated as to his repeated questioning. This is your first child going to school. I think it's reasonable to have some strong feelings about this. (Criterion 1) Your strong emotions as a parent can impact your parenting behaviors, like being short with Jordan. (Criterion 2) I am wondering if it would be helpful to start today by discussing your feelings around Jordan's start to school and how they may affect your parenting behaviors. (Criterion 3)

EXAMPLE RESPONSES TO ADVANCED-LEVEL CLIENT STATEMENTS FOR EXERCISE 3

Example Response to Advanced Client Statement 2

We can have many feelings all at once. From what you're describing it sounds like you were feeling excited about how well Jessica played at the park, then became angry once she had a tantrum, and then started to feel guilty about your angry response. I can get how you had all of those feelings. (Criterion 1) It sounds like your anger escalated to the point that you screamed. When our emotions become really heightened, it can affect how we respond to tough situations our child may put us in, like how to respond to a tantrum. (Criterion 2) Have you noticed how when you are angry, your response may be different from when you are calm? I am wondering if this may be worth exploring more. (Criterion 3)

Example Response to Advanced Client Statement 3

It sounds like you became angry at Jackson bothering you and then started feeling embarrassed by your reaction. This can be common for parents, and experiencing some emotions in these moments makes sense. (Criterion 1) Our emotions, like the anger you felt from being interrupted as well as the guilt you felt after you yelled, can impact how we respond, like yelling at him when angry and having difficulty focusing when embarrassed. (Criterion 2) I am wondering if it would make sense to start the session by exploring more about how your emotions may be impacting how you react to and parent Jackson? (Criterion 3)

Example Response to Advanced Client Statement 4

It sounds like you are feeling guilty about not believing in your son and are now anxious about him going to camp. I can understand having a number of strong feelings related to this. (Criterion 1) When we have intense emotions, evidence shows that these emotions can actually affect how we parent, like not allowing our child to do something because of our own worries. (Criterion 2) Given how intense your guilt and anxiety seem, before we discuss your plans, do you think it would be helpful for us to explore your emotions as they relate to parenting? (Criterion 3)

Example Response to Advanced Client Statement 5

It sounds like you are having a few different feelings—you feel guilty about your response to Andreas and then maybe you feel some sadness when you think about your parenting skills. That is completely understandable. (Criterion 1) Parenting doesn't occur in an emotional vacuum, so when we experience a lot of our own feelings when parenting, it can affect our responses. (Criterion 2) I am wondering if it would make sense to explore this further and talk about other situations in which your emotions may have impacted your response to Andreas. (Criterion 3)

Teaching Parents How to Provide Praise

Preparations for Exercise 4

1. Read the instructions in Chapter 2.

2. Download the Deliberate Practice Reaction Form and the Deliberate Practice Diary Form at https://www.apa.org/pubs/books/deliberate-practice-behavioral-parent-training (see the "Resources" tab; also available in Appendixes A and B, respectively).

Skill Description

Skill Difficulty Level: Beginner

The main purpose of the praise skill is to teach parents to strategically increase behaviors they want from their children via verbal reinforcement. In our experience, parents often begin behavioral parent training (BPT) wanting to learn how to decrease or stop their children's negative behavior, often through punitive techniques. Instead, BPT programs initially focus on teaching parents positive strategies, such as praise, to help increase desired, prosocial behaviors that they want their children to perform (e.g., Barkley, 2013; Kazdin, 2005; McNeil & Hembree-Kigin, 2010). Praise teaches children the behaviors their parents wish to see more of, and children are likely to respond to positive feedback about behaviors their parents appreciate. Furthermore, parents typically begin BPT once interactions about their child's behavior have become routinely negative. Implementing punishment at the onset may further exacerbate this negative pattern of interaction, while praise begins to cultivate a positive interaction by pointing out what the parents think their child is doing well. In addition, learning how to provide effective praise is easier than successfully implementing punishment strategies. Therefore, clinicians can explain to parents that BPT focuses on initially teaching positive parenting skills before disciplinary strategies, which they will subsequently learn once they have some practice with positive parenting skills.

https://doi.org/10.1037/0000484-006

Deliberate Practice in Behavioral Parent Training, by M. D. Terjesen, H. B. Vidair, P. S. Ohr, O. A. Walsh, T. Rousmaniere, and A. Vaz

Clinicians should explain to parents that praise can be used as a strategic method for increasing the behavior they want to see from their child. To achieve this, parents can be taught to identify a negative behavior they wish to change and then identify the positive opposite of that behavior (Kazdin, 2005). For example, if a parent wants their child to stop interrupting, the positive opposite would be for the child to wait quietly until the parent finishes speaking. When they see their child engage in the positive opposite behavior, they should provide praise for it. The praise should be specific, often referred to in BPT programs as *labeled praise*, so the child knows exactly what the praise is for (McNeil & Hembree-Kigin, 2010). In addition, the parent should praise their child immediately, so the behavior is immediately reinforced. Furthermore, parents should initially praise this behavior every time they see it. Lastly, parents should ensure they sound enthusiastic while praising, as well as genuine about how much they like the behavior (McNeil & Hembree-Kigin, 2010).

Recognizing any hesitations parents have about using the praise skill is important and part of treatment acceptability. For example, we have found parents sometimes do not like the idea of praising their child because they think the child should behave as expected without reward. Parents can be validated for thinking this way while pointing out that unfortunately, their child is not performing the desired behavior at this time. Praising this behavior as described here is likely to increase the behavior moving forward. Much like we have communicated in Chapter 1 of this volume, the last criterion of some BPT skills expresses the expectation that the clinician will assess for treatment acceptability. For the praise skill, we decided to focus on asking parents how helpful they find the skill as well as their willingness to try it.

After the clinician has taught the parent how to provide praise, related homework can be assigned (see Exercise 12). The clinician can check on the parent's homework practice the following week and troubleshoot any difficulties.

Examples of the praise skills range in difficulty so clinicians can practice initial mastery of this skill, as well as its use in more challenging interactions with parents. We have structured these examples so that in the beginner difficulty level, the parent has recently started therapy and is interested in learning how to improve their child's behavior. For the intermediate difficulty level, parents have tried praising their child but are not seeing desired improvements. Finally, in the advanced difficulty level, the parent hesitates or has concerns about using praise to facilitate behavioral change. Several later skills directly build on the praise skill, including positive attention (Exercise 5), planned ignoring (Exercise 6), communication (Exercise 7), positive incentives (Exercise 8), and homework planning (Exercise 12).

SKILL CRITERIA FOR EXERCISE 4

1. Provide psychoeducation about the importance of praise for increasing a desired behavior or the positive opposite of the undesired behavior.
2. Teach the parents how to provide praise (i.e., specific, immediate, every time, with enthusiasm) and provide an example of how to use praise in the situation described.
3. Ask the parents questions that reflect treatment acceptability (e.g., how helpful they find the skill and their willingness to try it).

Examples of Therapists Teaching Parents How to Provide Praise

Example 1

CLIENT: [*pleading*] I keep giving Lydia a sticker when she does what I ask, and I say "nice job" or "I'm proud of you," but I really don't want to have to bribe my child to do things that she should be doing. There has to be a better way.

THERAPIST: It sounds like you are on the right track, and though it feels like bribery, research shows that praising Lydia for doing what you ask is strategic because providing praise will make her likely to continue to comply. (Criterion 1) One change I'd suggest is being specific about what behavior your praise is for. In addition, you want to provide the praise immediately after she does what you ask—frequently and with enthusiasm. For example, if you tell her to put away her markers and she does so, you could say "Nice job putting your markers away!" or "I'm so proud of you for putting your markers away when I told you to!" (Criterion 2) How helpful does this sound? Would you be willing to try it? (Criterion 3)

Example 2

CLIENT: [*hopeless*] Zaynab just doesn't listen and continues to hit her younger brother, Hassan. She's 5 and thinks that she is the parent. I can tell her "no hitting" over and over, but she still does it. I am at a loss.

THERAPIST: Research shows you can reduce the hitting, the behavior you don't want, by identifying and praising the positive opposite of that behavior. This will make behavior you want more likely to reoccur. (Criterion 1) When you praise, you want to do so immediately—whenever you see the behavior—and enthusiastically. Also be specific about the behavior you are praising. In this case, the positive opposite of Zaynab hitting her brother could be keeping her hands to herself. Each time you notice her doing this when she would typically hit her brother, say something right away, like, "Wow, I love how you are keeping your hands to yourself while you play with Hassan!" (Criterion 2) Does this seem helpful? Can we have you experiment with praise this week? (Criterion 3)

Example 3

CLIENT: [*exasperated*] You have told me to praise Brandon, but when he does four bad things and one good thing, how am I supposed to praise him? Like he always takes his tablet out when he isn't supposed to. He might listen to my reasoning for why he should put it away, but then he goes right back to playing his games!

THERAPIST: We find praising behavior we want rather than focusing on behavior we don't want makes it more likely for us to increase desired behavior. (Criterion 1) It can help to praise the one good thing you see right away, every time you see it. You also want to be specific and genuinely point out what you like about Brandon's behavior. If he keeps taking out his tablet when he is not supposed to and says he doesn't want to turn it off, but pauses his game when you speak, you can say, "I really appreciate you pausing your game to have this conversation. It feels good to see you are listening to me." (Criterion 2) Does that seem useful? Would you be open to practicing this? (Criterion 3)

INSTRUCTIONS FOR EXERCISE 4

Step 1: Role-Play and Feedback

- The client says the first beginner client statement. The therapist **improvises** a response based on the skill criteria.
- The trainer (or, if not available, the client) provides **brief** feedback based on the skill criteria.
- The client then repeats the same statement, and the therapist again improvises a response. The trainer (or client) again provides brief feedback.

Step 2: Repeat

- Repeat Step 1 for all the statements **in the current difficulty level** (beginner, intermediate, or advanced).

Step 3: Assess and Adjust Difficulty

- The therapist completes the Deliberate Practice Reaction Form (see Appendix A) and decides whether to make the exercise easier or harder or to repeat the same difficulty level.

Step 4: Repeat for Approximately 15 Minutes

- Repeat Steps 1 to 3 for at least 15 minutes.
- The trainees then switch therapist and client roles and start over.

➡ **Now it's your turn! Follow the exercise instructions.**

Remember: The goal of the role play is for trainees to practice improvising responses to the client statements in a manner that (a) uses the skill criteria and (b) feels authentic for the trainee. **Example therapist responses for each client statement are provided at the end of this exercise. Trainees should attempt to improvise their own responses before reading the examples.**

BEGINNER-LEVEL CLIENT STATEMENTS FOR EXERCISE 4

Beginner Client Statement 1

[Annoyed] Every night it's a struggle to get Evan to brush his teeth before bed. He knows by now that it has to get done—he's 4 years old—but he doesn't like to get up from the couch to do it! How can I get him to do this every night?

Beginner Client Statement 2

[Confused] Nia has been insisting on bringing her toys into the playground. I'm fine with that, as long as she is willing to share. Sometimes she does, but other times she tells the other kids they're her toys and they can't touch them. I know she's only 3 and doesn't fully understand sharing her belongings. What can I do to make her more willing to share?

Beginner Client Statement 3

[Curious] I know a lot of parenting programs for little kids focus on praise for good behavior, which makes sense to me. But how can I use praise with my 9-year-old to get them to behave better, like when I want them to clean up their toys?

Beginner Client Statement 4

[Frustrated] Soraya takes so long to get ready for school. I get that at 12 she wants to look good, but other people need to get in the bathroom, and she just takes her sweet time in there! I've told her to get ready faster, and she does the first day I say it, but then falls right back into her old pattern. How can I get her to speed up more consistently?

BEGINNER-LEVEL CLIENT STATEMENTS FOR EXERCISE 4

Beginner Client Statement 5

[Excited] Get this: I noticed Sam putting a pile of his clean clothes in his drawers the other day. I didn't ask him to do that! He's usually the one leaving his clothes on the floor! Maybe now that he's planning to apply to colleges he wants to practice managing more on his own. I was so proud, but I didn't say anything because I wasn't sure if I should point it out. What do you think?

> **Assess and adjust the difficulty before moving to the next difficulty level (see Step 3 in the exercise instructions).**

INTERMEDIATE-LEVEL CLIENT STATEMENTS FOR EXERCISE 4

Intermediate Client Statement 1

[Hopeless] Four is such a hard age. Leo just doesn't listen when I tell him to stop in the playground. He will play nicely on the slide. But as soon as the big kids come out of the building, he climbs up the slide with them, no matter how many times I tell him to stop! I just want him to slide down the regular way before he gets hurt, but it feels impossible.

Intermediate Client Statement 2

[Skeptical] Oliver, my 9-year-old, really makes a mess when he is eating. Occasionally he will clean up the crumbs but not if he's eager to play or watch TV. I even told him this morning that I like when he cleans and to please do so, but he didn't. Are you sure that praise will get him to clean up after himself more regularly?

Intermediate Client Statement 3

[Cynical] You're telling me to praise Lucy, and I do. I always tell her things like she's pretty and so smart for an 11-year-old. I don't think it helps her behave though. Like I need her to stop finishing her homework last minute. So how is praise supposed to help?

Intermediate Client Statement 4

[Concerned] I really want Maya to stop staying up so late on her phone. She really needs her sleep because her high school starts early in the morning. She does this most nights. I've learned it doesn't help to berate her about it. So last night she actually went to bed on time, and I said, "Thank goodness, you finally did something I said!" But I don't think she appreciated this, either. I don't know what to do.

Intermediate Client Statement 5

[Impatient] We've been trying to get Lani to pack her backpack on the nights before school. But she is not that motivated, even though she's already 14. I know she has done it some nights, but I'm not sure how often. Once I did see her do it, and I told her I was proud of her for getting her bag together. But there are still times when she's running late in the morning putting her stuff together. How can I get her to make getting ready the night before a habit?

> **Assess and adjust the difficulty before moving to the next difficulty level (see Step 3 in the exercise instructions).**

ADVANCED-LEVEL CLIENT STATEMENTS FOR EXERCISE 4
Advanced Client Statement 1
[Stubborn] I am a believer in hard work, so I don't like setting the stage at 3 years old that Carlos is going to get praise for anything he does. It's like everyone getting a trophy for participating in his soccer class. I want to save compliments for something exemplary.
Advanced Client Statement 2
[Assertive] Shira is already 7. She should know she can't speak to us disrespectfully. For example, we will tell her it's time to take a bath, and she will often talk back, saying she doesn't have to. Shouldn't we start by punishing her for that?
Advanced Client Statement 3
[Arrogant] Certainly by the time I was 9, I knew not to mess with my parents! My siblings and I were terrified to disobey them. Just one of my mother's looks would have me do what she expected, as I knew if I didn't, I'd get a whooping! But nowadays we aren't supposed to spank our kids. So how can I get Mara to follow directions just by praising her?
Advanced Client Statement 4
[Despondent] It's really hard to imagine finding something to praise about Jordan's current homework habits. Now that he's in 10th grade, the work is harder, so it's even more important that he sit down and get it done. But do you think he cares? If he doesn't care, how can I?
Advanced Client Statement 5
[Doubtful] Kierra is 17 and still living under our roof but thinks she can use our credit card without our permission and go out whenever she wants. I am not sure I can sound enthusiastic about anything she does. How will I get the words out of my mouth?

> 👆 **Assess and adjust the difficulty here (see Step 3 in the exercise instructions). If appropriate, follow the instructions to make the exercise even more challenging (see Appendix A).**

Example Therapist Responses: Teaching Parents How to Provide Praise

Remember: Trainees should attempt to improvise their own responses before reading the examples. **Do not read the following responses verbatim unless you are having trouble coming up with your own!**

EXAMPLE RESPONSES TO BEGINNER-LEVEL CLIENT STATEMENTS FOR EXERCISE 4
Example Response to Beginner Client Statement 1
One thing research has found effective is praising a child for behavior we want to see more of, or the positive opposite of the problematic behavior. With Evan, this would be getting up to brush his teeth. (Criterion 1) Effective praise involves labeling the positive opposite you want to see every time it happens. It's best if praise immediately follows the behavior. Kids also find it rewarding when their parents sound really enthusiastic. Every time Evan goes to brush his teeth more quickly than usual, I want you to sound excited right away, labeling what he is doing, like, "That's awesome that you are getting up to brush your teeth when I asked!" (Criterion 2) Do you think this could help? Would you be willing to attempt this for homework? (Criterion 3)

EXAMPLE RESPONSES TO BEGINNER-LEVEL CLIENT STATEMENTS FOR EXERCISE 4

Example Response to Beginner Client Statement 2

It can help to focus on praising the behavior you want to increase, as research shows emphasizing a child's positive behavior will get you better results than saying no to the negative behavior. (Criterion 1) The best praise specifically describes what you like about what your child is doing, in an enthusiastic tone. It is best to provide praise as soon as you see the behavior you want, and at first, every time she does it. This means the next time you see Nia share a toy, you'll want to make a big deal about it. You can say, "Great job sharing your toys, Nia!" Keep highlighting it when you see it. (Criterion 2) Do you think that would be helpful? Can we try it? (Criterion 3)

Example Response to Beginner Client Statement 3

Glad you asked! Praise can be useful for increasing positive behavior at any age. We identify a problematic behavior, like not cleaning up, and praise its positive opposite, cleaning, which can help make it more likely to happen again. (Criterion 1) Look for this behavior every time it happens and praise it immediately. Be specific about exactly what behavior you are praising and make sure to sound enthusiastic. Look for a time they put a toy away and praise it right away, like, "Wow, Charlie, I love how you are putting those Legos away so nicely!" Continue to praise each piece they put in the box. (Criterion 2) How helpful does that sound? Would you be willing to look for times to praise them this week? (Criterion 3)

Example Response to Beginner Client Statement 4

It sounds like you have already taken the first step, which is to identify the positive opposite of the behavior you dislike, her time in the bathroom. Praising the positive opposite of this behavior—getting ready quickly—makes it likely it will increase. (Criterion 1) Let's have you praise Soraya every time she does this, as soon as she comes out. Specify exactly what you like about her behavior and sound thrilled about it. How about looking for times when she comes out of the bathroom quickly and saying, "I really love how you got ready so quickly today so you can get to school on time!" as soon as she exits? (Criterion 2) Do you think experimenting with this could help? If so, would you try it this week? (Criterion 3)

Example Response to Beginner Client Statement 5

It's so great that you noticed Sam's positive behavior of putting the clothes away, as the positive behavior is exactly what we want you to point out! Doing so can help make this behavior occur more often. (Criterion 1) Effective praise involves communicating what you specifically liked in an excited tone and praising the behavior as soon as possible, every time you notice it. How would you feel about saying, "Wow, Sam, I was so proud of you for putting your clothes in your drawers!" You could even say it tonight while saying it more immediately in the future, since we want you to say it right away each time. (Criterion 2) What are your thoughts about the usefulness of this? Would you agree to try it? (Criterion 3)

EXAMPLE RESPONSES TO INTERMEDIATE-LEVEL CLIENT STATEMENTS FOR EXERCISE 4

Example Response to Intermediate Client Statement 1

Our urge is to tell kids what we want them to stop doing. In contrast, researchers have found it is more helpful to praise what we want them to do, as this is more likely to increase the behavior we like. (Criterion 1) Praise should specifically explain what we like and be given immediately, every time they behave well, and sound enthusiastic. Before the big kids come and as soon as he starts going down, say, "Leo, I really love how you are going down the slide the right way!" Be sure to sound thrilled and say this each time. (Criterion 2) Do you think this has any potential to help? Can we make this your homework? (Criterion 3)

EXAMPLE RESPONSES TO INTERMEDIATE-LEVEL CLIENT STATEMENTS FOR EXERCISE 4

Example Response to Intermediate Client Statement 2

It's great that you praised Oliver for cleaning up, as we know praising behavior we want gives us the best chance of increasing it. (Criterion 1) Let's take a look at how you can make it work. Praise is most effective when it occurs immediately after the behavior you want to increase. It also helps to specify the exact behavior, every time you observe it. And you want to sound enthusiastic. So next time you notice Oliver cleaning up crumbs, let's have you immediately praise him for this specific action. You can practice sounding enthusiastic and praise him each time he cleans up. (Criterion 2) Does this sound like a good plan? If so, could we have you try it this week? (Criterion 3)

Example Response to Intermediate Client Statement 3

It's wonderful that you compliment her; however, praise works best when you use it to try to increase a specific behavior. It helps to think of behavior you do not like and identify the positive opposite. (Criterion 1) Once you identify a behavior to increase, you praise its occurrence immediately and enthusiastically, every time you see it. It's also important to specify the behavior you want so Lucy knows exactly what you like. Let's try to find a time when Lucy finishes her homework in a timely manner and make a big deal about it right away, like "Nice job finishing your homework already!" You would repeat this every time she did so. (Criterion 2) Does this sound helpful? Are you willing to try it? (Criterion 3)

Example Response to Intermediate Client Statement 4

I think you're right, it doesn't help to berate her. Praising a teen's desired behaviors gives us a better chance of increasing them than criticizing undesired behaviors. (Criterion 1) Great job pointing out when Maya went to bed on time. We want to praise behavior we want immediately, and every time it happens. It sounds like your comment was a bit sarcastic, which I can understand, but this won't change her behavior. Remember, praise works best when given enthusiastically. It also helps to label exactly what she did that you liked. Next time you could say, "I'm really proud of you for going to bed on time since you'll be less tired in the morning!" (Criterion 2) Do you think this could help? Would you be open to testing it out? (Criterion 3)

Example Response to Intermediate Client Statement 5

I love how you praised Lani for getting her bag together one night. As we know, praising behavior we want gives us a great chance of increasing it. (Criterion 1) You said you aren't sure how often she does this. Praise is most likely to help increase a behavior if it is given every time. We also want praise to be immediate, specific, and said enthusiastically. How about looking for times she puts her bag together at night? You would praise her immediately, each time it happens. This could sound like, "You did such a great job packing up your bag the night before school!" (Criterion 2) Do you see how this could help her form a helpful habit? Would you be willing to try this? (Criterion 3)

EXAMPLE RESPONSES TO ADVANCED-LEVEL CLIENT STATEMENTS FOR EXERCISE 4

Example Response to Advanced Client Statement 1

Our goal is to use praise strategically for specific behaviors you want. Even though you have concerns about praise, psychologists find this is the best way to see more of the behavior you want. (Criterion 1) This will likely work if you praise this behavior each time it occurs by specifically labeling what Carlos did to earn the praise. This should happen as soon as you see the behavior and said with enthusiasm. Let's say you wanted Carlos to run after the soccer ball more. Every time he did, you would immediately shout out praise, like "Great job running after the ball, Carlos!" (Criterion 2) Do you think this could be more helpful than giving everyone a trophy? Are you willing to give praise a shot? (Criterion 3)

EXAMPLE RESPONSES TO ADVANCED-LEVEL CLIENT STATEMENTS FOR EXERCISE 4

Example Response to Advanced Client Statement 2

Punishment is a normal urge, yet research shows using praise to increase positive behaviors works better than using punishment to try to decrease problematic behaviors. We can praise the positive opposite of the problematic behavior. (Criterion 1) It helps to be specific about what behavior the praise is for, and to praise as often as the behavior occurs and as close to the behavior as possible. You will also want to be enthusiastic with your praise. You said Shira "often" talks back. I wonder if you can find times when she readily goes to take a bath to say, "I love how willing you are to take a bath today!" (Criterion 2) Do you think it could be worth starting off with some praise like this? Can we try it? (Criterion 3)

Example Response to Advanced Client Statement 3

The good news is research has found that we can get kids to do what we expect more easily through the use of praise than through spanking or other punishments. (Criterion 1) Praise is best delivered with enthusiasm, as soon as you see the desired behavior, every time you see it. In addition, your praise should specify the exact behavior. So if you need Mara to listen more, let's hold off on punishment for now and have you praise when she follows your directions by saying stuff like, "I'm so glad you're following my directions, Mara!" right away, and each time it happens. (Criterion 2) I wonder, do you think this could help? Are you willing to try this? (Criterion 3)

Example Response to Advanced Client Statement 4

It can be hard to find something to praise, and yet praising positive behaviors like sitting down and getting homework done will make them more likely to happen again. (Criterion 1) Let's find something specific to praise, like maybe Jordan occasionally sits down to start his homework. We can have you remark how much you like this as soon as he does it, any time you see him sit, even for a minute. As hard as it is, I'd also like you to sound enthusiastic, to give it the best chance of it working. How about saying something such as, "Nice job sitting down to start your homework!" (Criterion 2) Could starting like this help? I wonder if you'd be willing to see what it feels like. (Criterion 3)

Example Response to Advanced Client Statement 5

For sure, that's tough. We want to find some positive behavior, as praising the opposite of what is problematic can help get more of the behavior you want. (Criterion 1) Once you identify a positive opposite, you will want to provide specific praise every time it happens, as soon as you see it. Let's get as close to enthusiasm as we can. Ultimately, we want praise to sound authentic. We can look for times Kierra asks for money or to go somewhere and have you respond, "It feels good to have you ask my permission to pay for that" or "to do that." (Criterion 2) Would statements like this help you feel genuine without going overboard? Would you be willing to start by looking for specific behaviors to praise? (Criterion 3)

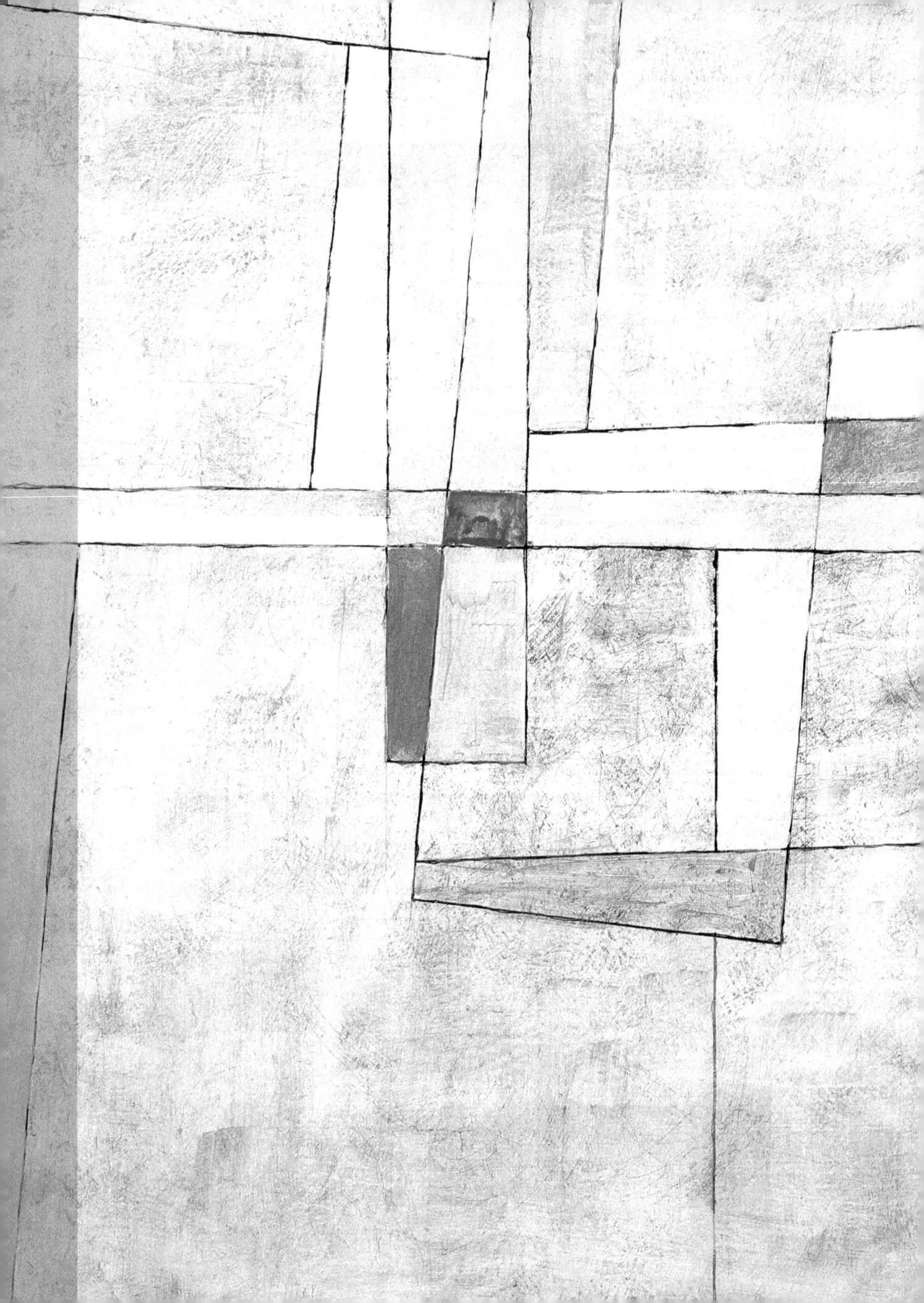

Teaching Parents to Provide Positive Attention

Preparations for Exercise 5

1. Read the instructions in Chapter 2.

2. Download the Deliberate Practice Reaction Form and the Deliberate Practice Diary Form at https://www.apa.org/pubs/books/deliberate-practice-behavioral-parent-training (see the "Resources" tab; also available in Appendixes A and B, respectively).

Skill Description

Skill Difficulty Level: Intermediate

The goal of using the positive attention skill in behavioral parent training (BPT) is to shift parents' attention from their child's negative behaviors to positive behaviors (McNeil & Hembree-Kigin, 2010). Children are eager for their parents' attention, even if they are obtaining attention for negative behavior. It is typical for parents to comment and provide attention when their child is not behaving rather than when the child is behaving appropriately. Parental attention can be so powerful that even reprimanding negative behavior provides the child with attention that can increase the likelihood of them misbehaving again. We can teach parents to focus on "catching their child being good," which means making an effort to look for when their child is behaving well, even for a few seconds, and then acknowledging they like this behavior, verbally or nonverbally (Barkley, 2013). For example, a parent can say, "Wow, you're cleaning up all of your blocks!" and give their child a thumbs up. Parents can also provide labeled praise (Exercise 4). At the same time, we ask parents to try to refrain from commenting on their child's mild negative behaviors. If children learn they can receive parental attention from engaging in positive as opposed to negative behavior, it makes it more likely that the positive behavior will occur again. Parents are subsequently taught how to

https://doi.org/10.1037/0000484-007

Deliberate Practice in Behavioral Parent Training, by M. D. Terjesen, H. B. Vidair, P. S. Ohr, O. A. Walsh, T. Rousmaniere, and A. Vaz

actively ignore mild negative behaviors (Exercise 6). Taken together, paying positive attention to behaviors they like and ignoring behaviors they do not appreciate differentially reinforces children's positive behavior (McNeil & Hembree-Kigin, 2010).

Teaching parents to focus on the child's positive behavior can also improve the parent–child relationship (McNeil & Hembree-Kigin, 2010). Parents can be instructed to join their child in an activity that their child enjoys or of their child's choosing. They can do this one-on-one for as little as 5 and up to 20 minutes per day (Barkley, 2013; McNeil & Hembree-Kigin, 2010). The goal is for the parent to acknowledge or praise specific things they like about their child's behavior—and their child in general—during the activity. They can also describe what their child is doing to show they are fully focused on their child's actions. Parents should refrain from giving commands or criticism and limit questions during these interactions. When tension between a parent and child is particularly high, positive interactions may start with only a brief comment or nonverbal affirmation and increase as interactions improve. Inducing positive interactions where the child leads the activity and the parents pay attention to the child's interests can help improve how the child feels about themselves, increasing their confidence (McNeil & Hembree-Kigin, 2010).

As we reviewed in the introductory chapter to this volume, the last criterion of some BPT skills involves assessing treatment acceptability. For the positive attention skill, we have chosen to highlight asking parents about self-efficacy, as well as their willingness to try it.

Once the clinician teaches the parent how to engage in positive attention, they can assign it for homework (Exercise 12). The following week, the clinician can check in with the parent about their practice of the skill and troubleshoot any issues that arose.

Client prompts for the beginner difficulty level of this skill each present a parent early in the treatment process and describe being stuck in a pattern of focusing on their child's negative behaviors rather than any positive behaviors. For the intermediate level of difficulty, although the stage of treatment is similar, the parent is particularly concerned about the quality of their relationship with their child. Finally, in the advanced difficulty level, the parent has been trying to focus more on positive behaviors yet faces a barrier (logistical or psychological) that may make application of this skill challenging. When practicing clinician responses, you should assume parents have already mastered praise (Exercise 4) because it is relevant for the skill of positive attention. Skills that subsequently build off positive attention include planned ignoring (Exercise 6) and homework planning (Exercise 12).

SKILL CRITERIA FOR EXERCISE 5

1. Provide psychoeducation on shifting attention from unwanted behaviors to attention toward desired behaviors.

2. Teach the parents how to "catch their child being good" (e.g., behavioral descriptions, nonverbal affirmations) using the described situation as an example, while avoiding comments about undesired behaviors.

3. Ask the parents questions that reflect treatment acceptability (e.g., is the skill understandable, are they willing to try it).

Examples of Therapists Teaching Parents to Provide Positive Attention

Example 1

CLIENT: [*confused*] It's like whenever I decide to do something I enjoy, like cooking, Kai immediately interrupts me, and it's almost never to tell me something good. I give him plenty of attention and just want to know what I am doing wrong.

THERAPIST: I am not sure you are doing anything wrong. We are going to want you to shift your attention from Kai's negative behaviors, like interrupting, to behavior you want to see, which can help obtain the results you are hoping for. (Criterion 1) Imagine taking a magnifying glass and finding small opportunities to point out his good behavior while avoiding commenting on negative behaviors. For example, if you are cooking, look for a short time where Kai is able to occupy himself, give him a thumbs up, and say something like, "I love how you're playing while I cook right now!" Then try not to comment on moments he interrupts you. (Criterion 2) Do you think you can do this? Might this be something we could start with? (Criterion 3)

Example 2

CLIENT: [*frustrated*] When playing together, I get really frustrated when Lucas doesn't do things as they are supposed to be done. This could be when he makes no effort to color within the lines or doesn't follow the directions when putting the rocket ship together. Playing with him is supposed to be a good form of attention, but good for who? I feel like I have to repeatedly tell him, or really correct him, when he is not doing what is expected. Then he just gets annoyed with me, and it takes the fun out of playing together.

THERAPIST: Moving your attention during play from Lucas's negative behaviors to positive behaviors you want can help you increase those behaviors. It can also help improve your relationship and how he feels about himself. (Criterion 1) We can work on catching times Lucas is being good or engaging in behaviors you want, while ignoring problematic behaviors. Look for times he is making an effort coloring or complying with directions, even briefly. Then enthusiastically describe his behavior, saying something like "Wow, you are coloring in the lines!" And give him a big smile. Then don't comment when he is off task. (Criterion 2) Do you believe you can do this? Is that something you are willing to try? (Criterion 3)

Example 3

CLIENT: [*shocked*] I never thought my 12-year-old daughter would speak to me the way that she does. It is so disrespectful. I yell back at Alana, and she just gets even more nasty. It seems to be in a never-ending cycle. Then she just sits in front of the TV watching a show. There has to be a better way for us to interact. This can't be fun for her either, and I am always waiting for the nastiness to start.

THERAPIST: Shifting your focus from Alana's disrespectful comments to any times where she speaks to you in a calmer tone can help improve how she speaks to you over time, which can improve your interactions more generally. (Criterion 1) This is called "catching your child being good," or finding positive moments and praising her rather than reacting to her negative behavior. Look for times she is speaking calmly, even if fleeting, and say, "I really like how you used a calm tone when you explained you were upset. It helped me understand how you were feeling." Yet ignore any negative comments. Perhaps also briefly sit next to her while she watches her show. (Criterion 2) Does this idea sound feasible for you? Would this be something you would try? (Criterion 3)

INSTRUCTIONS FOR EXERCISE 5

Step 1: Role-Play and Feedback

- The client says the first beginner client statement. The therapist **improvises** a response based on the skill criteria.
- The trainer (or, if not available, the client) provides **brief** feedback based on the skill criteria.
- The client then repeats the same statement, and the therapist again improvises a response. The trainer (or client) again provides brief feedback.

Step 2: Repeat

- Repeat Step 1 for all the statements **in the current difficulty level** (beginner, intermediate, or advanced).

Step 3: Assess and Adjust Difficulty

- The therapist completes the Deliberate Practice Reaction Form (see Appendix A) and decides whether to make the exercise easier or harder or to repeat the same difficulty level.

Step 4: Repeat for Approximately 15 Minutes

- Repeat Steps 1 to 3 for at least 15 minutes.
- The trainees then switch therapist and client roles and start over.

→ Now it's your turn! Follow the exercise instructions.

Remember: The goal of the role play is for trainees to practice improvising responses to the client statements in a manner that (a) uses the skill criteria and (b) feels authentic for the trainee. **Example therapist responses for each client statement are provided at the end of this exercise. Trainees should attempt to improvise their own responses before reading the examples.**

BEGINNER-LEVEL CLIENT STATEMENTS FOR EXERCISE 5

Beginner Client Statement 1

[Weary] Stella, my 6-year-old, always wants my attention. She constantly wants me to look at what she's playing with, and if I don't, she behaves badly—like she'll throw a ball in the house even though I've told her not to a million times. I am so tired of this. How do I balance giving her the attention she wants with getting her to follow the rules?

Beginner Client Statement 2

[Uncertain] It's hard to get Dylan ready for preschool in the morning. He waits for me to tell him to get out of bed and go eat his cereal multiple times. I think he likes that I have to keep coming back in his room. I keep telling him I can't go back into his room and that if he keeps this up, he'll lose his tablet, but he keeps doing it. I feel stuck.

Beginner Client Statement 3

[Worried] Zoe is so social, and I think she's better at communicating than many other 9-year-olds! But she tries to talk to people when they are in the middle of talking to someone else. As her parent, I feel it's my job to stop her, but she just gets mad at me every time I bring it up. I don't want to make her feel bad. What do you think I can do?

BEGINNER-LEVEL CLIENT STATEMENTS FOR EXERCISE 5

Beginner Client Statement 4

[Ashamed] I'm at a loss with Aidan. He should still want to play with his toys—he's only 8! But he will often come into the house after school and only want to watch TV. I always make suggestions about ways we could play together instead, and he repeatedly says he doesn't want to. Then I feel like a bad mom for not being able to get him off a screen. What can I do to get him to listen to me about this?

Beginner Client Statement 5

[Angry] I don't know how many times I've told Delilah to clean up her room! She tells us teenagers are allowed to keep their rooms the way they want and that all we do is point out her problems. If her boyfriend comes over, she will clean it. But never for us!

✋ **Assess and adjust the difficulty before moving to the next difficulty level (see Step 3 in the exercise instructions).**

INTERMEDIATE-LEVEL CLIENT STATEMENTS FOR EXERCISE 5

Intermediate Client Statement 1

[Annoyed] When Sadie plays on her tablet, she constantly comes over to me and wants me to pick a game for her to try. But the whole point is to give her something to do while I'm working. I keep telling her now that she is 4, the tablet is for her to use by herself, and to stop annoying me already! I'm so stressed because I want to have a good bond with her, but I need her to give me a break!

Intermediate Client Statement 2

[Sad] When Arina turned 12, we got her a cell phone like her friends have. The problem is now she spends more time on her phone than with our family. Every time I bring this up, she snaps at me and says to leave her alone. Occasionally she will come home after school and want to chat, but it's often when I am busy and she just goes right to her cell. I keep telling her that if she keeps this up, we will take her phone back. But is there anything I can do to get her to talk with me more?

Intermediate Client Statement 3

[Pensive] I realize I'm criticizing Elaina's actions more and more. It's because she hasn't been behaving well since she started middle school. She comes in, sits down, and gives us such an attitude. She's also rude to us in the mornings. I keep saying I don't like how she's been treating us. But it just continues and is getting worse.

Intermediate Client Statement 4

[Pleading] I want Desmond to spend time hanging out with me, but at 16, he seems to care more about his friends. Now when he's home, he wants to play video games with his friends online. He says I nag him about it when he's playing near me in the living room, but I just want him to spend time with me. Instead we end up in a back-and-forth until we are yelling and slamming doors. Is there anything I can do?

INTERMEDIATE-LEVEL CLIENT STATEMENTS FOR EXERCISE 5

Intermediate Client Statement 5

[Angry] Now that Kelly drives, I don't mind them using the car. But they are very demanding. They tell us to give them gas money and yell at us when the car isn't available. I told them how dare they speak to us like that, but it's like the more angry I sound, the more they give us a hard time about using the car. I'm just looking for a way to restore civil communication about this.

> **Assess and adjust the difficulty before moving to the next difficulty level (see Step 3 in the exercise instructions).**

ADVANCED-LEVEL CLIENT STATEMENTS FOR EXERCISE 5

Advanced Client Statement 1

[Overwhelmed] My newborn takes up a lot of my time, and then I have to keep asking Sandro to behave himself. I get that he's only 4 years old and having a sibling in the house is a big change, but I need him to act right while I'm nursing and changing the baby. How can I get him to behave and still have a good relationship with him while we all adjust to the new baby?

Advanced Client Statement 2

[Contempt] I know we talked about paying attention to Lily's good behaviors, but she really doesn't have any. She fights me on any single thing I say. I've never heard of such a stubborn 7-year-old. She just doesn't deserve me noticing anything good about her.

Advanced Client Statement 3

[Complaining] I just don't see how paying positive attention to Isabella is going to help with the problem here. Her middle school teachers give so much homework! She really can't handle all the work and complains every step of the way. I'm put in the position of arguing with her to do her homework or pushing her to drill flash cards while she complains about not liking school. It has really negatively affected our relationship. Do you think there is anything I can do to get her to stop complaining?

Advanced Client Statement 4

[Disgusted] How am I supposed to pay positive attention to Martin when I know he's been lying to me? I know he doesn't want to hear me talk about it, but I can't help it. A 15-year-old should realize when they're just bad at lying. He's sick of being around me at all. Well, the feeling is mutual. We don't have any positive moments together anymore. Just tension.

Advanced Client Statement 5

[Hopeless] Teenage Rita is a whole different animal than kid Rita. She has been challenging what I say so much that I can't say anything nice to her. She finds a way to turn any feedback I give her, positive or negative, into an argument. Like she knit a beautiful scarf, and I told her I really liked it, but she just went on about how I never take her to the store for yarn. I don't know how I'm supposed to point out anything good about her behavior when she won't take it in.

> **Assess and adjust the difficulty here (see Step 3 in the exercise instructions). If appropriate, follow the instructions to make the exercise even more challenging (see Appendix A).**

Example Therapist Responses: Teaching Parents to Provide Positive Attention

Remember: Trainees should attempt to improvise their own responses before reading the examples. **Do not read the following responses verbatim unless you are having trouble coming up with your own!**

EXAMPLE RESPONSES TO BEGINNER-LEVEL CLIENT STATEMENTS FOR EXERCISE 5
Example Response to Beginner Client Statement 1
We want you to give her attention—we just want you to focus on the behaviors you want. Moving your attention away from Stella's negative behaviors to her positive behaviors will make her more likely to engage in positive behaviors in the future. (Criterion 1) We can start with you "catching her being good," which means looking for positive behaviors she's doing and making a big deal about them while refraining from mentioning problematic behaviors. Find moments to watch her and comment on how well she is playing, even joining her play for 5 to 20 minutes a day, while not commenting on the ball throwing right now. (Criterion 2) Is this something you think you can accomplish? Would you be open to attempting this? (Criterion 3)
Example Response to Beginner Client Statement 2
Shifting your attention to behavior you would like to see from Dylan while not responding to unwanted behavior can help increase the behavior you are aiming for. (Criterion 1) I'd like you to find times he is doing some of what you want and really acknowledge it. This means trying to find even 5 seconds when he does what you want while dropping the focus on misbehavior, for now. For example, if he gets out of bed more quickly than usual one day, make a big deal about it. Say something like, "Look at you getting out of bed like I told you to!" (Criterion 2) Do you think you could do this? Would you be open to experimenting with this strategy? (Criterion 3)
Example Response to Beginner Client Statement 3
It can help to move your focus from the times Zoe is interrupting to the times she is behaving in a socially appropriate way, as paying attention to a child's behaviors can actually help increase them. (Criterion 1) Let's have you focus on catching times she is communicating appropriately and give her some positive attention in that moment. You can let problematic behaviors go right now. In other words, let's have you catch the times she is communicating appropriately and point it out, like, "Aw Zoe, you waited your turn to talk!" and give her a hug, while not pointing out when she's interrupting. (Criterion 2) How doable does this idea sound to you? Does it seem feasible this week? (Criterion 3)
Example Response to Beginner Client Statement 4
Studies have shown that parents can most likely improve behavior by paying more attention to their children's desired behaviors than their undesired behaviors. (Criterion 1) This means "catching their child being good," or acknowledging something positive that their child is doing that is the opposite of the undesired behavior. How about we have you look for times Aidan shows any interest in interacting with you, even briefly? Then you could respond positively, saying you love spending time with him, without bringing up the TV. (Criterion 2) Does that strategy seem possible for you? Is it something you would be willing to practice? (Criterion 3)

**EXAMPLE RESPONSES TO BEGINNER-LEVEL
CLIENT STATEMENTS FOR EXERCISE 5**

Example Response to Beginner Client Statement 5

Even though the natural urge is to point out Delilah's problematic behavior, turning your attention to any positive behaviors you see rather than behaviors you don't want can improve your interactions over time. (Criterion 1) You can search for times she does what you want and make sure to express how wonderful it is, verbally and with your body language, instead of pointing out your concerns. How about noticing a time she does clean her room and saying, "Your room looks really great like this!" with a genuine tone and a big smile while refraining from commenting that you wish she cleaned up all the time. (Criterion 2) Do you think you can do that? Would you be willing to try it? (Criterion 3)

**EXAMPLE RESPONSES TO INTERMEDIATE-LEVEL
CLIENT STATEMENTS FOR EXERCISE 5**

Example Response to Intermediate Client Statement 1

If we ignore behaviors we don't want and comment positively on behaviors we want to see, over time we can get more behaviors we want. Acknowledging the times Sadie acts positively can also help you strengthen your bond with her. (Criterion 1) We can have you do this by catching times she is behaving positively and ignoring times she is annoying you. Let's have you look for moments when she is able to play alone on her tablet and tell her you appreciate her playing independently. Then offer to look at it when you have time and show interest for five minutes. Try not to respond to her requests while you are working. (Criterion 2) Does this sound manageable for you? Could we have you try it? (Criterion 3)

Example Response to Intermediate Client Statement 2

Paying attention to behaviors you want instead of ones you don't want can help make positive behaviors more likely to occur. Giving Arina positive attention can also help improve your interactions over time. (Criterion 1) The goal is to find times when she is "acting good," or the way you want her to behave, and respond positively, verbally or even without words. But you wouldn't mention any negative behaviors. Try highlighting times she does chat with you, like saying "I'm so glad we were able to spend time talking!" You can make eye contact and summarize her points to show you are really listening. And you would not mention her phone. (Criterion 2) Would you be able to carry out this plan? Is it something we could have you aim for this week? (Criterion 3)

Example Response to Intermediate Client Statement 3

Focusing on Elaina's negative behaviors may unfortunately be increasing them. Research shows that switching your attention to any positive behaviors you see can help increase them and even decrease unwanted behavior. This can also improve the quality of parent–child relationships. (Criterion 1) You can accomplish this by searching for small moments where Elaina is kind or neutral and share how you appreciate them. For now, you'd aim to ignore when she has an attitude. So if she comes in, sits down, and doesn't say much, you can say, "I like sitting with you." You could also pat her shoulder. But avoid commenting when she sounds rude. (Criterion 2) Do you believe you could do this? Would you be willing to test it out? (Criterion 3)

EXAMPLE RESPONSES TO INTERMEDIATE-LEVEL CLIENT STATEMENTS FOR EXERCISE 5

Example Response to Intermediate Client Statement 4

It can help to switch your attention to times Desmond is acting the way you want, instead of belaboring times he is not. Letting him know when you like his behavior can build upon your relationship and increase behavior you want over time. (Criterion 1) We can have you notice any time he behaves how you like and acknowledge this while ignoring other behaviors. Let's practice not "nagging" him for his video game use, as he calls it. How about catching him playing his video game and saying you enjoy watching him? You can say you'd love to learn and observe him for 10 minutes, pointing out his impressive moves. (Criterion 2) How do you feel about your ability to join him? Would you try it for homework? (Criterion 3)

Example Response to Intermediate Client Statement 5

We find when parents move their attention from behaviors that are problematic to their child's positive behaviors, they are likely to see an increase in behaviors they want. Pointing out Kelly's positive behaviors could also make them feel good and improve your communication. (Criterion 1) We call this "catching your child being good," or catching times they communicate the way you want and positively acknowledging it. I'd like you to look for times Kelly speaks in a positive or neutral way. When you notice this, try making eye contact, nodding, and responding thoughtfully to show you are engaged. However, avoid commenting on times they make demands. (Criterion 2) Do you think you can do what I am suggesting? Can we have you try it as an experiment? (Criterion 3)

EXAMPLE RESPONSES TO ADVANCED-LEVEL CLIENT STATEMENTS FOR EXERCISE 5

Example Response to Advanced Client Statement 1

We can have you draw your attention toward Sandro's good behavior while letting bad behavior go. Giving your attention to behavior you want has been found to increase good behavior. This can also help him feel good about himself and his relationship with you. (Criterion 1) We can have you make a big positive deal about brief times he behaves while you tend to your baby and ignore problematic behaviors. You can say things like, "Sandro, I love watching you play nicely with your toy while I feed the baby!" while ignoring negative comments. While the baby naps, you can play a game he chooses, giving him your full attention. (Criterion 2) Do you believe you can handle this? Would you be willing to try? (Criterion 3)

Example Response to Advanced Client Statement 2

As we discussed, the purpose of shifting your attention from Lily's negative behaviors to any positive behavior is to increase the chance of seeing more positive behavior over time. Looking for positives can help her feel good as well, which can improve the quality of your interactions. (Criterion 1) Let's start by taking a magnifying glass to Lily and catching any time she is doing something other than fighting with you. (Criterion 2) This can even be a few seconds where she is listening after you say something. You can say, "I love it when you listen to what I'm saying." (Criterion 2) I know this is new—can you see yourself doing this? Would you be willing to try this? (Criterion 3)

EXAMPLE RESPONSES TO ADVANCED-LEVEL CLIENT STATEMENTS FOR EXERCISE 5

Example Response to Advanced Client Statement 3

It's easy to focus on wanting to reduce Isabella's negative behaviors, like complaining about homework, but research shows shifting attention to positive behavior can help increase behaviors you want. Highlighting positives can also help improve your relationship. (Criterion 1) You can do this by catching her engaging in positive behavior and pointing it out rather than commenting on negative behavior. For example, look for a moment she is doing homework without complaining and tell her how proud you are of her, yet ignore any complaints. You can also add a daily, 5-minute special time together, where she chooses something fun to do and you share positives about her. (Criterion 2) Do you think you could manage these ideas? Would you be open to doing so? (Criterion 3)

Example Response to Advanced Client Statement 4

Although hard, shifting your attention from negative behavior like lying to any positive behavior you see at other times can help reduce tension and start to repair your relationship. It can help increase positive behaviors you are hoping for while reducing behavior you don't want. (Criterion 1) We could have you catch times Martin behaves at all, particularly when he tells the truth, even for something benign, while avoiding talking about lying. So if he tells you he doesn't like the potatoes you made, while somewhat critical, you could say, "Got it, I appreciate you being honest about the potatoes" as genuinely as possible. (Criterion 2) Do you see yourself being able to pull this off? Do you think we can work toward your attempting this? (Criterion 3)

Example Response to Advanced Client Statement 5

We know moving your focus from negative to positive behavior can help you start to see more of the behaviors you want. The same is true for your relationship. It might not seem like Rita is taking in what you say, but she might still feel good about herself, and this can start to improve your interactions. (Criterion 1) I'm curious what will happen if you comment on things you like about her, while ignoring negative responses. You can say, "Wow, I'm really impressed with how you knit that scarf!" And say you would love to watch her knit, if she would be willing, but don't respond to any argumentative responses. (Criterion 2) Can you imagine doing this? Are you open to trying? (Criterion 3)

Teaching Planned Ignoring With Positive Attention

Preparations for Exercise 6

1. Read the instructions in Chapter 2.

2. Download the Deliberate Practice Reaction Form and the Deliberate Practice Diary Form at https://www.apa.org/pubs/books/deliberate-practice-behavioral-parent-training (see the "Resources" tab; also available in Appendixes A and B, respectively).

Skill Description

Skill Difficulty Level: Intermediate

There are many reasons or functions for why some children may misbehave. These are addressed in Exercise 2. One of the more frequent reasons is that children receive attention for their problematic behaviors. The goal of using planned ignoring in behavioral parent training (BPT) is to give parents a tool to decrease problematic attention-seeking behaviors by removing the attention they have been giving to those behaviors. One example of attention-seeking behavior is the child who shows a clear pattern of loud complaining and disrespectful language when they want their parents to give them a snack. If the parent consistently attends to their problematic behaviors by getting them the snack, they are reinforcing those behaviors in that the child learns that being loud and disrespectful gets them what they want.

When children no longer receive attention for those particular behaviors, they will eventually extinguish. In applied behavior analysis, the term *extinction* refers to discontinuing rewarding a behavior that has previously been rewarded (Kazdin, 2008). The theory and practice of extinction is based on the premise that children with a challenging behavior that is maintained by attention will change that behavior when the reinforcing component (i.e., attention) is removed. As a parent intervention strategy, planned ignoring has been widely shown to be effective in reducing rates of problematic

https://doi.org/10.1037/0000484-008

Deliberate Practice in Behavioral Parent Training, by M. D. Terjesen, H. B. Vidair, P. S. Ohr, O. A. Walsh, T. Rousmaniere, and A. Vaz

attention-seeking behaviors in children (Kazdin, 2017). A challenge for many parents is that sometimes ignoring the behaviors of their children can be quite difficult. Further, because the child has a history of having their negative/maladaptive behavior reinforced by receiving attention, when parents make efforts to extinguish this behavior by withholding attention, the intensity level of the child's behavior may increase in the child's effort to gain that reinforcer (i.e., attention). BPT clinicians should stress to parents the importance of not giving attention in these moments because doing so strengthens negative behavior and teaches children that gaining attention may require a stronger level of negative behavior.

When teaching planned ignoring, it is important for clinicians to listen to the parent's description of their concerns and propose that the function of their child's behavior is attention. All the examples described in this exercise are attention-driven behaviors. Planned ignoring is only effective if the function of the child's behavior is to gain attention.

After proposing that attention is serving to maintain the child's problem behaviors, clinicians should explain why planned ignoring can decrease attention-seeking behaviors. Although it is understandable that youth seek parental attention, what matters is how children go about gaining the attention they seek. Many lack the ability to differentiate between positive attention, commonly expressed by parental praise, and negative attention, often given as a reprimand. This means that if a child is loud and disrespectful and the parent's immediate reaction is to stop everything and attend to what they want, the child is reinforced even if a reprimand or consequence from the parent accompanies the attention. As long as the child gets what they want (i.e., attention), the inappropriate behaviors are strengthened and will likely continue and increase in the future. Planned ignoring helps stop this pattern. Planned ignoring does not end with the ignore (Kazdin, 2017). Giving immediate verbal or nonverbal positive acknowledgment when the child engages in behaviors that are the positive opposite to the problem behaviors during the described situation is critical. In addition, consistently giving positive attention to all appropriate child behaviors throughout the day not only increases appropriate behavior but also enhances the parent–child relationship (see Exercise 5).

Planned ignoring starts with the clinician explaining what it is and advising parents not to respond by giving attention if their child continues to use those behaviors. Therapists work with parents regarding what they are to communicate to their child and make clear that they still care about their child even if they are not responding to their behavior and to specify positive-opposite behaviors that they will respond to. For example, "When you complain loudly and use disrespectful language when you want a snack, I will not respond to you. If you use a calm, respectful tone, I will start responding again." Parents are taught exactly how to ignore their child, including looking the other way to avoid eye contact, being silent and resisting arguing if provoked, and considering beforehand different activities they can engage in while ignoring, such as doing a brief task, reading, or listening to music. Parents are told to ignore until the behavior stops and then reengage by praising the positive behaviors they want to see. Importantly, consistency is stressed because once the process of ignoring is in progress, any parental attention given to the behavior can actually reinforce it further (Kazdin, 2005). For parents who experience strong emotions, suggestions are made to practice mindfulness, by, for example, counting their breaths (see Exercise 10).

The beginner level focuses on demonstrating and practicing an understanding of planned ignoring. Although this skill may sound relatively straightforward, there are challenges that make it difficult to implement. The intermediate level focuses on clinicians teaching parents how to continue using planned ignoring when there are moderate challenges, such as an extinction burst, which is a temporary increase in the behavior at the start of planned ignoring, as the child increases the behaviors that worked in the past before giving up. Another challenge is a lack of consistency between partners, which needs to be addressed because consistency is very important with this approach. The advanced level focuses on teaching therapists to help parents when the function of the behavior is not clear or is concerning, such as when the child expresses intense anger during ignoring and is physically aggressive or becomes despondent and uses statements suggestive of self-harm. When this occurs, parents are instructed to use other behavioral parenting techniques—for example, consequence interventions (see Exercise 9) or active listening skills to communicate empathy and understanding (see Exercise 7).

As we reviewed in Chapter 1, many BPT skills incorporate assessment of treatment acceptability. In this exercise, therapists should assess the parents' willingness to try planned ignoring paired with positive attention or whether there are barriers they foresee to using the suggested strategies. For example, "Are you willing to do planned ignoring with positive attention over the next week?" or "Do you foresee any reasons why this would be difficult for you to do?" Once the clinician teaches the parent how to use planned ignoring, they can assign it for homework (see Exercise 12). The following week, the clinician can check in with the parent about their practice of the skill and troubleshoot any issues that arose.

SKILL CRITERIA FOR EXERCISE 6

1. Propose the function of attention for the child's behavior in the described situation.
2. Explain why planned ignoring can be effective and how it can be used in the described situation.
3. Ask the parent at least one question regarding treatment acceptability (e.g., do they believe that the approach will be effective, are they willing to try the skill, do they anticipate any barriers).

Examples of Therapists Teaching Planned Ignoring With Positive Attention

Example 1

CLIENT: [*despair*] My 14-year-old, Abby, says that I'm an awful cook, and at least 4 days out of the week she won't eat dinner unless it's takeout from one of her favorite restaurants. If I make dinner instead of giving in to her, she screams that I am the worst mother. The more I argue and try to reason with her, the louder she screams, and when it gets really bad, I have to give in. She is so annoying. She makes me go out, even at 9 p.m. when I'm tired.

THERAPIST: It sounds like the function of Abby's screaming and disrespect is to get your attention, and it sounds like she gets it, which reinforces or strengthens her behavior. By changing your response to Abby's demands you'll be altering the reinforcers that impact her behavior. (Criterion 1) Planned ignoring involves the deliberate removal of attention to inappropriate child behaviors when the function is to gain parental attention. In this situation, remove your attention from Abby's inappropriate behavior immediately. Return your attention only when she is no longer behaving inappropriately and immediately praise her for the change in her behavior. By positively acknowledging flexible and respectful behavior, you will start seeing decreased screaming and disrespect. (Criterion 2) Would planned ignoring be a strategy you'd be willing to use? Do you foresee any difficulties? (Criterion 3)

Example 2

CLIENT: [*perplexed*] My 10-year-old, Ali, makes loud noises and bangs on my desk when I tell him I can't stop working to play with him. Ali and I have really bonded over superheroes, but I often work from home and can't just stop everything to play with him. For the past 2 weeks, I've tried using planned ignoring the way you described, but Ali's loudness is interfering with virtual meetings, and I'm concerned I will lose my job. In fact, for the past 3 days, he has gotten even louder, so I'm not sure that taking my attention away is working. Should I continue ignoring Ali if it's getting worse?

THERAPIST: From your description, the function of Ali's loud noises and banging is to get your attention. (Criterion 1) Although you've noticed an increase, deliberately removing attention is still the best technique, and temporary increases are not unexpected. This temporary spike is called an extinction burst and often occurs at the start of planned ignoring. Ali has been relying on loud noises and banging to get his way, and he will continue this until he learns he will not gain your attention unless he changes his behavior. Giving any attention will accidentally teach Ali that behaving even worse is a way to get you to stop working and attend to him, so be consistent. (Criterion 2) Do you think you can continue using planned ignoring? Do you believe that this is helpful? (Criterion 3)

Example 3

CLIENT: [*embarrassed*] It's like Nia, my 5-year-old, only behaves this way when others are around. She acts like a holy terror and has a devilish smile when doing it. I can't tell you how many times I have to stop what I'm doing and just deal with her tantrums, such as screaming that I had to get her favorite fast food for dinner when her cousins visited, as I was cooking dinner. Last week she got "ill" at her brother's school play and had me and all the grandparents cater to her, and we missed the play. It's crazy how she runs this family, but when she flashes her smile, we all laugh. I've taken her to the doctor and there's no medical concerns, so it really is intentional.

THERAPIST: When Nia tantrums or complains about feeling ill you stop what you're doing to give her attention. Since you've ruled out medical concerns, it seems the goal of her behavior is to get what she wants and avoid activities that don't revolve around her, like when you're attending to her brother. (Criterion 1) Planned ignoring, the deliberate removal of your attention when Nia is behaving inappropriately, will reduce her attention-seeking behaviors. Avoid mistakenly reinforcing her by laughing when she gives her "devilish smile" after misbehaving. Instead positively reinforce behaviors that are appropriate, such as being patient. (Criterion 2) Might this be something we could start with? Do you foresee any obstacles? (Criterion 3)

INSTRUCTIONS FOR EXERCISE 6
Step 1: Role-Play and Feedback
• The client says the first beginner client statement. The therapist **improvises** a response based on the skill criteria.
• The trainer (or, if not available, the client) provides **brief** feedback based on the skill criteria.
• The client then repeats the same statement, and the therapist again improvises a response. The trainer (or client) again provides brief feedback.
Step 2: Repeat
• Repeat Step 1 for all the statements **in the current difficulty level** (beginner, intermediate, or advanced).
Step 3: Assess and Adjust Difficulty
• The therapist completes the Deliberate Practice Reaction Form (see Appendix A) and decides whether to make the exercise easier or harder or to repeat the same difficulty level.
Step 4: Repeat for Approximately 15 Minutes
• Repeat Steps 1 to 3 for at least 15 minutes.
• The trainees then switch therapist and client roles and start over.

> **Now it's your turn! Follow the exercise instructions.**

Remember: The goal of the role play is for trainees to practice improvising responses to the client statements in a manner that (a) uses the skill criteria and (b) feels authentic for the trainee. **Example therapist responses for each client statement are provided at the end of this exercise. Trainees should attempt to improvise their own responses before reading the examples.**

BEGINNER-LEVEL CLIENT STATEMENTS FOR EXERCISE 6
Beginner Client Statement 1
[Stressed] My 5-year-old, Tonya, has a lot of trouble sharing and taking turns with toys. Just the other day, we were building with Legos and I picked up a yellow Lego. Tonya screamed that they were her Legos and wouldn't stop yelling until I put it down. I told her that she has to learn how to share and that if she didn't, I'd give her Legos away. I didn't really mean it, and I never give her stuff away because I can't afford to keep getting her new stuff. Unfortunately, nothing has changed. And now she's started screaming at her younger brother if he even looks at her toys. I'm worried this is getting worse and she won't be invited for playdates.
Beginner Client Statement 2
[Exasperated] Restaurant time is a disaster for my family. When Elijah, my preschooler, is finished eating, he wants to leave—even if no one else is finished. He whines and tries pulling me away from the table. If that doesn't work, he crawls under the table and shrieks. Coloring books, which I bring to distract him, stopped working. Lately, when I can't take it anymore, I pick him up and leave the restaurant and wait in the car for the others to finish. In 2 months, we're having a big party in an expensive restaurant for my father. Should I forget about taking Elijah? Help!

BEGINNER-LEVEL CLIENT STATEMENTS FOR EXERCISE 6

Beginner Client Statement 3

[Annoyed] My 11-year-old, Kelvin, whines and cries when I tell him he has to wait until he finishes his homework before playing video games. He's driving me crazy, and I can't help my 8-year-old twins with their homework because Kelvin is so darn loud. I know I shouldn't, but I've started to let him play anyway just to shut him up. The problem is that Kelvin starts his homework so late now, and he doesn't always finish it because he says he's too tired and needs to go to bed. What am I going to do?

Beginner Client Statement 4

[Frustrated] My 14-year-old, Barbie, says she has to have the latest styles no matter what the cost or she won't be popular. In the store I try to reason with her, but she doesn't listen. The more I try to reason with her, the louder she screams, and when it gets really bad, I have to give in. Help me—I'm going broke.

Beginner Client Statement 5

[Angry] Amari, my 16-year-old, is very disrespectful to me when I listen to my music in the car. He says I'm an idiot for listening to an oldies station and asks me to—well, actually demands—that I change the station. I tell him that it's my car and therefore my music, but then he starts singing his music and keeps getting louder and louder and louder until I have to turn his station on or risk getting into an accident because I get so agitated that I start shaking. I'm thinking of buying earplugs so I don't have to listen to his music!

> Assess and adjust the difficulty before moving to the next difficulty level (see Step 3 in the exercise instructions).

INTERMEDIATE-LEVEL CLIENT STATEMENTS FOR EXERCISE 6

Intermediate Client Statement 1

[Perplexed] You've told me to use planned ignoring when Kalani, my 5-year-old, starts whining when I'm on the phone. I've been trying, but I don't think I'm getting through to her. As she's whining, I glare at her in a very obvious way, thinking she'll get the message that I'm ignoring her—she doesn't. I shake my head "no" and whisper "quiet," but she keeps whining. I don't know how else to show that I'm ignoring her. Any suggestions?

Intermediate Client Statement 2

[Irritated] When Drake cried and wouldn't sleep in his own room after his dad, Joe, moved out, I thought nothing would work. You taught me to use planned ignoring 3 months ago, and he's been sleeping in his own bed ever since. I thought we got past it. Unfortunately, ever since he started sleepovers with his dad, which began 2 weeks ago when he turned 7, he's been arguing and whining when I put him to bed. I've started planned ignoring again, but I don't think it's working. I asked Drake what happens at bedtime with his dad. He says he got upset once but he doesn't anymore because his dad lets him sleep with him. Will planned ignoring help if only I do it?

Intermediate Client Statement 3

[Resignation] I noticed the change in Noah when he started middle school a month ago. He came home and went to the den to play video games. After an hour of playing, I reminded Noah that it was time for his younger sister to play. He went ballistic on me, screaming that I was ruining his life, running up to his room, and slamming the door. That came out of nowhere! This happens almost every day now. I've tried ignoring him, but he screams that I'm an awful mother and ruining his life, so I let him play. I want to ignore him like you said but I don't want to ruin his life. Maybe I am the worst mother in the world.

INTERMEDIATE-LEVEL CLIENT STATEMENTS FOR EXERCISE 6

Intermediate Client Statement 4

[Desperate] I started the planned ignoring technique you taught me when Rachel asks over and over when I'm going to take her and her friends to the mall. She annoys the heck out of me. I take them every weekend because, clearly, 12-year-olds love to get dropped off on their own. I've been good at the ignoring part, but it's the giving praise part for positive behavior that's rough. Unfortunately, there is absolutely nothing for me to praise because from the time she wakes up at 9 until we leave after lunch she will not stop asking—she's like a broken record. Do you have any other tricks I can try before I lose my mind?

Intermediate Client Statement 5

[Perplexed] If you could give a prize for "high school senior with the worst attitude," it would go to my stepson Chris. His mother and I have attempted using planned ignoring to decrease eye-rolling, back talk and disrespect, and constant arguing. We know how to withdraw our attention from Chris when he shows those behaviors. We've become better at recognizing positive opposite behaviors, and we know it's important to praise Chris when we catch him being prosocial. The problem is that praising Chris gets him really angry.

✋ **Assess and adjust the difficulty before moving to the next difficulty level (see Step 3 in the exercise instructions).**

ADVANCED-LEVEL CLIENT STATEMENTS FOR EXERCISE 6

Advanced Client Statement 1

[Concerned] How do I know if I should continue using planned ignoring for CJ's escalating aggressive behavior? When we started parent training a few weeks ago, CJ had just turned 4, and he was throwing toys and pushing us away when he was angry, especially in response to the word "no." Ignoring him seems to make him angrier. He is now hitting us when he can't get his way, and I'm worried he may accidentally hurt the baby. What should I do?

Advanced Client Statement 2

[Guilty] Mealtime has always been a battleground with Jazmine. She's 8 and only eating bland foods. Two weeks ago, I decided to serve her a variety of foods at dinner instead of giving her only what she wants. That really backfired! She's spitting food out and gagging and making other disgusting noises until I serve her what she wants. I was using planned ignoring for when she interrupts me when I'm working. I hoped it would work for eating, but I don't know. Should I continue ignoring her? I had an eating disorder when I was in college. Do you think this is the start of an eating disorder and I'm hurting her by ignoring her? What if she doesn't eat anything for dinner?

Advanced Client Statement 3

[Angry] You taught me to use planned ignoring, and it works. His arguing has definitely decreased, and he hardly interrupts me when I'm busy. But there's no way I'm not going to react when Liam disrespects me if I won't do what he wants, especially in public. He's only 9 years old, and I don't know how he learned some of the disgusting names he calls me. I know that I should ignore him, but I can't because he makes me so angry!

ADVANCED-LEVEL CLIENT STATEMENTS FOR EXERCISE 6
Advanced Client Statement 4
[Anxious] The rule is, when it's 9 p.m., my daughter Sheinelle's phone gets put in my locked drawer until morning. I was ignoring her meltdowns when I started the rule, but she's been swearing at me and threatening to break every phone in the house if I don't let her have hers all night. One night after she threatened to destroy my phone, I went to lock it in the drawer. She pushed me away from the drawer quite aggressively, and I almost fell, which scared me. Maybe I should just let her have her phone all night. She's almost 15 and promised to turn it off before going to bed, which might work. What do you think I should do?
Advanced Client Statement 5
[Exasperated] I've been using planned ignoring for Moe's whining and constant bickering when I tell him to stop playing video games at 10 p.m. He complains that he's almost 17 and I'm treating him like he's a baby, but he does eventually comply with my rules. Using planned ignoring has changed several of Moe's attention-seeking behaviors throughout the day, such as interrupting me when I'm busy or demanding that I watch television with him. The reason I'm calling you up before our session is because Moe told me he's going to cut himself unless I let him play video games until midnight. Is this another attention-seeking behavior or should I be concerned?

> Assess and adjust the difficulty here (see Step 3 in the exercise instructions). If appropriate, follow the instructions to make the exercise even more challenging (see Appendix A).

Example Therapist Responses: Teaching Planned Ignoring With Positive Attention

Remember: Trainees should attempt to improvise their own responses before reading the examples. **Do not read the following responses verbatim unless you are having trouble coming up with your own!**

EXAMPLE RESPONSES TO BEGINNER-LEVEL CLIENT STATEMENTS FOR EXERCISE 6
Example Response to Beginner Client Statement 1
Tonya's screaming enables her to keep something she believes belongs to her. Threatening to give away toys and not following through reinforces her screaming. (Criterion 1) An effective approach that encourages sharing is planned ignoring of inappropriate behaviors, paired with praise for positive opposites. Praise daily for spontaneous sharing and model this while playing with Tonya. When modeling, avoid touching her toys by using your own. After 2 weeks, continue modeling and briefly touch Tonya's toys, praising her for remaining calm. If Tonya screams, ignore by removing eye contact and continue playing with your toys. Only return attention and give praise when Tonya is calm, telling her you can continue playing together now that she's quiet. (Criterion 2) Is this something you're willing to do? Do you foresee any difficulties? (Criterion 3)

EXAMPLE RESPONSES TO BEGINNER-LEVEL CLIENT STATEMENTS FOR EXERCISE 6

Example Response to Beginner Client Statement 2

The behaviors you described function as attention-seeking. When whining alone doesn't work Elijah escalates to get you to leave with him. (Criterion 1) When done consistently, planned ignoring extinguishes attention-seeking disruptive behavior by withdrawing attention from disruptive behaviors and giving attention to positive behaviors. To prepare for planned ignoring in public, make clear to Elijah before leaving home what you expect of his behavior and what he can expect of yours. Throughout the meal ignore disruptive behaviors and frequently acknowledge positive behavior, such as sitting and talking quietly. Consistency for both praise and ignoring is critical. Since Elijah is young and being in public may be overstimulating, having him stretch his legs or going on brief walks with him is helpful. (Criterion 2) What do you think? Would this be helpful to address his behavior? (Criterion 3)

Example Response to Beginner Client Statement 3

Kelvin's whining and name-calling takes attention away from the twins and gets you to let him play video games. Giving him what he wants strengthens these behaviors. (Criterion 1) Planned ignoring is an extinction strategy that teaches children that engaging in disruptive attention-seeking behaviors won't get them what they want. First, explain that Kelvin needs to wait until you're free and then ask you respectfully to play video games with him. If Kelvin waits and asks respectfully, play with him when you're finished with the twins. If he is rude, ignore his effort to gain your attention and instead respond to the twins by praising them for respectful behavior. Remember to praise Kelvin throughout the day when he is patient and respectful. (Criterion 2) What do you think? Do you foresee any barriers to doing this? (Criterion 3)

Example Response to Beginner Client Statement 4

The function of Barbie's screaming is to get what she wants, and she gets it when you reinforce screaming by giving in. Changing your response, which alters the reinforcers that influence her behavior, reduces screaming. (Criterion 1) Planned ignoring involves the deliberate removal of attention to inappropriate child behaviors when the function is to gain something. Here in this situation, immediately remove your attention when Barbie is screaming. It's challenging not to give in, but return your attention only when she's no longer screaming. Give her positive attention, such as praise, for the change in her behavior. By being consistent and positively acknowledging appropriate behavior, you will start seeing decreased screaming. (Criterion 2) What do you think? Is planned ignoring a strategy you'd be willing to use? (Criterion 3)

Example Response to Beginner Client Statement 5

Amari's singing and name-calling gets your attention, the function, and you switch to his music station. Amari has learned that amping up his annoying behaviors will yield a reward. For some teens, agitating a parent is also reinforcing, further strengthening annoying behaviors. (Criterion 1) Ignoring annoying behaviors and praising positive opposites, a technique called planned ignoring, communicates that annoying behavior will not get a rise out of you. Before your next car ride, tell Amari you won't react to attempts to get you to change the station. Praise all positive opposite behaviors during the car ride. (Criterion 2) Are you willing to do your best to pay attention to Amari's quiet and respectful behaviors before, during, and after car rides? Can you consistently ignore annoying behaviors? (Criterion 3)

EXAMPLE RESPONSES TO INTERMEDIATE-LEVEL CLIENT STATEMENTS FOR EXERCISE 6

Example Response to Intermediate Client Statement 1

The "why" of Kalani's whining is to get your attention. You're trying to use planned ignoring, but glaring and whispering to Kalani are likely maintaining whining. (Criterion 1) Planned ignoring requires you to completely withdraw attention from Kalani's whining, while fully attending to positive behaviors. First, remind Kalani to show quiet behavior whenever you're on the phone. Suggest activities she can do independently. If she's quiet while you're on the phone, give nonverbal positive attention, such as a thumbs up. Ignore whining by intentionally looking away and only talking to the caller. End the call when she is quiet for at least 5 seconds to teach her that hanging up is not connected to attention-seeking behavior. (Criterion 2) Is this something you think may be effective? Do you see any barriers to doing this? (Criterion 3)

Example Response to Intermediate Client Statement 2

It seems like an increase in Drake's nighttime attention-seeking behaviors coincides with Joe reinforcing whining by allowing him to sleep with him. (Criterion 1) While consistency between households in ignoring attention-seeking behavior and attending to positive behavior is preferred, conflicts are often inevitable. Yet planned ignoring can still be effective in your home if we troubleshoot. First, discuss with Joe the importance of reducing nighttime attention-seeking behaviors. If agreeable, I can teach Joe planned ignoring by instructing him to immediately remove his attention when Drake whines at bedtime, returning attention and praising immediately when Drake's tone is positive and Drake sleeps in his own bed, and giving positive attention throughout the day for positive tone. If Joe is not agreeable, inform Drake about the different nighttime rules. Be patient and consistent as Drake learns which rules apply to Joe's household and which apply to yours. (Criterion 2) What do you think? Would you be willing to try this with Drake? Can you see any difficulties with doing this? (Criterion 3)

Example Response to Intermediate Client Statement 3

Sounds like Noah's intense interest in video games, typical of early adolescents, is a challenge. Understandably, the "why" of his disruptive behavior and hurtful words is to get more video game time. (Criterion 1) Research shows planned ignoring—taking attention away from disruptive behaviors and giving attention to positive behaviors—can decrease problematic behavior even in particularly challenging situations. First, developing video game rules with input from Noah is important. Next, continue taking your attention away from him completely when he becomes disruptive and won't follow the rules. Return attention as soon as he follows the rules and positively acknowledge appropriate behaviors, such as calming. Importantly, remind yourself that Noah's hurtful talk is his way of getting what he wants. (Criterion 2) Do you think that this would be helpful? Do you foresee any reasons why this would be difficult for you to do? (Criterion 3)

Example Response to Intermediate Client Statement 4

I'm proud you're using ignore skills to address Rachel's relentless questioning and I hear your frustration identifying positive behaviors. As we discussed, she does this because she has a hard time waiting to get what she wants, and, yes, preteens do love being on their own. (Criterion 1) It's great you want to learn to recognize positive opposites, since studies show that ignoring problem behaviors while acknowledging positive ones are both critical for planned ignoring. For now, pay close attention to Rachel whenever she has to wait for what she wants and create a list of positive behaviors. For example, does she remain calm even though her insistence is annoying? Next time, we'll role-play giving positive attention during the described situation. (Criterion 2) Are you willing to try this? Is there any part of this which may be difficult for you? (Criterion 3)

EXAMPLE RESPONSES TO INTERMEDIATE-LEVEL CLIENT STATEMENTS FOR EXERCISE 6

Example Response to Intermediate Client Statement 5

Learning to withdraw attention and recognize positive opposites isn't easy, and I'm happy that you've both worked hard to develop these skills. Unfortunately, it's not unusual for teens to get angry and become disrespectful in reaction to praise. Likely, his hurtful behaviors help him avoid feeling uncomfortable. (Criterion 1) Planned ignoring, which requires not responding to Chris's disrespect while attending to positive opposites, has a strong research base for effectiveness with teens. Our next step in learning this technique is to explore alternatives to verbal praise since that's a barrier. In similar described situations, when you notice positive opposite behavior, try using nonverbal reinforcers, such as a thumbs up, smiling and head nodding, or patting him on the back. (Criterion 2) Is this something that you think would be helpful? Are you willing to try this over the next week? (Criterion 3)

EXAMPLE RESPONSES TO ADVANCED-LEVEL CLIENT STATEMENTS FOR EXERCISE 6

Example Response to Advanced Client Statement 1

You're teaching CJ to deal with strong emotions, and this is challenging. The function of hitting is likely a temporary escalation of attention-seeking and should decrease. (Criterion 1) I'm suggesting you continue planned ignoring. Remember to consistently ignore problem behaviors and consistently praise positive opposites. However, this doesn't mean you should turn away from CJ's unsafe behaviors. In the described situation, you can intervene if CJ is hitting by blocking his way. The moment he shows any positive opposite behavior, such as keeping his arms still, pour on the praise. You and CJ can practice calmly breathing together during times he's experiencing strong emotions. (Criterion 2) Are you willing to try this? Do you think that this would be helpful or do you perceive any barriers to doing this? (Criterion 3)

Example Response to Advanced Client Statement 2

Jazmine's disruptive behavior enables her to get her way at mealtime. It's important to avoid reinforcing these attention-seeking behaviors if you want to decrease the behaviors that interfere with healthy eating. (Criterion 1) Planned ignoring is helpful for the type of eating-related concerns you describe. Not responding when she spits out food or gags and consistently praising positive behaviors can decrease stress at mealtimes. Explain to Jazmine at a calm time before mealtime that you will remove your attention when she is disruptive during meals. Removing attention includes not giving direct commands to eat while piling on positive attention for both food- and non–food-related appropriate behaviors, especially spontaneous healthy eating. (Criterion 2) Do you think this would work to address her behaviors? Are you willing to see how Jazmine reacts to this approach? (Criterion 3)

Example Response to Advanced Client Statement 3

I hear your anger. No one likes to be disrespected, especially in public. Yet Liam is likely disrespectful because he has learned from your reaction that you will attend to him. (Criterion 1) My goal is to decrease Liam's hurtful talk by having you continue using planned ignoring, which research has determined is effective in reducing the type of behavior you are concerned about. Ignore disruptive behavior and attend to positive behavior. Explain to Liam that it's not okay to be disrespectful and that you will not react to his name-calling but will react to respectful language. I'll teach you how to manage your own strong feelings in public, such as taking calming breaths. (Criterion 2) What are your thoughts? While challenging now, do you think this could work? Are you willing to continue to apply it and do you foresee any barriers to continuing with this technique? (Criterion 3)

EXAMPLE RESPONSES TO ADVANCED-LEVEL
CLIENT STATEMENTS FOR EXERCISE 6

Example Response to Advanced Client Statement 4

The escalation of disruptive behavior is not surprising, given Sheinelle's strong reliance on her phone. She's learned that the more disruptive she is, the more likely it is that you will give her what she wants. (Criterion 1) Utilizing planned ignoring will get Sheinelle to comply with your phone rules. It's important to ignore her attempts to get access to a phone even if her disruptive behavior is escalating. Consistently attending to positive behaviors throughout the day is critical if planned ignoring is to be effective. I recommend all cell phones get locked away by 9 p.m. for this to be effective. Once Sheinelle learns that her disruptive behavior will not get her access to a phone, you can develop reasonable phone rules to maintain her change. If Sheinelle pushes you again, you can use active listening, in which you give Sheinelle the opportunity to share her view. Nonjudgmental responding by repeating her view communicates to Sheinelle you are listening and understand her. Additionally, explaining the rationale for phone rules is a way to address continued aggressive behavior in this skill domain. (Criterion 2) Although this may be hard at the start, are you willing to try this plan? With continued effort, do you think this would work? Do you see any barriers? (Criterion 3)

Example Response to Advanced Client Statement 5

For many teens, the function of threatening self-harm is to gain something. Since Moe has a pattern of using disruptive behaviors to gain more gaming time, threatening self-harm may be another attempt to get what he wants. (Criterion 1) When attention-seeking is clearly established as the function after a careful assessment, planned ignoring would require you to not give in to Moe's threat since this may reinforce and increase his use of self-harm threats. This doesn't mean you disregard him. It's important for him to know you're listening but will not increase screen time in reaction to his threat. In this situation, I would sit down with Moe and develop reasonable guidelines for gaming that include ways of earning extra gaming time for positive opposite behaviors. (Criterion 2) Do you think this would be helpful? Are you willing to try this? Anything that you can think of that would make this difficult to do? (Criterion 3)

Teaching Parents About Effective Communication

Preparations for Exercise 7

1. Read the instructions in Chapter 2.

2. Download the Deliberate Practice Reaction Form and the Deliberate Practice Diary Form at https://www.apa.org/pubs/books/deliberate-practice-behavioral-parent-training (see the "Resources" tab; also available in Appendixes A and B, respectively).

Skill Description

Skill Difficulty Level: Intermediate

The goal of teaching communication skills in behavioral parent training (BPT) is to help parents recognize and change ineffective communication strategies they use to gain child compliance. At the beginner level of this BPT exercise, we teach parents the characteristics of effective commands and in which situations to use them to increase child compliance (McNeil & Hembree-Kigin, 2010). We then introduce the communication strategy of compromise and problem solving at the intermediate and advanced levels (Barkley & Robin, 2014; Greene & Ablon, 2006).

The important first step to increase compliance is teaching parents the basics of how to make effective commands (Kazdin, 2008; McNeil & Hembree-Kigin, 2010). This starts with giving parents the rationale for why we recommend using "direct commands," which research has deemed to be more effective than "indirect" commands (McNeil & Hembree-Kigin, 2010). This is followed by teaching parents to recognize the features of a direct command so that they will be more likely to choose and use this communication strategy.

Effective commands are specific and direct, not vague. They are positively stated and tell the child what to do rather than what not to do—for example, "Please sit down in that chair" rather than "Stop running around the room." Parents are instructed

https://doi.org/10.1037/0000484-009

Deliberate Practice in Behavioral Parent Training, by M. D. Terjesen, H. B. Vidair, P. S. Ohr, O. A. Walsh, T. Rousmaniere, and A. Vaz

to tell, not ask, their child what they want them to do using a neutral voice. Starting with the word *please* is respectful and sets the stage for a calm, nonjudgmental tone. Furthermore, making sure the command is developmentally appropriate is critical for gaining compliance in young children, who need to be given one command at a time. Recalling a string of commands may be difficult for children. Giving multiple commands simultaneously, such as "Sit down in the chair near the table, put the crayons in the box, and take out the cars so we can play" can make it difficult for the parent to determine whether the child has complied (McNeil & Hembree-Kigin, 2010).

Effective commands for emerging and older adolescents should take into account that teens are striving for autonomy, and parents require an additional skill set appropriate for this developmental stage. Parents of teens are taught when to give commands and when to use an alternate communication strategy. They are taught to give commands calmly and respectfully and to be aware of their communication patterns that contribute to teen noncompliance and increase family conflict. To reduce the ineffective use of commands, parents are taught to give indirect commands that suggest flexibility in compliance and save nonnegotiable commands for situations with safety concerns. It is also helpful for parents to give a reason or rationale along with their command. Giving a reason before giving the command will increase compliance and reduce the adolescent's attempts to negotiate or delay compliance. Helping parents develop effective rule setting also establishes effective communication and helps children clearly understand behavior guidelines and expectations (Kazdin, 2008). Regardless of the age, when children and teens comply with effective commands and set rules, it is essential that parents consistently follow up with praise and positive regard.

At the intermediate difficulty level, we teach parents other effective communication skills to be used as an adjunct to commands. An effective technique is a problem-solving communication approach that involves teaching parents several steps in problem solving including problem definition, brainstorming of possible solutions, negotiation, decision making about a solution, and implementation of the solution (Barkley & Robin, 2014). At this level, we introduce challenging situations as we help parents consider how to integrate giving effective commands with problem solving to gain compliance from their child when parents think there is room for negotiation. Additional problem-solving communication strategies are taught to parents at the advanced difficulty level of this exercise to help them address the experience and expression of strong emotions in children that may reduce compliance. Situations introduced at this level depict conflict caused by lack of parental perspective-taking and misunderstandings, especially when trying to gain compliance from dysregulated youth. We point out the conflict to parents and instruct them to speak to their child in an even tone of voice and actively pay attention to their child (e.g., putting away electronics). We instruct parents to summarize what their child is saying using their own words while avoiding judgment and checking back with the child to see if their perspective is correct (Greene & Ablon, 2006). In situations when parents struggle with perspective and misunderstanding, it is especially important to use effective commands and problem-solving skills that involve negotiation, as well as active listening to gain compliance and improve the parent–child relationship.

As we highlighted in Chapter 1, many BPT skills incorporate assessment of treatment acceptability. In the communication skill, we chose to assess the parents' willingness to try the communication strategies and the feasibility as to whether they foresee any barriers to using the suggested communication strategies, asking questions such as "Is this something you think you can do?" or "Are there any roadblocks that may make this strategy difficult to use?"

SKILL CRITERIA FOR EXERCISE 7

1. Provide the parent with information to help identify ineffective communication patterns.
2. Explain the communication skills relevant for the parent. Communication skills used in this exercise include the following:
   - Effective commands
   - Rule setting
   - Problem solving (negotiation)
   - Problem solving (active listening)
3. Teach the parent how to apply these skills to specific situations.
4. Ask the parent questions that reflect treatment acceptability (i.e., are they willing to try the skill, do they anticipate any barriers).

Examples of Therapists Teaching Parents About Effective Communication

Example 1

CLIENT: [*frustrated*] I just can't get my 7-year-old to do what I want without yelling. I probably ask Suri four or five times to start her homework, and then she only does it when I yell at her. I hate that this is the kind of parent that I have become.

THERAPIST: It sounds like Suri is noncompliant to your requests to do homework; you describe yelling and asking her multiple times, and it's not working. (Criterion 1) Giving effective commands begins with giving direct commands, which make it clear to Suri that she is being told, not asked, to do her homework. Effective commands are positively stated and given in a respectful tone. (Criterion 2) In the current situation, when telling Suri to do homework, say, "Please do your homework now." When Suri complies, remember to give praise such as "Great job doing your homework!" (Criterion 3) Is this something you are willing to do, and do you see any barriers to doing it? (Criterion 4)

Example 2

CLIENT: [*angry*] Somewhere along the line, my 16-year-old, Max, has developed the belief that our home is a democracy and there shouldn't be rules he doesn't agree with. So he doesn't follow the rules we've set and questions them. He doesn't seem to care and will even tell me to calm down. He says I am making a big deal out of nothing. That really sets me off. I just want him to do what he is supposed to when asked without it leading to an argument each time. Which communication strategy should I use?

THERAPIST: Max is questioning rules, and you're wondering what strategies to use in specific situations to gain his compliance. (Criterion 1) The best treatment strategy is using direct commands when compliance is imperative and indirect commands when optional and to involve Max in problem solving to communicate that his opinion counts. (Criterion 2) To give a direct command, use wording such as "To keep your laptop from breaking, please put it in your desk drawer at bedtime." When compliance is preferred but not essential, give an indirect command, which is a request rather than a demand, using wording such as "How about putting away your clothes?" Problem solve with Max by brainstorming the importance of each rule or command and use negotiation to decide which are imperative and which are flexible. (Criterion 3) Is this helpful? Are there barriers that may make this strategy difficult to use? (Criterion 4)

Example 3

CLIENT: [*exasperated*] The fight over Jade's phone was frankly ridiculous. She's supposed to turn the phone in at 7 p.m. if she doesn't start her homework. It was 7:30. I said: "Can you please give me that phone now?" and she just went into her room and locked the door, so I ignored her for the night. The other night, I shut off her phone's WiFi access and she screamed that she needs her phone, and I don't understand her. She slammed the door to her room, so I didn't bother going in to talk to her. She finally started her homework but didn't finish until almost 10. I'm afraid that tonight will be the same story. How can I just get my 12-year-old to do what I ask and to talk to me?

THERAPIST: It sounds like you're using indirect commands such as "Can you . . . ," which imply a choice when really compliance is imperative. Additionally, you and Jade avoid talking when she is experiencing strong emotions, and this is something you'd like to change. (Criterion 1) For this, using an effective command, and communicating that you are actively listening to Jade's perspective to promote problem solving in establishing rules, is the best approach. (Criterion 2) Start by saying, "Since homework is important and your feelings are important, we talked and came up with homework rules." Then use a direct command to follow the rule that is in effect. Until Jade complies, restate at reasonable intervals a direct, positive, unambiguous command to follow the rule you both established well in advance of 7 p.m., such as "The rule is to finish your homework if you want to keep WiFi access after 7 p.m., so please begin your homework now." (Criterion 3) Are you willing to try this? Let me know if you foresee any roadblocks I can help you with. (Criterion 4)

INSTRUCTIONS FOR EXERCISE 7

Step 1: Role-Play and Feedback

- The client says the first beginner client statement. The therapist **improvises** a response based on the skill criteria.
- The trainer (or, if not available, the client) provides **brief** feedback based on the skill criteria.
- The client then repeats the same statement, and the therapist again improvises a response. The trainer (or client) again provides brief feedback.

Step 2: Repeat

- Repeat Step 1 for all the statements **in the current difficulty level** (beginner, intermediate, or advanced).

Step 3: Assess and Adjust Difficulty

- The therapist completes the Deliberate Practice Reaction Form (see Appendix A) and decides whether to make the exercise easier or harder or to repeat the same difficulty level.

Step 4: Repeat for Approximately 15 Minutes

- Repeat Steps 1 to 3 for at least 15 minutes.
- The trainees then switch therapist and client roles and start over.

> **Now it's your turn! Follow the exercise instructions.**

Remember: The goal of the role play is for trainees to practice improvising responses to the client statements in a manner that (a) uses the skill criteria and (b) feels authentic for the trainee. **Example therapist responses for each client statement are provided at the end of this exercise. Trainees should attempt to improvise their own responses before reading the examples.**

BEGINNER-LEVEL CLIENT STATEMENTS FOR EXERCISE 7
Beginner Client Statement 1
[Annoyed] Seth, my 7-year-old, does not like to put on his sneakers. Every morning I say "Let's put your sneakers on" or "How about putting your sneakers on?" Seth just doesn't listen. I know he's capable of putting on his sneakers because he does it when he wants to. When I tell him to do it, he runs around the house screaming "no, noo, nooo." I have to shut the door and hold him down to put on his shoes, which is not much fun for either of us and doesn't work. Can you help?
Beginner Client Statement 2
[Frustrated] I give up. Going food shopping with Angel is a horror show. He touches everything and runs around the store, screeching as he runs. I keep telling him not to run, to stop touching everything, to quit screeching and to just behave, but he acts as if I don't exist. If you don't help me, I'm going to give up on going shopping until he goes to college, which is a long way off since he's in kindergarten.
Beginner Client Statement 3
[Sad] She never used to be this sneaky. Solana started middle school, and our relationship changed. Right now, what gets me most upset is when I ask her who she's going to be with after school, and she says "friends" instead of telling me who. When I respond with "Why aren't you telling me who?" she says it's not important. But it's important to me because I want to make sure she's safe.
Beginner Client Statement 4
[Annoyed] I can't get Lev to do his one chore of the day without him stalling for so long that I end up doing it. The other day, I started out nicely with "How about taking out the garbage?" He said "Later," which is his usual response. I waited about 30 minutes and asked again. "Don't you think you should be taking out the garbage now? It's getting late." He responded with "Later." His last chance was before bedtime. I asked one more time: "Are you going to take the garbage out or, as usual, not do what I ask you to do? You're so lazy." He didn't bother saying "later" but rolled his eyes and ignored me. I did it myself.
Beginner Client Statement 5
[Angry] The argument was all about cleaning her room. I told Aliyah, "Let's get your room cleaned up sometime today." She nodded her head. I look in an hour later, and she's Zooming with her new high school friend. I say, "Didn't I tell you to clean your room? It's a mess." She says, "I did. I put my books on my desk." So I say, "What about your clothes? They're all over the floor. Are you blind?" Then we ended up arguing about how I didn't tell her I also wanted her clothes put away and if I wanted her room clean, I should clean it myself, which I did.

🛈 **Assess and adjust the difficulty before moving to the next difficulty level (see Step 3 in the exercise instructions).**

INTERMEDIATE-LEVEL CLIENT STATEMENTS FOR EXERCISE 7

Intermediate Client Statement 1

[Resigned] My preschooler, Felicia, doesn't like when I leave her to go shopping, even when my mom watches her. I know she loves her grandma, but recently when I tell her to stay home and play with Grandma she says no and that I'm the only one she wants to play with, so I end up staying home and we all play together.

Intermediate Client Statement 2

[Stressed] Every morning and evening, I tell my 7-year-old, Deniz, "We want your breath to smell clean so please brush your teeth." I don't know why I bother telling him so nicely because he always says no and tries to run out of the room, so I hold him down and do it for him even though he screams. What an awful way to start and end our day. He says the toothpaste tastes gross and makes him feel icky even though we've tried every flavor under the sun. And that's not the only thing he's overly reactive to. He avoids certain foods and doesn't like wearing certain clothing. What should I do?

Intermediate Client Statement 3

[Resignation] Yoni is my middle-schooler who says no to all my attempts to have him go to birthday parties with his friends from school. He complains about wanting friends but refused to attend the party of our next-door neighbor after I told him he would lose screen time for a month unless he went. Of course I didn't mean it since screen time makes him happy.

Intermediate Client Statement 4

[Compassionate] Roni complains that every rule I make is unfair. They are particularly noncompliant when it comes to my rule that no friends are allowed in their room after 10 p.m. even on the weekend. Roni ignores my direct commands to have their friend leave, and sometimes the friend stays until midnight, which I guess is not too unusual for two 17-year-olds. Roni says I'm not sensitive to their need to have a friend to talk to and that leaving at 10 p.m. is so old school. Am I really being insensitive and unreasonable? I like to go to bed by 10 p.m. and I feel uncomfortable having someone else in their room. Should I compromise? I love Roni and want a good relationship with them.

Intermediate Client Statement 5

[Disappointed] Jin does not listen to me when it comes to participating in social activities at our church. Every Wednesday there's a social group for teens. Jin has attended this group since middle school. Now in high school she says it's not her thing and refuses to go, even though I tell her she must go because it connects us to our heritage, which is an important family value. She still refuses to go, claiming that it's not one of her values. This makes me so sad. I want her to stay connected to our heritage, but I don't want to force her. How should I handle this?

Assess and adjust the difficulty before moving to the next difficulty level (see Step 3 in the exercise instructions).

ADVANCED-LEVEL CLIENT STATEMENTS FOR EXERCISE 7

Advanced Client Statement 1

[Hopeless] I have three children under age 5. Jimmy is my oldest and he's 4. Ben and Jen are my 3-year-old twins. Jimmy gets very angry very quickly when the twins grab his toys. He screams at them, pushes them down, and has even spit at them. I tell him, "Please be nice to the twins." But he doesn't listen. I ask him if he can "share," but he says, "It's not fair. Those are my toys." I try putting him in his room for a time-out, but he starts crying and says he's sorry for being bad and why won't I listen to him. I feel so hopeless.

Advanced Client Statement 2

[Frustration] My 12-year-old daughter, Vega, is glued to TikTok. Before going to bed, she spends 2 hours looking at it. I told her she can't look at TikTok anymore except on the weekends, but I find her hiding under the covers looking at it anyway on her iPad. I took her iPad away a week ago, and she had the most intense meltdown ever. She cried for 2 hours straight, then finally fell asleep, but I heard her crying throughout the night and she was exhausted the next day. Since then, she hasn't spoken to me respectfully. She argues and screams, saying I don't understand what it's like to be her, that I've ruined her life and she hates me. Can you help me?

Advanced Client Statement 3

[Stressed] Mark has a new middle school friend, Henry, and was spending weekends at his house, but we put a stop to it. I found out from a friend that Henry's father has a gun and Henry knows how to get into the lockbox and sometimes takes it out with Mark there. Two weeks ago, I told him the rule was no more spending time in Henry's house until we know it's safe, although Henry can come over to our house. Mark flipped out on me—even left the house—and I had to go out looking for him. Now he barely talks to me or his mom and says he's a prisoner in his own home. He quit basketball, saying we may be able to force him to stay at home, but we can't make him do everything. I'm not sure what to do.

Advanced Client Statement 4

[Frustrated] Mei refuses to stay on her high school tennis team, so I had to take matters into my own hands. She says the thought of her friends and family looking at her and expecting her to win is too painful and she feels hopeless. She's been playing since freshman year and was just put on the varsity team. I told her the rule is you never give up on a sport, especially in the middle of the season, and she has to continue to get a scholarship. This was last week. Since then, she's been playing tennis, but I see her briefly, only at breakfast and dinner. The rest of the time, she's in her room and I hear her crying. She won't let me in but continually texts me that I don't know what it's like to be her and that I'm stealing her identity. Can you help?

Advanced Client Statement 5

[Despair] Jett, my 13-year-old, tells me every day that she hates me because I won't allow her to be in a relationship with a 16-year-old "friend" she met online. I'm really worried about her safety and that she'll sneak out to meet up with him. She argues with me about everything and curses at me constantly, even in public. She claims I'm ruining her life by treating her like a baby. I love her and want to keep her safe, so I lock up her electronics at night, which is just making things worse. How can I keep her safe but not ruin her life—how can I make things better again? What can I do?

🛑 **Assess and adjust the difficulty here (see Step 3 in the exercise instructions). If appropriate, follow the instructions to make the exercise even more challenging (see Appendix A).**

Example Therapist Responses: Teaching Parents About Effective Communication

Remember: Trainees should attempt to improvise their own responses before reading the examples. **Do not read the following responses verbatim unless you are having trouble coming up with your own!**

EXAMPLE RESPONSES TO BEGINNER-LEVEL CLIENT STATEMENTS FOR EXERCISE 7
Example Response to Beginner Client Statement 1
Seth won't put his sneakers on, and from your description, holding him down isn't an effective strategy. (Criterion 1) Since Seth is developmentally capable of putting on his sneakers, I suggest you start with using a direct command to make it clear that you expect Seth to follow through. The commands you describe using are indirect, which are less effective because it implies Seth has a choice. Use direct commands only when putting on sneakers is imperative, such as when you must leave the house. (Criterion 2) Using a calm tone, say, "It's time to go out. Please put on your sneakers." Giving Seth a reason to put on his sneakers will help with compliance. Using the word *please* helps you deliver the command in a polite manner. If Seth complies, say, "Great job listening! Now we can go outside." For noncompliance, put his sneakers on unemotionally, ignoring all attention-seeking behaviors, and remember to use a direct command the next time you need him to put on his shoes. (Criterion 3) What do you think of this approach, and are you willing to try it? (Criterion 4)
Example Response to Beginner Client Statement 2
Shopping with Angel is hard because he doesn't stay near you, keep his hands to himself, or uses a quiet voice, and it's difficult to tell whether he's compliant since you give him multiple vague commands. (Criterion 1) Effective commands are clear and given one at a time. They positively state what to do and include a reason. (Criterion 2) In the situation you described, start by giving a single command with a reason for one behavior you would like to change. Say "Shopping will be quicker if you stay right by my side." Give continuous verbal and nonverbal praise for compliance. On subsequent shopping trips, once Angel is consistently compliant with staying by your side, you can give him a direct command for keeping his hands to himself. (Criterion 3) Are you willing to try this the next time you go shopping? (Criterion 4)
Example Response to Beginner Client Statement 3
It's typical for preteens to interpret questioning and limit setting as an invasion of privacy, even though, from your perspective, you're asking because you care. (Criterion 1) Giving a command with the expectation that it's imperative to comply is recommended for situations in which there is an issue of safety, especially for teens, and from your description, safety is a concern in this situation. (Criterion 2) To get Solana to comply, give a command containing a reason or rationale for complying with your directive. Approach Solana in a calm time and tell her, "Knowing who you are with when you're not home helps me keep you safe. I'll do my best to consider your privacy when it's not a matter of safety. For now, I need you to either text or call me after school and let me know who you are with." (Criterion 3) Can you do this? (Criterion 4)

EXAMPLE RESPONSES TO BEGINNER-LEVEL CLIENT STATEMENTS FOR EXERCISE 7

Example Response to Beginner Client Statement 4

Lev has learned that noncompliance will enable him to avoid taking out the garbage because you'll do it for him. To gain compliance, I can help you with the type of command you give and how you respond to noncompliance. (Criterion 1) First, your command needs to be direct, not indirect. (Criterion 2) Here, instead of "How about taking out the garbage?" which implies choice, say calmly, "Taking out the garbage is your chore. Please take it out now." If he is noncompliant, after waiting 5 seconds repeat the command verbatim, ignoring any problematic behaviors (see Exercise 6 on planned ignoring). If he is compliant, whether immediately or after 5 seconds, say "Thank you for doing what I told you to do." If he is still noncompliant 5 seconds after the second command, say "You have a choice, either you take the garbage out now or you lose half an hour of your screen time tonight." (Criterion 3) Do you foresee difficulty doing this? (Criterion 4)

Example Response to Beginner Client Statement 5

It sounds like your commands suggest Aliyah has a choice, and she's learned to avoid cleaning because she knows you'll do it. For Aliyah, it's worth the argument. (Criterion 1) Being very specific with Aliyah and the time frame will increase compliance. Use negotiation problem solving to decrease arguments by deciding together what needs to be cleaned and why. (Criterion 2) To start, problem solve with Aliyah by deciding which two or three cleaning tasks are reasonable for her to do so that friends can visit. Then calmly and nonjudgmentally give Aliyah this direct command: "For your room to be clean enough for friends to visit, please put your clothes in the closet, your books on the shelf, and your dirty laundry in the bin by the end of an hour." Repeat the command verbatim after 15 minutes if she hasn't started. If she doesn't comply, give her the information that her room needs to be cleaned before she has friends over and don't clean the room for her. (Criterion 3) How do you feel about trying this approach? What do you see as barriers? (Criterion 4)

EXAMPLE RESPONSES TO INTERMEDIATE-LEVEL CLIENT STATEMENTS FOR EXERCISE 7

Example Response to Intermediate Client Statement 1

It sounds like you tell Felicia to stay home and play with her grandma, but she complains and you give in, which strengthens noncompliance. A function of this behavior at her age may be anxiety as well. (Criterion 1) Our goal is to develop a plan that starts with a direct command and allows for problem solving to negotiate how much time Felicia will be separated from you to address her anxiety. (Criterion 2) First, problem solve with Felicia how much time is reasonable for you to be away. Then tell Felicia, "I'm going to the store and will be gone for 1 hour instead of the 2 hours I'm usually gone. That's the amount of time it takes for you to watch your favorite television show. Please watch television with Grandma while I'm gone, and I will be back when the show is over." Praise her when you return, regardless of her reaction while you were gone. (Criterion 3) Tell me your thoughts. Do you think it will work? (Criterion 4)

EXAMPLE RESPONSES TO INTERMEDIATE-LEVEL CLIENT STATEMENTS FOR EXERCISE 7

Example Response to Intermediate Client Statement 2

It sounds like Deniz is noncompliant to brushing his teeth, despite you giving him an effective command. Some children are temperamentally overreactive to tastes and other sensory stimuli, and part of Deniz's oppositionality may be related to that. (Criterion 1) Coming up with a plan to improve Deniz's compliance requires both an effective command and problem solving a compromise that takes into consideration Deniz's temperament. (Criterion 2) After having Deniz decide which toothpaste tastes the "least icky," tell him you are going to put a very small amount on the toothbrush, and he will help you decide how much. This is followed by a direct command to "Please brush your teeth while I count to five." Remember to praise Deniz's attempts consistently. (Criterion 3) What do you think? (Criterion 4)

Example Response to Intermediate Client Statement 3

It sounds like you've been giving Yoni direct commands, which have not been effective because, even with the threat of losing screen time, he doesn't comply. Yoni may not be motivated to comply because he knows you won't take away screen time. Also, he may not comply even though he says he wants more friends and doesn't want to lose screen time because social situations make him anxious. (Criterion 1) The best approach is to use an effective command that makes it clear you expect Yoni to comply with your command while problem solving how much time he has to remain at the party. (Criterion 2) Together with Yoni when he is calm, negotiate how much time is reasonable for him to spend at the party. Then give him a direct command to spend that amount of time or he will lose screen time. Make sure you remove screen time if he is noncompliant. (Criterion 3) Is this something you are willing to try? (Criterion 4)

Example Response to Intermediate Client Statement 4

It seems as if you're considering a compromise since maintaining a relationship with Roni is important to you and they've shared that from their perspective this rule seems unfair. (Criterion 1) Problem solving is a communication strategy that will help you and Roni brainstorm how to make a rule that makes sense for both of you and will earn Roni's compliance. (Criterion 2) The first step is to define the problem, which is that Roni wants their friend to stay later than 10 p.m. because it's not that late for a teen and you would like them to leave at 10 p.m. so you can go to sleep. Together brainstorm a solution and then negotiate. Perhaps having Roni's friend stay 1 hour later and you staying up 1 hour later is an acceptable solution for both of you. (Criterion 3) What do you think? (Criterion 4)

Example Response to Intermediate Client Statement 5

Jin is seeking autonomy and searching for values in line with her own identity. Telling her to attend a social group based on your values results in noncompliance and causes conflict. (Criterion 1) Problem solving is helpful when families are in conflictual situations and parents see room for compromise. (Criterion 2) To do this, find a quiet time for you and Jin to clarify what each of you wants. It sounds like you would like her to continue attending the social group and she would like to leave the group. Brainstorm solutions to come up with a compromise that works for both of you, such as having Jin comply with attending once monthly for 3 months. At the end of 3 months, review the solution and either continue or renegotiate. (Criterion 3) Do you see any roadblocks to engaging in problem solving? (Criterion 4)

EXAMPLE RESPONSES TO ADVANCED-LEVEL
CLIENT STATEMENTS FOR EXERCISE 7

Example Response to Advanced Client Statement 1

Jimmy says sharing his toys is unfair and you're uncertain how to address his strong emotions and increase sharing and gentle behaviors. Using commands and consequences alone doesn't seem to be working. (Criterion 1) I'm suggesting three communication strategies to help you. (Criterion 2) Negotiation problem solving requires you and Jimmy to choose and place three special "nonsharing" toys in a box. Next, use active-listening problem solving to calmly tell Jimmy, "I see how upset you feel when told to share. You can play with your special toys if your feelings get too big." When Jimmy needs to share, use this effective command, "This is a sharing toy. Please play gently with the twins." Immediately and consistently reinforce sharing and gentle behavior. For problematic behaviors validate Jimmy's feelings and direct him to his special toys. (Criterion 3) Are you willing to try this approach? (Criterion 4)

Example Response to Advanced Client Statement 2

Disengaging from TikTok is a challenge for Vega and using commands and consequences isn't enough. Vega's emotional reaction is strong as you've noticed arguments and disrespect, and Vega feels you don't "get" her. (Criterion 1) In this situation using rule setting as well as negotiation and active-listening problem-solving techniques helps set reasonable expectations and reduces strong emotions. (Criterion 2) Since attempts to talk with Vega are met with screaming, text to meet and hear her view. Show you're actively listening by repeating her perspective, and negotiate to develop reasonable TikTok viewing rules. For example, "I understand that TikTok is important to you. The rule is, before bed you can use TikTok for 1 hour and then you have 1 hour of nonscreen activity, such as listening to music, or you will lose TikTok privileges for today and tomorrow." (Criterion 3) Are you willing to keep working with me to learn these strategies? (Criterion 4)

Example Response to Advanced Client Statement 3

To keep Mark safe, you've set a firm rule that he can't go to Henry's house, but it's impacting your relationship. You're wondering how to keep Mark safe and still respect his need for autonomy, which he's strongly asserting. (Criterion 1) Problem solving to negotiate reasonable and clear rules and using active listening is the suggested approach. (Criterion 2) To start, allow Mark to go over Henry's house when there's adult supervision. Consider easing restrictions when Mark agrees to ongoing conversations with you about safety. Use active-listening communication skills during discussions and consider compromises for increasing the time Mark can be at Henry's house. Showing Mark you are listening will decrease his resistance to engaging with you and give him a nugget of hopefulness. Understanding each other's perspective will help both you and Mark deal with strong emotions. Taken together, these strategies will repair your relationship. (Criterion 3) Do you think continuing to learn this approach will be useful? (Criterion 4)

Example Response to Advanced Client Statement 4

You want Mei to continue tennis to help finance college. Mei views tennis as painful, and she feels hopeless. Your differing perspectives are creating conflict in your relationship. (Criterion 1) To help Mei, I suggest compromising on the rules that contribute to her hopelessness and brainstorming other ways to finance college. (Criterion 2) Text her suggesting that the two of you talk in person, which allows for eye contact and other nonverbal ways of communicating empathy. Share your views and ask if she understands how you feel. Using negotiation problem solving, develop a new rule in which Mei continues tennis until the end of the season, with you helping her manage stress by practicing calm breathing together. When the season is over, there is no rule for her to continue unless it's something she wants. (Criterion 3) Are you willing to use these strategies to learn how to help Mei with stress, such as calm breathing? (Criterion 4)

**EXAMPLE RESPONSES TO ADVANCED-LEVEL
CLIENT STATEMENTS FOR EXERCISE 7**

Example Response to Advanced Client Statement 5

While setting limits on online relationships may keep Jett safe, her intense negative
reaction concerns you and is damaging your relationship. Many parents struggle with this.
(Criterion 1) I suggest you approach this situation using compromise and understanding.
As part of negotiation problem solving, together with Jett, research how teens can
communicate safely online to establish helpful rules. (Criterion 2) To start, discuss the risks
and how strangers may identify as a teen but actually be older and dangerous. To decrease
strong emotions, give Jett the opportunity to express how she feels and communicate to
her using active-listening skills that you care and need to keep her safe. Together set clear
guidelines for her online activities, such as monitoring interactions. Compromise about
her continuing to communicate with her male online friend, by arranging to meet him.
(Criterion 3) Are you willing to try this challenging approach? Please let me know if you
foresee any barriers that I can help you with. (Criterion 4)

Teaching Parents How to Implement Positive Incentives to Bring About Behavioral Change

Preparations for Exercise 8

1. Read the instructions in Chapter 2.

2. Download the Deliberate Practice Reaction Form and the Deliberate Practice Diary Form at https://www.apa.org/pubs/books/deliberate-practice-behavioral-parent-training (see the "Resources" tab; also available in Appendixes A and B, respectively).

Skill Description

Skill Difficulty Level: Intermediate

The purpose of the positive incentive skill in behavioral parent training (BPT) is to increase a desired child behavior through the implementation of a tangible reward or privilege subsequent to the performance of the behavior. This can be done through the development of a contingency, or "if–then" plan, which means if a child performs a specific behavior, then they receive a reward or privilege. A reward can be a tangible item the child is motivated to earn, like stickers, a small toy, or money. A privilege involves the child earning an activity they want to do, such as going to a special event with friends or use of a cell phone. Positive incentives can be helpful when praise (as described in Exercise 4) is not sufficient for increasing the desired child behavior (Barkley, 2013).

To implement the positive incentive skill, parents are first instructed to identify at least one specific, measurable positive behavior they wish to increase. Like with the praise skill, this may entail having them describe a negative child behavior they wish to decrease and helping them identify the positive opposite of that behavior. The clinician should assess if the child will likely be able to perform the behavior at this time or if the behavior should first be broken down into smaller steps and shaped over time (e.g., doing homework independently vs. completing some of it independently and some of it with help). Once a parent has a feasible positive behavior in mind, the clinician

https://doi.org/10.1037/0000484-010

Deliberate Practice in Behavioral Parent Training, by M. D. Terjesen, H. B. Vidair, P. S. Ohr, O. A. Walsh, T. Rousmaniere, and A. Vaz

can brainstorm ideas for rewards or privileges the child can earn, based on what the child likes. It is important to consider what incentives will be developmentally appropriate for the child (e.g., stickers for a preschooler, seeing a movie with friends for an adolescent). It can be useful for the parent and/or the therapist to involve the child in identifying the rewards and/or privileges. This ensures it is clear what the child will be motivated to earn. It can also give the child a sense of autonomy and control over the contingency plan. Other ideas include having the parent observe items or activities the child is drawn to, asking the teacher what engages their child, or asking their child to select ideas from a list of possible incentives.

Some tangible rewards and privileges can be offered immediately after each instance of the desired child behavior. Initially, parents can either be specific about what the reward or privilege will be each time or, to prevent loss of interest, provide a variety of incentive options and let the child choose one each time the desired behavior occurs. Parents might even surprise their child with a different reward they know their child likes each time they earn something. For larger rewards or privileges, it is common to give the child points or chips each time the wanted behavior occurs, allowing the child to exchange these short-term earnings for a larger incentive later (for specific steps, see Barkley, 2013).

To implement positive incentives successfully, it is important for the clinician to help the parent be clear about how they would know if the child engaged in the specific behavior required as part of the contingency plan, as well as the exact reward or privilege paired with the behavior. Similarly, the child should understand the specific behavior expected, as well as the reward or privilege paired with the behavior. Any ambiguity about how to know if the behavior was performed or if an incentive should be granted can lead to confusion and conflict. With older children, it can help to write and sign a behavioral contract with each family member's responsibilities listed so that everyone can be clear about the contingency plan ahead of time (e.g., Barkley & Robin, 2014).

Once the child is regularly performing the desired behavior, the incentive can be phased out. In other words, the parent should not anticipate providing a reward or privilege for any given behavior forever. At times, once a child has mastered a behavior, the parent can make the contingency plan more challenging by increasing the complexity of the behavior needed or adding on other behaviors needed to earn the incentive. For example, imagine a contingency plan that requires a child to comply with brushing their teeth with parental assistance to earn a sticker. Once the child is regularly doing this, the parent might transition to having the child brush their teeth on their own to earn a sticker or to brushing their teeth and brushing their hair to earn a sticker.

As we discussed in Chapter 1, the final criterion of some of the BPT skills involves the clinician evaluating treatment acceptability. In the positive incentive skill, we focus on willingness to attempt the skill as well as potential obstacles.

Once the clinician teaches a parent how to initiate a contingency plan with a positive incentive, they can ask the parent to initiate the plan for homework during the week (see Exercise 12). The clinician should review how the homework went during the next session and either address any barriers the parent faced or help modify the plan so that it is more effective (e.g., more feasible for the family, more motivating to the child).

Similar to prior skills, the examples of positive incentive skills provide a range in difficulty so that clinicians can practice using them in situations with varying levels of difficulty. The beginner difficulty level represents the early period of treatment, when the parent aims to learn strategies to improve their child's behavior. The statements at the intermediate difficulty level involve times when the parent struggles to set up effective positive incentives or considers punishment when a positive incentive could be effective. Finally, statements at the advanced difficulty level focus on times the parent has concerns about implementing positive incentives. When practicing clinician responses, proceed as if parents have already learned how to praise their children (Exercise 4). Subsequent skills that build off positive incentives include when to use consequence interventions (Exercise 9) and homework planning (Exercise 12).

SKILL CRITERIA FOR EXERCISE 8

1. Provide psychoeducation about using positive incentives (tangible rewards and/or privileges) to increase a desired behavior.

2. Teach the parent how to set a contingency (reward/privilege) for performing a desired behavior (if–then). Example rewards and privileges include the following:
   - A specific tangible reward (e.g., stickers, a small toy, money)
   - A privilege such as an activity the child desires to do (e.g., going out with friends, screen time)
   - A choice from a variety of tangible rewards or privilege options
   - Points, chips, or checks that can be earned toward a larger incentive

3. Generate an idea for a reward or privilege based on the situation described.

4. Ask the parents questions that reflect treatment acceptability (e.g., willingness, anticipation of barriers).

Examples of Therapists Teaching Parents How to Implement Positive Incentives to Bring About Behavioral Change

Example 1

CLIENT: [*confused*] I want to reward Lorraina for following house rules like coming home on time, but all she seems to want are gift cards for her gaming system. I don't understand this and won't buy those, but I don't know what else to do. I need her to come home at a reasonable hour.

THERAPIST: While ultimately what you offer Lorraina is up to you, strategically we have the best chance of getting her to behave the way you want if we offer her an incentive, or something she wants to receive. (Criterion 1) This is called a contingency. In other words, we could come up with a plan indicating that if she behaves the way you expect, then she would earn a reward. The reward is contingent on her behavior. (Criterion 2) For example, you could say that if she makes curfew four out of five times this week, you will reward her with a $20 gift card for her games. (Criterion 3) Would you be willing to try this? Do you foresee anything getting in the way? (Criterion 4)

Example 2

CLIENT: [*critical*] I don't think what I am asking of Nathaniel is too difficult. He's 9 years old already! We have a schedule for the nighttime routine as to what he is expected to do and when he is expected to complete it. No matter what, though, he doesn't stick to it. It shouldn't be this tough to get him to listen.

THERAPIST: One strategy would be to give Nathaniel the opportunity to earn rewards or privileges if he completes the nighttime routine. This would increase the likelihood that he will do what you expect. (Criterion 1) We call this setting up a contingency plan. You would want to be clear about what behaviors are expected and what rewards or privileges he could receive in return. (Criterion 2) Let's say there are three tasks you want him to complete each night. You could give him a token for each task. Those tokens add up and can be exchanged for a reward or privilege at the end of the week, or you could have a bunch of potential rewards and let him choose how to spend his tokens over time. What do you think he would find rewarding or motivating? (Criterion 3) Are you willing to try this? Do you anticipate any problems following through? (Criterion 4)

Example 3

CLIENT: [*exhausted*] No matter what, homework completion is always a nighttime battle. There is always something else that my kids want to do instead of their homework. Franchesca is only 6 but copies her older sister, getting distracted by one thing after another and saying she will do her homework in a little while. They both put it off and put it off until I raise my voice at the end of the night and then they do it. There has to be a better way. I am exhausted by these fights.

THERAPIST: We could likely get your kids to do their homework if they could earn a reward or a privilege. Research shows that offering a child an incentive to perform a behavior makes it more likely they will do it. (Criterion 1) We could come up with what we call a contingency, meaning if your children do something you need them to do, then they can get something they want. (Criterion 2) For example, let's suppose that Franchesca always wants to watch TV when she gets home from school. We might say if she completes her math homework after eating a snack, then she can watch a 30-minute TV show of her choosing. (Criterion 3) Is this something we could have you try this week? Is there anything that might interfere with this plan? (Criterion 4)

INSTRUCTIONS FOR EXERCISE 8
Step 1: Role-Play and Feedback
• The client says the first beginner client statement. The therapist **improvises** a response based on the skill criteria.   • The trainer (or, if not available, the client) provides **brief** feedback based on the skill criteria.   • The client then repeats the same statement, and the therapist again improvises a response. The trainer (or client) again provides brief feedback.
Step 2: Repeat
• Repeat Step 1 for all the statements **in the current difficulty level** (beginner, intermediate, or advanced).
Step 3: Assess and Adjust Difficulty
• The therapist completes the Deliberate Practice Reaction Form (see Appendix A) and decides whether to make the exercise easier or harder or to repeat the same difficulty level.
Step 4: Repeat for Approximately 15 Minutes
• Repeat Steps 1 to 3 for at least 15 minutes.   • The trainees then switch therapist and client roles and start over.

> **Now it's your turn! Follow the exercise instructions.**

Remember: The goal of the role play is for trainees to practice improvising responses to the client statements in a manner that (a) uses the skill criteria and (b) feels authentic for the trainee. **Example therapist responses for each client statement are provided at the end of this exercise. Trainees should attempt to improvise their own responses before reading the examples.**

BEGINNER-LEVEL CLIENT STATEMENTS FOR EXERCISE 8

Beginner Client Statement 1

[Aggravated] Jake won't turn off the TV when we tell him it's time. We've told him that watching too much isn't good for a 4-year-old's brain. But he continually asks for 5 more minutes and gets upset when we turn it off. We just want him to comply without the back and forth.

Beginner Client Statement 2

[Irritated] I want Eleanor to brush her hair in the morning. She's 5 years old and knows by now that this is what we need to do before going to school. I explain this to her every day, but it's like she doesn't care. What can I do?

Beginner Client Statement 3

[Curious] Lark gets home from school and just plays video games all afternoon. They used to love to draw, but now they grab the controller the moment they walk in the door. I know there are other kids in middle school who do this, but I want them to do other things! Do you think there is any way I could motivate them to go back to drawing?

Beginner Client Statement 4

[Concerned] Jenna still doesn't get herself up in the morning, and she's a senior in high school! She relies on me to tell her to get up multiple times before she even sits up in bed. I want her to learn to wake up on her own before she goes away to college this fall. How do you think we can tackle this?

Beginner Client Statement 5

[Motivated] Now that Darrell is 15, his schoolwork is harder, and he really needs to spend time studying for tests ahead of time. But he would rather be on screens with his friends and leave all the work for the last minute. Then he gets really stressed out! We want to find a way to encourage him to start studying a few days in advance.

🛑 **Assess and adjust the difficulty before moving to the next difficulty level (see Step 3 in the exercise instructions).**

INTERMEDIATE-LEVEL CLIENT STATEMENTS FOR EXERCISE 8

Intermediate Client Statement 1

[Skeptical] Eddie isn't like other 3-year-olds. He isn't motivated by stickers or M&M's to comply when I tell him to do something, like be gentle with the cat. I also can't get him a huge gift every time he does what I ask. So I'm not sure how to reward him.

Intermediate Client Statement 2

[Bitter] I don't understand. I tell Maria she is so lucky that we give her so many toys. She's luckier than most 8-year-olds. But then she won't stop playing with her toys to get in the bath when we tell her to. Should I take away some of her toys?

INTERMEDIATE-LEVEL CLIENT STATEMENTS FOR EXERCISE 8

Intermediate Client Statement 3

[Amused] Cassandra keeps leaving her empty juice boxes laying around the house instead of putting them in the recycling bin. We told her she won't get any candy if she keeps this up. But it's hard to follow through on that punishment because we eat candy in the house, too.

Intermediate Client Statement 4

[Helpless] You know, I've offered Randall rewards for listening when I say, "Finish your homework," but he says he doesn't want them. You would think a 13-year-old would want some extra screen time, but he doesn't seem interested. I'm at a real loss as to how to get him to comply.

Intermediate Client Statement 5

[Discouraged] Now that Lee is driving, I have tried giving him points each time he brings the car home with a full tank of gas in it. But inevitably I forget to track the points, and then he argues about how many he has. It's just too hard to stick to.

> Assess and adjust the difficulty before moving to the next difficulty level (see Step 3 in the exercise instructions).

ADVANCED-LEVEL CLIENT STATEMENTS FOR EXERCISE 8

Advanced Client Statement 1

[Hostile] I don't like the idea of giving Wendy stickers every time she does something we need her to do. At 5 years old, she should just be doing what we tell her to do without getting rewarded all the time!

Advanced Client Statement 2

[Anxious] I'm worried about incentivizing Michael. If I give him ice cream for putting his toys away, will he learn an unhealthy eating habit? I don't like the idea of him learning to reward himself with food.

Advanced Client Statement 3

[Disgusted] Larissa thinks now that she's in junior high, she should be able to get an allowance when she is doing well in school. But even if she does well, she is so rude to us that I don't want to give her my money. Why should we reward that attitude?

Advanced Client Statement 4

[Self-righteous] When I was growing up, I didn't get points or presents from my parents for doing what I was supposed to do. I just knew I had to do it, so I did. Crystal is 15 years old. She needs to learn that there are things she has to do in life, like coming home when she's supposed to, or she will face consequences.

Advanced Client Statement 5

[Outraged] You mentioned positive incentives, but James doesn't deserve any. He keeps asking me to go to a concert next month with his friends, but I told him I won't let him do anything else unless he helps out around here! He's 16. He could at least do something small, like take out the garbage!

> Assess and adjust the difficulty here (see Step 3 in the exercise instructions). If appropriate, follow the instructions to make the exercise even more challenging (see Appendix A).

Example Therapist Responses: Teaching Parents How to Implement Positive Incentives to Bring About Behavioral Change

Remember: Trainees should attempt to improvise their own responses before reading the examples. **Do not read the following responses verbatim unless you are having trouble coming up with your own!**

EXAMPLE RESPONSES TO BEGINNER-LEVEL CLIENT STATEMENTS FOR EXERCISE 8
Example Response to Beginner Client Statement 1
We could probably motivate Jack to turn off the TV when you tell him to by letting him know he can earn a reward for doing this right away. (Criterion 1) We would have you explain that if he turns off the TV as soon as you tell him it's time, then he can earn a reward. We refer to this if–then statement as a contingency. (Criterion 2) As an example, let's suppose that Jake often asks for an extra story at bedtime. Here, you could tell him if he turns off the TV as soon as he is told to, then he can have an extra story at bedtime. (Criterion 3) Would you be open to trying this as an experiment? Are there any obstacles you imagine running into? (Criterion 4)
Example Response to Beginner Client Statement 2
There is substantial evidence showing that rewarding a child for a behavior increases the likelihood they will perform that behavior. (Criterion 1) A contingency plan involves deciding what type of reward or privilege your child can earn if she does the behavior you want. (Criterion 2) What about telling Eleanor she can earn a quarter for every morning she brushes her hair before school? At the end of the week, if this is something she likes, you can take her to the store with the quarter toy vending machine to use what she has earned. Or you could consider other rewards that she finds motivating. (Criterion 3) Is this something you would want to try to do this week? Do you anticipate any barriers? (Criterion 4)
Example Response to Beginner Client Statement 3
We can set up a plan where Lark knows they can earn a reward or privilege for spending time drawing. Research indicates having an incentive based on what your child likes increases the chance they will engage in the behavior you want them to. (Criterion 1) Let's have you set up something called a contingency plan, meaning that if Lark spends time drawing, they can earn a reward. (Criterion 2) How about if Lark draws for half an hour, then they can earn an hour of video game time? If they do this three times in a week, you will give them money toward a new video game. (Criterion 3) Would you be willing to try this type of plan? What could get in the way of carrying it out? (Criterion 4)
Example Response to Beginner Client Statement 4
Research shows we can increase the chance of someone behaving the way we want them to by offering an incentive, like a reward or privilege. (Criterion 1) I would like us to work on a contingency plan, which means coming up with something Jenna likes that she would be able to earn if she got up on her own. (Criterion 2) We can start with you calling up to her room once. Do you think she would be motivated to do this if you made her breakfast each time she was successful in the beginning? (Criterion 3) Could you see yourself trying something like this? What might get in the way? (Criterion 4)

EXAMPLE RESPONSES TO BEGINNER-LEVEL
CLIENT STATEMENTS FOR EXERCISE 8

Example Response to Beginner Client Statement 5

A good, evidence-based way to encourage an increase in Darrell's studying earlier is to find something he would find rewarding for doing so. (Criterion 1) A contingency plan is a plan to provide a reward or privilege for engaging in a desired behavior. (Criterion 2) What if you tell Darrell that any day he studies for a half hour during the week before an exam, you will let him stay on screens for an extra half hour? We can define what studying would look like and when he can start screen time, then write up a contract you can both sign to hold each of you accountable. (Criterion 3) Would you commit to experimenting with this idea this week? What problems might you encounter? (Criterion 4)

EXAMPLE RESPONSES TO INTERMEDIATE-LEVEL
CLIENT STATEMENTS FOR EXERCISE 8

Example Response to Intermediate Client Statement 1

A child does need to feel motivated by a reward or privilege to increase the behavior you want to see, yet you are not expected to provide a big present each time. (Criterion 1) I would like to find something that motivates Eddie to be gentle with your cat. Instead of a reward, we can set up what is called a contingency plan for complying where he can earn a privilege. (Criterion 2) Assuming that there is an activity that Eddie likes to do with you, like playing board games, perhaps you can communicate that if he is gentle with the cat three times in one afternoon, then could he earn playing a game of his choice with you? (Criterion 3) Would you be open to this? What are some challenges you may run into? (Criterion 4)

Example Response to Intermediate Client Statement 2

Research shows that offering a reward or privilege for increasing a behavior you want is actually more effective than punishment. (Criterion 1) Let's start developing a contingency plan, which is a plan for what Maria can earn if she gets into the bath when you tell her to do so. (Criterion 2) For example, given that she really enjoys her toys, what about buying a bunch of inexpensive bath toys and telling her that each time she gets into the bath as soon as she is supposed to, she can choose one? (Criterion 3) Is this something you would be open to doing this week? Can you think of anything that could get in the way? (Criterion 4)

Example Response to Intermediate Client Statement 3

As tempting as punishment is, it is more realistic and effective to incentivize Cassandra's putting the juice boxes in the recycling bin with a reward or privilege. (Criterion 1) We can create what we call a contingency plan, where if she does what you expect, then she earns something she likes. (Criterion 2) For example, if she throws a juice box away, she can earn a piece of her favorite candy, which you would be the one to give her. (Criterion 3) Are you willing to try this? What could get in the way of following through with this plan? (Criterion 4)

Example Response to Intermediate Client Statement 4

You are on the right track, in terms of trying to incentivize Randall with a reward to increase the chance he finishes his homework. (Criterion 1) It sounds like we have to figure out what type of reward or privilege would motivate him, as screen time is not working. This is what we call a contingency plan, or earning a reward or privilege he would like in exchange for getting his homework done. (Criterion 2) How about we have you explain that you want to help motivate him to finish his homework by letting him earn something he really likes? He can even have a menu of different reward options to choose from. (Criterion 3) Would you be willing to discuss this idea with Randall? Do you predict any challenges when trying to work on this with him? (Criterion 4)

EXAMPLE RESPONSES TO INTERMEDIATE-LEVEL CLIENT STATEMENTS FOR EXERCISE 8

Example Response to Intermediate Client Statement 5

I am glad to hear you are trying to incentivize Lee's filling the gas tank, because providing a reward or privilege for this behavior gives you the best chance of it occurring more often. (Criterion 1) It sounds like you have tried to develop a contingency plan, meaning if he fills the gas tank, then he earns points. (Criterion 2) If it is too hard to track points over time, perhaps we could think of a reward or privilege Lee would want to earn each time he brings the car home. (Criterion 3) Would you be willing to work on this new type of plan? Do you see any challenges with rewarding him each time instead of with points? (Criterion 4)

EXAMPLE RESPONSES TO ADVANCED-LEVEL CLIENT STATEMENTS FOR EXERCISE 8

Example Response to Advanced Client Statement 1

Right, it is important to make sure rewards or privileges are only strategically provided for a few of Wendy's positive behaviors that you wish to increase. (Criterion 1) I am thinking we can figure out something called a contingency. This means identifying a few specific behaviors you want Wendy to do. If she does one of these behaviors, then she can earn a reward. (Criterion 2) Let's identify two or three specific behaviors you want her to do, which can lead to a sticker or something else she likes. (Criterion 3) Would you be willing to implement a plan like this? What might prevent you from moving forward with this? (Criterion 4)

Example Response to Advanced Client Statement 2

Strategically providing rewards and privileges has been shown to increase a desired child behavior, like putting toys away. (Criterion 1) Given your concern about giving Michael ice cream every day, we can set up a type of plan called a contingency plan where each day provides an opportunity for him to earn a point toward a larger reward. (Criterion 2) For example, if he puts his toys away one evening, then he earns one point. Perhaps earning four out of five points during the week can add up to going for ice cream on Friday after school. (Criterion 3) Would you be open to attempting this next week? I am wondering if you can imagine any obstacles to this plan. (Criterion 4)

Example Response to Advanced Client Statement 3

I agree, rewards and privileges should not be given for a rude attitude. They can, however, be useful for incentivizing specific behaviors you want to increase. (Criterion 1) I am wondering if we can come up with what is called a contingency, meaning if Larissa speaks to you politely, then she can earn something. (Criterion 2) We can define what Larissa speaking politely would sound like, as well as how much allowance she could earn for this. Then you call tell her that if she speaks this way, then she can earn money. (Criterion 3) Do you think you would be willing to create contingencies like this? Can you foresee any barriers? (Criterion 4)

Example Response to Advanced Client Statement 4

Some things you want Crystal to do, like come home when she is supposed to, are not happening. Research shows the first step for increasing a behavior is to provide a reward or privilege. (Criterion 1) We could start working on improving her behavior by setting up what we call a contingency, or a plan where her engaging in a behavior you want leads to a privilege she is hoping for. (Criterion 2) For example, if Crystal comes home on time three days out of the week, you could grant her the privilege of going with her friends to the mall. (Criterion 3) Could we try this and see what happens? What might prevent you from moving forward with this plan? (Criterion 4)

**EXAMPLE RESPONSES TO ADVANCED-LEVEL
CLIENT STATEMENTS FOR EXERCISE 8**

Example Response to Advanced Client Statement 5

It is difficult to want to provide positive incentives when James isn't helping around the house, yet rewards or privileges can be used strategically to increase behaviors you want. (Criterion 1) We refer to this as a contingency plan. You can pick a behavior you want to increase, like taking out the garbage, and tell James every time he does this, you will note his effort, which will earn him points toward a larger privilege. (Criterion 2) In other words, if he takes out the garbage one day, then he can earn a check mark toward the concert. Over time, the checks add up, and we can decide how many checks mean he attends the show. He can be involved in that decision, and we can sign a contract spelling out what each of you committed to so expectations are clear. (Criterion 3) Are you willing to implement this in time for the concert? Could anything get in the way? (Criterion 4)

Teaching Parents About Consequence Interventions

Preparations for Exercise 9

1. Read the instructions in Chapter 2.

2. Download the Deliberate Practice Reaction Form and the Deliberate Practice Diary Form at https://www.apa.org/pubs/books/deliberate-practice-behavioral-parent-training (see the "Resources" tab; also available in Appendixes A and B, respectively).

Skill Description

Skill Difficulty Level: Advanced

The goal of teaching consequence interventions in behavioral parent training (BPT) is to give parents options to decrease disruptive behaviors by delivering consequences that are effective, while also being respectful and developmentally appropriate. When parents want to decrease a problematic behavior and the use of positive reinforcement of appropriate opposite behaviors has not worked, BPT clinicians discuss the application of imposing a consequence on the child. Choosing the right consequence needs careful thought, including developmental considerations (e.g., time-out is most appropriate for younger children) as well as what the negative behavior was (e.g., noncompliance to direct commands, rule breaking, and harmful behaviors). As a parent intervention strategy, consequence strategies have been shown to be effective in reducing rates of disruptive behaviors in children (Michelson et al., 2013).

For a consequence to be effective, the clinician needs to determine the specific behaviors that need to change for both child and parent, which is the first criterion of this exercise. Examples of disruptive child behaviors that can be addressed using consequences include the child who says "no" to direct commands, the emergent adolescent who breaks a house rule, and the teen who threatens parents when they believe their autonomy is being challenged by parental restrictions (Kazdin, 2005).

https://doi.org/10.1037/0000484-011

Deliberate Practice in Behavioral Parent Training, by M. D. Terjesen, H. B. Vidair, P. S. Ohr, O. A. Walsh, T. Rousmaniere, and A. Vaz

Examples of ineffective parent behaviors that can be targeted by clinicians include the parent who gives in to their child's noncompliance, which reinforces the child's disruptive behaviors, and the parent who gives an unreasonable consequence, which increases disrespectful and defiant behavior, resulting in a strained parent–child relationship or no relationship at all.

For the second criterion, we focus on educating parents about consequence strategies and instruct them on how to use a variety of consequence strategies. Educating parents involves explaining to them why consequences are effective for the disruptive behaviors described and communicating that consequence interventions are categorized as taking something desirable away to reduce the occurrence of disruptive behavior or adding a reasonable consequence to decrease disruptive behavior. The use of consequence interventions effectively reduces disruptive behaviors if given correctly. However, although many parents are eager to learn how to "punish" their child because they view it as the solution to their child's problem behaviors, delivering consequences for inappropriate behavior should not be the core of a behavioral parenting program (Kazdin, 2008).

In this exercise, parents are taught how to choose reasonable consequences that can effectively decrease problem behaviors and, in some cases, provide a learning experience, as well as how to combine punishment with a positive incentive (see Exercise 8) that acknowledges positive opposites of disruptive behavior or other desirable behaviors that compete with the undesired behavior (Lieneman & McNeil, 2023). For example, a learning experience is provided when the child who breaks a rule is given a choice between losing an hour of screen time—an example of a reasonable response cost—and doing a chore from a list of helpful chores generated by ideas from both the parent and the child—a reasonable consequence. Parents may also be taught to combine a response cost, such as losing friend privileges, with earning back some of those privileges using an incentive system (Kazdin, 2008).

Finally, to make learning move from more conceptual to procedural, the clinician teaches the parent how to use consequence interventions. We offer definitions and examples of a few different consequence strategies that the BPT clinician may use in response to the situation described by the parent. Time-out, a consequence for noncompliance that is appropriate for younger children, is explained to parents as the removal of their child from all types of desirable reinforcement (including parent attention) for a specified, short period of time (e.g., 3 minutes) in a time-out chair or space. Importantly, the time-out environment should be safe so that parents can see their child in the chair but not make eye contact. Parents are told to start time-out with a single direct command (Exercise 7) and follow through with enthusiastic labeled praise for compliance (Exercise 4) or a warning for noncompliance. Time-outs are ended only after the child is quiet for a few seconds to learn that time-out ends for calm, quiet behavior, which also provides a learning experience for the child (Lieneman & McNeil, 2023).

Another consequence, response cost, involves a reasonably time-limited removal of an important privilege or possession, which, when connected to the behavior, can also make it a learning experience. For example, taking away laptop privileges for a day may be taught as a consequence for not turning the laptop off when told to, in which case the consequence is logically related to the problematic behavior. Taking a toy away when the child won't sit quietly during dinner is also a response cost, but the consequence is not related to the behavior. Parents are also taught to recognize consequences that occur as a function of the child's misbehavior, which they themselves don't deliver but nevertheless would serve to decrease problematic behavior.

As an example, a teen losing laptop access because they threw the laptop on the floor when angry and it broke is receiving a natural consequence.

A consequence that parents are frequently taught to give is a reprimand after misbehavior, either verbal (e.g., "Being rough with your brother is not nice") or nonverbal (e.g., giving a stern look after a misbehavior). Giving a reprimand refers to the addition of a reasonable consequence to decrease inappropriate behavior. Another consequence taught to parents that is used to change behavior is assigning their child extra activities or undesirable or tedious chores after they engage in problematic behaviors. For example, a child using disrespectful language may be assigned a chore such as folding the laundry or a more challenging chore such as cleaning the basement. Grounding is a consequence in which teens have restricted access to reinforcing activities. For example, as a consequence for missing curfew, a parent would be taught to limit their child's time with friends to only in school for 2 weeks and to assign daily chores. Parents are also taught how to use choices when delivering consequences after the child engages in problematic behavior, such as saying, "You have a choice. Either you clean up the basement or you lose an hour of screen time tonight." In this case, the child is choosing between the positive punishment consequence of doing a disliked chore or the negative punishment consequence of losing screen time.

There are several situations in which parents would consider the use of consequences to reduce noncompliance to direct commands, rule breaking, and harmful behaviors. The beginner level will focus on teaching clients to understand and practice administering/selecting basic consequences for noncompliance with direct commands. The intermediate level will focus on teaching clients how to use consequences with rule breaking and difficult problem behaviors. The advanced level will focus on teaching clients how to use consequences with serious disruptive behaviors or in special situations.

As we reviewed in Chapter 1, several BPT skills include the assessment of treatment acceptability. In the consequence intervention skill, we focus on examining parents' willingness to implement consequences, as well as any perceived barriers, as our fourth criterion. Overall, using consequences is effective when used correctly, sparingly, and as just one component of a multifaceted BPT program that has positive parenting as the centerpiece. Incorporating positive parenting strategies such as positive attention (Exercise 5), effective commands (Exercise 7), and positive incentives (Exercise 8) into consequence strategies is essential for consequential interventions to be effective.

SKILL CRITERIA FOR EXERCISE 9

1. Provide the parent with information to help identify which inappropriate behaviors from the child should receive a consequence as well as which parent responses to those behaviors are ineffective.
2. Explain which consequence would be effective in the described situation. Example consequences include the following:
   - Response cost or privilege loss
   - Verbal or nonverbal reprimand
   - Chore assignment
   - Time-out
3. Teach the parent how to implement the consequence.
4. Ask the parent questions that reflect treatment acceptability (e.g., are they willing to try the skill, do they anticipate any barriers?).

Examples of Therapists Teaching Parents About Consequence Interventions

Example 1

CLIENT: [*frustrated*] The house rule is that Mason, my 5-year-old, has to sit at the kitchen table for at least 15 minutes when meals are served. He finishes his food within 5 minutes and then typically stands on his chair, bangs on the table, and throws his utensils on the floor. He makes mealtime miserable for everyone, so I let him leave the table. I know this sounds awful, but I enjoy meals so much more once he leaves. I need help.

THERAPIST: It sounds like Mason has learned to ignore your house rule because there's no consequence. By letting him leave the table, he avoids something he dislikes, which strengthens problem behaviors. (Criterion 1) Start with a reprimand such as "Throwing your fork on the floor is not acceptable." Next, use response cost—the loss of privileges, which decreases problem behaviors. (Criterion 2) Tell Mason he loses a privilege for mealtime disruptive behavior and clearly define these behaviors. Explain what privilege he'll lose, such as 15 minutes of video gaming. Clearly define what positive opposite behaviors you'd like to see, such as sitting in his seat or using utensils appropriately, and praise positive opposite behaviors consistently. Should he misbehave, repeat the reprimand and remind him which behaviors will result in losing gaming time and which won't. If he continues, tell Mason he's lost his privilege. (Criterion 3) Are you open to trying this? What might get in the way? (Criterion 4)

Example 2

CLIENT: [*perplexed*] Romola, my 10-year-old daughter, loves to watch TikTok videos. It's at the point where she's refusing to shut it off when I tell her to do her homework. I tell her over and over again that she has to listen to me, but she doesn't turn it off even if it means she won't have enough time to get her homework done. This is happening more often, and twice this week she was too tired to finish her homework. I know this is wrong, but I don't want her to get in trouble with her teacher, so on those 2 days I finished her homework for her. How do I deal with this?

THERAPIST: Romola's noncompliance is a growing concern, and it's good you realize that finishing homework for her isn't effective because it enables her to continue doing what she wants without consequences. (Criterion 1) Giving logical consequences for Romola's problem behaviors is a place to start. A reasonable consequence would be restricting access to TikTok on school days for homework noncompliance. (Criterion 2) If Romola doesn't comply with your direct command to do homework, tell her she'll lose TikTok access for the rest of the day. If she is noncompliant, you may want to place her electronics in a locked drawer until she finishes her homework, only giving monitored access to electronics for homework. (Criterion 3) Are you willing to try using this consequence? Do you foresee a problem with this? (Criterion 4)

Example 3

CLIENT: [*sad*] Help! I'm living with identical bullies. My teenage twins argue over just about anything. When their disagreements get really intense, they call each other names and say they hate each other. When I ask them what's up, they both say they are just so angry even though they won't say what they're angry about. I've tried ignoring them or being the voice of reason, but neither are working. They weren't always like this, and I want it to go back to them caring about each other.

THERAPIST: Sibling arguments are often accepted as a normal family occurrence and downplayed by parents. It sounds like you recognize that ignoring them isn't working and want to learn how to reduce conflict. (Criterion 1) An effective intervention starts with implementing consequences immediately after the intense arguing. (Criterion 2) In advance and with input from your teens to provide a learning experience, determine reasonable consequences for arguing. Calmly review the rules of acceptable behavior, giving examples of respectful language. Explain that it's not okay to express anger by being disrespectful, and they will be given the decided-on consequence, such as a chore, for hurtful language. Be consistent and for chore noncompliance, give a choice of doing the chore or losing a privilege. At the same time, positively acknowledging all respectful and helpful sibling interactions you notice, such as sharing, would be important. (Criterion 3) Is this something you would try? What barriers might you encounter? (Criterion 4)

INSTRUCTIONS FOR EXERCISE 9

Step 1: Role-Play and Feedback

- The client says the first beginner client statement. The therapist **improvises** a response based on the skill criteria.
- The trainer (or, if not available, the client) provides **brief** feedback based on the skill criteria.
- The client then repeats the same statement, and the therapist again improvises a response. The trainer (or client) again provides brief feedback.

Step 2: Repeat

- Repeat Step 1 for all the statements **in the current difficulty level** (beginner, intermediate, or advanced).

Step 3: Assess and Adjust Difficulty

- The therapist completes the Deliberate Practice Reaction Form (see Appendix A) and decides whether to make the exercise easier or harder or to repeat the same difficulty level.

Step 4: Repeat for Approximately 15 Minutes

- Repeat Steps 1 to 3 for at least 15 minutes.
- The trainees then switch therapist and client roles and start over.

Now it's your turn! Follow the exercise instructions.

Remember: The goal of the role play is for trainees to practice improvising responses to the client statements in a manner that (a) uses the skill criteria and (b) feels authentic for the trainee. **Example therapist responses for each client statement are provided at the end of this exercise. Trainees should attempt to improvise their own responses before reading the examples.**

BEGINNER-LEVEL CLIENT STATEMENTS FOR EXERCISE 9

Beginner Client Statement 1

[Irritated] Getting Sarita to clean up her toys is impossible. I tell her to put her Legos in the closet and she ignores me. When I threaten to punish her if she doesn't put her puzzles on the shelf, she rolls her eyes and tells me to do it myself. This happens every single day when I tell her to clean up. Even though she is only 4, she seems like a teenager. Is this the start of her disobeying everything I ask her to do? How do I get her to listen to me when I tell her what to do?

BEGINNER-LEVEL CLIENT STATEMENTS FOR EXERCISE 9

Beginner Client Statement 2

[Baffled] My 6-year-old son, Anthony, is known as the "no" man. He says no to everything I tell him to do even though I use the direct commands you taught me. I tell him, "Please sit at the table to eat" or "Please share your crayons with your sister." He says "no." He wins all our battles by saying "no." I don't bother repeating myself anymore because he'll just ignore me, but I know that's wrong. What's my next step?

Beginner Client Statement 3

[Vulnerable] Nate is the master of noncompliance. When I tell him "We're going to the park so please put your sneakers back on," he screams "no!" If I repeat that, he lays down on the floor, kicking his feet around, saying I can't make him, and adding in a little bit of swearing, like saying "Hell no!" Time-out used to be effective when he was younger, but it hasn't worked more recently, since he's too big for me to carry onto the chair. I feel helpless because the more I tell him he has to do things "or else" the more he tantrums, so I just walk away.

Beginner Client Statement 4

[Puzzled] According to my teenager, Angelica, keeping her room messy is not a crime. Maybe I'm overreacting, but when I tell her that I can barely open her door because of all the crap on her floor, and she's dismissive and gives me the middle finger, then I get angry. I'm sure there're bugs at the bottom of her pile of leftover food! What can I do to get her to clean up her room? I swear, she was never like this before high school. Suddenly I'm the enemy. I don't get it.

Beginner Client Statement 5

[Infuriated] Miquel, my 14-year-old, drives me crazy with his swearing. He doesn't swear at me or his mother, but he uses curse words frequently, such as "damn" or "crap." I've noticed that he doesn't swear when he gets angry or frustrated. It seems to me like he thinks it's cool or a grown-up thing to do. I'm worried that he'll swear in school and get suspended or that his younger brother will imitate him. This really bothers the crap out of me.

🤚 **Assess and adjust the difficulty before moving to the next difficulty level (see Step 3 in the exercise instructions).**

INTERMEDIATE-LEVEL CLIENT STATEMENTS FOR EXERCISE 9

Intermediate Client Statement 1

[Angry] The rule in our house is "anyone younger than 5 years has to be in bed by 7:30 p.m.," and that means Phillipa. She will do everything to avoid going to bed. Sometimes she's very sweet and says she'd like to help me sort the clothes. Other times, she's the devil in disguise, throwing things at me, running around the house, shouting "You can't make me." What can I do?

Intermediate Client Statement 2

[Ashamed] "Calm, gentle hands" is an important "rule" in our house because Mohammed, our 4-year-old, is anything but calm and gentle with his hands. He destroys toys, hits both me and my husband, and grabs his older sister's hair when they fight, which is very frequently. I'm keeping my fingers crossed that he doesn't start hitting her. I feel guilty saying this, but I look forward to those times Mohammed is out of the house because that's the only time life is calm and gentle in our house.

INTERMEDIATE-LEVEL CLIENT STATEMENTS FOR EXERCISE 9

Intermediate Client Statement 3

[Frustrated] Privacy is a big issue in our home. There are two rooms that are off limits, especially when I'm not home, my office and my bedroom. Somehow Gianna and her middle school friends often end up in these rooms. I remind her ahead of time that the "rule" is she is not to go in either room. Yet I often find them there when I get home or even when I'm home but in the backyard. I usually keep quiet because I don't want to embarrass her in front of her friends, but this is unacceptable. The other day I went into her room to talk to her and didn't think of knocking since I never have before. She screamed that I had no right to sneak into her room! I am so frustrated and almost punished her for life on the spot, but I didn't.

Intermediate Client Statement 4

[Exasperated] Daveed is only in middle school, but he has the bad attitude of a high schooler. His constant meanness and disrespect are breaking my spirit. I often have to remind him of the rule that he takes the garbage out to the curb on Mondays and Thursdays. His go-to is to grab the garbage, very obviously roll his eyes, and mutter under his breath "whatever" as he throws it out. Lately he's gone a little too far—giving me the finger and screaming that I should move my own lazy butt instead of bothering him. When I made it clear that I heard his insult, he threw the garbage bag onto the curb, and it spilled all over the place. He then kicked it around before cleaning it up poorly. We used to be so close. Why is this happening? What can I do?

Intermediate Client Statement 5

[Aggravated] Sasha missed their curfew by 2 hours. They didn't respond to any of my texts, and I was stressed all night until they came in at 2:00 a.m. I was furious and ended up grounding them for 2 months, which overlaps with the prom. Now I'm not sure what to do because this is their senior prom.

Assess and adjust the difficulty before moving to the next difficulty level (see Step 3 in the exercise instructions).

ADVANCED-LEVEL CLIENT STATEMENTS FOR EXERCISE 9

Advanced Client Statement 1

[Worried] Don't get me wrong, I love Seth, but sometimes he scares me. He goes from 0 to 100 in 5 seconds flat, and it's hard to predict what will set him off. For example, the other day I told him we were going with his cousin to the pool, something he typically enjoys. He started throwing his toys and kicking me, screaming that he wanted to go to the park and not the pool. When I said we could go to the park tomorrow he ran to the kitchen and got a knife out of the drawer. Luckily, I was able to get it from him and his baby sister was sleeping in the other room so he couldn't hurt her. He might only be 4 years old, but he's strong and very willful. How can I keep my family safe? How can I help Seth?

ADVANCED-LEVEL CLIENT STATEMENTS FOR EXERCISE 9

Advanced Client Statement 2

[Troubled] I'm heartbroken. For the past month, Emmy has been lying to me about where she goes with her middle school friends when they hang out Friday night. She says they are at a friend's house and that at least one parent is home and there are no boys. Well, yesterday my neighbor went to the mall and saw Emmy there with a bunch of her friends, both boys and girls. What hurts is the lying. I never told Emmy she couldn't hang out with boys. I was just worried about them being in the mall. I wonder what else she has been lying to me about?

Advanced Client Statement 3

[Concerned] We have told Javier what is expected when he is playing games online and someone invites him to have a private conversation. We informed him that we would be monitoring his online activity, and this is now the third time we found out he's been talking privately to someone else who claims they're also in middle school. Despite repeatedly explaining our concerns about his safety, we caught Javier sneaking out of the house this past Saturday at 10 p.m. We asked him if he was meeting his online friend, but he denied it and claimed he was taking a walk. Javier doesn't have many friends, and I don't want to take this medium away completely, but I'm not sure about his judgment and problem-solving ability.

Advanced Client Statement 4

[Perplexed] Bianca has really disappointed me. After all the talks I've had with her about the dangers of smoking and drugs, I caught her and her high school buddies vaping in the basement. I sort of flipped out and kicked her friends out and told her I don't want her hanging out with them anymore. It's been 2 days, and she tells me every chance she gets that I've ruined her life and she has no friends left. She's nasty to everyone in the house. She used to play with her younger brother and sister, but now she rolls her eyes at them. How can I fix this?

Advanced Client Statement 5

[Frustrated] My teenage son, Ephraim, has been watching soft pornography on his laptop. We found this out when my wife brought clean laundry into his room while he was in the bathroom and his laptop was left open. We confronted him, and he went ballistic. He threw his laptop against the wall, and now it's out getting fixed. He cursed us out, screaming that he hated us and that we weren't allowed in his room ever again. That was last week. He barely talks to us except to curse or say "leave me alone." We even took his phone away and said he wasn't getting it back for a month and only if he stopped disrespecting us. He said he didn't care about his phone or us and he wishes we were dead. We love him and don't know what to do.

> **Assess and adjust the difficulty here (see Step 3 in the exercise instructions). If appropriate, follow the instructions to make the exercise even more challenging (see Appendix A).**

Example Therapist Responses: Teaching Parents About Consequence Interventions

Remember: Trainees should attempt to improvise their own responses before reading the examples. **Do not read the following responses verbatim unless you are having trouble coming up with your own!**

EXAMPLE RESPONSES TO BEGINNER-LEVEL CLIENT STATEMENTS FOR EXERCISE 9
Example Response to Beginner Client Statement 1
You've described a pattern of noncompliance in clean-up situations that should be addressed before Sarita's noncompliance extends to other situations and becomes increasingly problematic. (Criterion 1) An effective consequence is response cost, which involves losing privileges for noncompliance. (Criterion 2) In the described situation, you would tell Sarita that if she doesn't put her Legos back in the cubby, you'll remove all of her toys for a half hour, a logical and reasonable consequence. Showing her a timer, explain she needs to comply by the time the timer goes off if she wants to continue playing with her toys. To build compliance, for 1 week give five effective toy clean-up commands daily. For each noncompliance, remove toys for a half hour. For continued noncompliance, after the first week pair response cost with an incentive, such as stickers when she complies. (Criterion 3) Are you willing to try this? (Criterion 4)
Example Response to Beginner Client Statement 2
Anthony has learned to ignore your commands because there's no consequence. Letting him get his way and avoid doing what he dislikes strengthens his noncompliance. (Criterion 1) Time-out is an effective consequence to increase compliance. (Criterion 2) Explain to Anthony he needs to follow your commands or sit quietly in a chair. After giving him a direct command, wait 5 seconds to see his response. For compliance, immediately say "Thank you for doing what I told you to do." For noncompliance give him this warning: "If you don't do what I told you to do, you'll have to sit in this chair until I say you can leave." If he is still noncompliant, gently guide Anthony to the chair. Once Anthony sits quietly for 3 minutes, approach and give him the same command that sent him to time-out. When he complies, praise him and allow him to resume a preferred activity. (Criterion 3) Tell me what you think about using this approach. (Criterion 4)
Example Response to Beginner Client Statement 3
You're giving effective commands, but Nate is not complying, and the lack of a consequence strengthens these behaviors. As Nate is now bigger, time-out is no longer possible. (Criterion 1) Response cost is an alternative consequence that requires you to take away a desired activity or object when Nate misbehaves. When clearly and consistently delivered, response cost improves compliance and ends coercive interaction by telling Nate he is losing a privilege for noncompliance and misbehavior. (Criterion 2) To start, develop a list of reinforcing activities meaningful to Nate if removed, such as block play before bedtime. If Nate does not put blocks away give him this choice: "Either you put the blocks away or you lose block play before bed." If Nate doesn't obey within 5 seconds, remind him about his choice. For continued noncompliance, tell Nate he's lost bedtime block time. Don't attend to disruptive behavior or allow block play before bed or you'll be reinforcing his problematic behaviors. (Criterion 3) Although this may be challenging to do, what do you think? Are you willing to try this? (Criterion 4)

EXAMPLE RESPONSES TO BEGINNER-LEVEL CLIENT STATEMENTS FOR EXERCISE 9

Example Response to Beginner Client Statement 4

For Angelica, keeping her room how she prefers may be her way of declaring independence. (Criterion 1) An effective intervention for this includes natural and logical consequences. Natural consequences are the results of behavior that happen without parent influence. Logical consequences are those imposed by parents that logically fit the misbehavior. (Criterion 2) If Angelica prefers to keep food in her room, she'll likely experience natural consequences of smells and bugs. Clothes on the floor will naturally remain dirty or tear and you'll logically not buy her new clothes until she cares for old clothes. Similarly, electronics may naturally break and logically not be replaced until she is careful with them. (Criterion 3) What do you think? Is this something you would consider doing? (Criterion 4)

Example Response to Beginner Client Statement 5

Miquel's swearing sounds like developmentally typical attempts to grow up. Addressing swearing before it generalizes, gets imitated by siblings, or is used to express anger makes sense. (Criterion 1) Response cost is an effective, time-limited consequence for swearing, which involves removing a privilege that is important and adding a learning experience connected to the behavior. (Criterion 2) To begin, tell Miquel that when he swears, he'll lose access to his phone until he can go without swearing for 2 hours. This consequence is meaningful, brief, and teaches self-control in the moment, a positive opposite to swearing. Using respectful language should be a rule for all family members, including parents. A family consequence for swearing may include having a "swear jar" that all family members contribute a dollar to for swearing. (Criterion 3) So, is this something you can see yourself doing? Do you see any barriers to doing this? (Criterion 4)

EXAMPLE RESPONSES TO INTERMEDIATE-LEVEL CLIENT STATEMENTS FOR EXERCISE 9

Example Response to Intermediate Client Statement 1

Phillipa's noncompliance seems related to the "battle" being more stimulating than her "boring" bed. (Criterion 1) An effective technique is response cost, which involves removing privileges logically related to bedtime delay. (Criterion 2) Have Phillipa choose a preferred activity to do with you at 7 p.m. in her bedroom, following the completion of established bedtime rituals. Set a timer to signal 5 minutes left of the preferred activity. At 7:30, if she starts delaying, firmly tell her she has a choice of losing time from a preferred activity the next day equal to the amount of time she delays or earning a sticker for a small reward the next day. Make sure to consistently remove time from her preferred activity the next day if that's her choice. Giving a firm choice between an incentive and a privilege loss is an important component of this strategy. Use planned ignoring for arguing. (Criterion 3; see also Exercise 6) Do you foresee any barriers to using this strategy? (Criterion 4)

Example Response to Intermediate Client Statement 2

Mohammed's aggressiveness is clearly disrupting your household. (Criterion 1) Time-out, a brief time in which access to stimulation is limited, can decrease aggressive behavior. (Criterion 2) Calmly explain to Mohammed the house rule that he'll get a time-out for hurtful behavior, clearly defining what you mean by hurtful behavior and describing positive opposite, gentle behavior. The next time he behaves aggressively say, "You broke the house rule by being hurtful, so you have to sit quietly in this chair until I say you can get off." If he remains in the chair for 3 minutes, say, "You've been sitting quietly in the chair and can now get off. Remember, if you're gentle you won't have to sit in time-out." If Mohammed will not take the time-out, say, "Either sit or lose one half-hour of game time." If he still resists, tell him he's lost his privilege. (Criterion 3) Tell me what you think about using this strategy. (Criterion 4)

EXAMPLE RESPONSES TO INTERMEDIATE-LEVEL CLIENT STATEMENTS FOR EXERCISE 9

Example Response to Intermediate Client Statement 3

Gianna's rule violation may be one way she's establishing independence, and breaking your rule in front of friends suggests peer approval is reinforcing this behavior. While Gianna isn't respecting your privacy, she's demanding you respect hers, which is frustrating but not surprising for her age. (Criterion 1) An effective intervention is writing a behavioral contract that includes family privacy rules, consequences for when Gianna breaks the rules, and how you'll balance respecting her privacy with the need to monitor her. (Criterion 2) In the situation you described, remind Gianna which rooms are off limits if her friends are over. A logical consequence can include not having friends over for a week or a loss of nighttime phone privileges with friends for 2 or 3 nights, which should be specified in the contract. (Criterion 3) How does that sound? (Criterion 4)

Example Response to Intermediate Client Statement 4

Behavior changes at Daveed's age are not surprising. They are often puberty-related, and may contribute to disrespectful behavior. Disrespect may signal independence-seeking or attention-seeking, and likely Daveed is struggling with strong emotions. (Criterion 1) While ignoring mild forms of disrespect such as eye rolling is recommended, ignoring substantial disrespect might lead to an escalation, and it also doesn't address emotional needs. An effective approach includes the consequence strategies of response cost and assigning a chore paired with positive attention, which you need to communicate clearly to Daveed. (Criterion 2) Explain that a respectful attitude is expected, even in the presence of strong emotions. When he is disrespectful, assign Daveed a predetermined chore to be done that day as a repair. For chore refusal or continued disrespect, use privilege loss, such as reduced screen time. Remember that frequent acknowledgment of positive opposite behaviors increases the effectiveness of this approach. (Criterion 3) I hope this is something you are willing to try. What do you think? (Criterion 4)

Example Response to Intermediate Client Statement 5

Sasha's escalating pattern of defiance by missing curfew and not communicating can become a serious behavioral problem. (Criterion 1) Grounding is a consequence in which teens have restricted access to reinforcing activities. (Criterion 2) To be effective, Sasha should start with limited access for 2 weeks, with daily "chores" assigned. Extended periods are unreasonable and increase defiance. Since you already set the consequence of 2 months, explain that the consequence for the remainder of time will be daily chores, and the time they are grounded will contract if they engage in positive behaviors and they could even earn back prom. Inform Sasha that if they miss curfew again, they'll have no access to friend privileges and limited access to electronics for 2 weekends and must complete several chores. Once grounding is over, remind Sasha of the behaviors that led to their grounding and what behaviors you want to see. (Criterion 3) I realize this is a complicated intervention. What are your thoughts? (Criterion 4)

EXAMPLE RESPONSES TO ADVANCED-LEVEL CLIENT STATEMENTS FOR EXERCISE 9

Example Response to Advanced Client Statement 1

Children are aggressive for several reasons, including poor emotion regulation, biological impulsivity, or learning that aggressiveness gets them what they want. For Seth, it may be all three, and if not addressed, it will worsen. (Criterion 1) Delivering consistent consequences will teach Seth skills to decrease aggression. (Criterion 2) Importantly, first, knives and other potential weapons should be secured out of Seth's reach. When aggressive, Seth should receive an immediate consequence, without warning. To avoid physicality, give Seth a choice of going to time-out on his own or removing a preferred toy or activity for an hour. If he is aggressive, a safe backup room can be used until he calms, followed by again being given a choice of time-out or privilege removal. (Criterion 3) This is an important yet difficult strategy to use. Are you willing to try this with Seth? (Criterion 4)

EXAMPLE RESPONSES TO ADVANCED-LEVEL CLIENT STATEMENTS FOR EXERCISE 9

Example Response to Advanced Client Statement 2

Emmy wants to socialize with her friends, and if that means going to the mall, and she's certain you'll say no, she's likely lying to get her way, a problematic behavior associated with increased independence-seeking in preadolescents. (Criterion 1) Behavior contracting with reasonable consequences and parent compromise would effectively address your concerns. (Criterion 2) To begin, develop a behavior contract together that includes reasonable consequences for lying behavior as well as parent compromises to acknowledge Emmy's independence-seeking. Include consequences for dishonesty, specifically losing the privilege of being with friends or losing phone time over the next weekend, or assigning a chore as reparation. Parent compromise may be a willingness to allow Emmy to go to the mall if she complies with certain expectations, such as checking in at intervals. (Criterion 3) Is this something you can see yourself doing? (Criterion 4)

Example Response to Advanced Client Statement 3

Javier is disregarding your guidelines for safe socializing online, and his leaving the house without permission has you concerned that poor judgment may put him at risk. (Criterion 1) When noncompliance and faulty decision making are related to safety, developing a behavioral contract that clearly describes expectations, and states both consequences for problem behavior and incentives for desired behavior, is recommended. (Criterion 2) First, involving Javier in the development of a contract would teach him good problem-solving skills and give him the opportunity to explain his behavior and his thinking. A reasonable consequence for noncompliance or risky behavior includes 2 days of limited and supervised online activity, which Javier receives access to only if he completes an assigned chore. (Criterion 3) Does this sound doable? (Criterion 4)

Example Response to Advanced Client Statement 4

Asserting independence from parents and gaining approval from friends are strong motivators for engaging in risky behavior. Your challenge is finding a balance between open communication and giving Bianca an unequivocal message that there are consequences. (Criterion 1) I would suggest the development of a behavioral contract with Bianca's input, stating reasonable consequences for problem behaviors and incentives for positive opposites. (Criterion 2) Calmly explain to Bianca that she'll be assigned a daily chore and will have no face-to-face access to friends for a week, which means Bianca will be limited to school and home. Repeat this consequence the following week but incentivize respectful language, no vaping, and doing chores by permitting Bianca weekend, in-home, monitored friend privileges. If concerns escalate, exploring factors that impact treatment effectiveness, such as addiction, is recommended. (Criterion 3) Please tell me your thoughts about this approach. (Criterion 4)

Example Response to Advanced Client Statement 5

On the one hand, Ephraim has been cursing and hurtfully excluding you, and understandably you'd like these behaviors to change. On the other hand, while engaging in a typical teen activity, he believes that his privacy has been invaded and he feels disrespected. (Criterion 1) Using response cost as an intervention to address Ephraim's disrespectful behaviors is recommended. Although Ephraim demonstrated heightened disrespect in reaction to your lengthy phone consequence and while he says he doesn't care, research on teen development suggests he does. (Criterion 2) First, define disrespect and its positive opposite. Next, remove phone privileges for 2 days and reinstate only for daily clearly, defined, positive opposite behaviors. Having to wait for his laptop to be repaired is also a powerful natural consequence that offers a learning experience. (Criterion 3) What do you think? (Criterion 4)

Providing Strategies for Parent Affect Management

Preparations for Exercise 10

1. Read the instructions in Chapter 2.

2. Download the Deliberate Practice Reaction Form and the Deliberate Practice Diary Form at https://www.apa.org/pubs/books/deliberate-practice-behavioral-parent-training (see the "Resources" tab; also available in Appendixes A and B, respectively).

Skill Description

Skill Difficulty Level: Advanced

The main purpose of this skill is for clinicians to acknowledge the parent's emotions and provide strategies the parent can use to help manage their strong emotions in the moment to address their child's behavior. As discussed in Exercise 3 (Identifying and Validating Parent Affect), parents will often report considerable emotional experiences within their role as parents (Rueger et al., 2011). Parents' emotional reactions model to their children how to regulate their own emotions and in turn affect how children develop their own emotional regulation strategies (Morris et al., 2017). Evidence suggests that parents with stronger emotion regulation skills engage in more positive parenting behaviors (Zimmer-Gembeck et al., 2022). Therefore, in addition to identifying and validating these emotional experiences, it is also critical for clinicians to provide parents with effective strategies to manage the intensity of their emotions in the moment. Of note, psychoeducation regarding the effects of emotions on parenting is not the main focus of this skill, as it is covered in Exercise 3; however, in practice, a combination of these skills may be warranted.

There are many evidence-based cognitive and behavioral strategies that parents can use when faced with strong emotions. We believe in providing parents with some psychoeducation about how emotions are a normal part of our lives and are expected

https://doi.org/10.1037/0000484-012

Deliberate Practice in Behavioral Parent Training, by M. D. Terjesen, H. B. Vidair, P. S. Ohr, O. A. Walsh, T. Rousmaniere, and A. Vaz

in the parenting process. Further, it is good to communicate that at times, our emotions become too strong and have a negative impact on our parenting choices. Decreasing the frequency, intensity, and duration of emotional experiences can help parents work toward finding more healthy emotions and, as a result, engage in more healthy and effective parenting behaviors. Cognitive restructuring—that is, identifying maladaptive thoughts and changing them to be more effective and helpful—includes strategies that can help to decrease the intensity of emotions (Leahy, 2017). Decreasing the intensity of emotional experiences may help parents use their behavioral parent training (BPT) skills more effectively (Hajal & Paley, 2020). Additionally, relaxation techniques such as deep breathing, visualization techniques, drinking cold water or splashing some on your face have also been shown to decrease the intensity of parental emotions (Sanders et al., 2007). By identifying emotional regulation strategies for parents, you as the clinician are helping the parents modulate their own affect, which may be both intense and negative; this can help them build a more trusting and close relationship with their child (Hajal & Paley, 2020).

Examples of this skill range in difficulty so clinicians can practice initial mastery, as well as its use in more challenging interactions with parents. At the beginner difficulty level, the parent's emotion is stated in the client prompt, and the clinician responds with one affect management strategy. In the intermediate level, the parent's emotion is stated in the client prompt, and the clinician responds with two affect management strategies. Finally, in the advanced difficulty level, parents do not explicitly state their emotional state but describe emotional behaviors that the clinician uses to identify their emotion or to discuss multiple emotions they are feeling; additionally, the clinician identifies two affect management strategies.

SKILL CRITERIA FOR EXERCISE 10

1. Acknowledges the parents' emotions.
2. Provide strategies parents can use to help manage their strong emotions. Example strategies include (a) examining maladaptive thoughts, (b) relaxation strategies (i.e., deep breathing, exercising), (c) journaling, (d) problem solving, (e) creating a schedule, (f) use of a mantra, (g) labeling of emotions, and (h) using breaks.
   - Beginner level: Identify one affect management strategy.
   - Intermediate and advanced levels: Identify two or more affect management strategies.
3. Invite parents to consider whether they believe that these strategies may work for them and discuss their willingness to address their emotions within treatment.

Examples of Therapists Providing Strategies for Parent Affect Management

Example 1

CLIENT: [*panicked*] I get so anxious and worried when I am away from her. Even though there is a school nurse and she is 10, she has severe allergies, and I worry constantly. I basically get no work done for the hours when she is out of my care.

THERAPIST: I can completely understand your feeling concerned about your daughter being in school with all her allergies and I hear that you get so worried, you're not able to get your work done. (Criterion 1) If you are having the thought that "my daughter is going to eat a peanut and end up in the hospital today," it may be really hard for you to focus on your work. If we can change the thought to "my daughter has an allergy, and there are steps in place with the school to limit her exposure to peanuts," it may open up some space in your brain to allow you to get work done. (Criterion 2) Do you think this is something that would be helpful and worth giving a try? (Criterion 3)

Example 2

CLIENT: [angry] His repeated errors in judgment when it comes to using social media infuriate me. He is 16 years old! We have had talk after talk about this, yet he goes back and does it again. I got so angry the other day, I threw his smartphone and smashed it. I know I shouldn't have done that, but I was so upset.

THERAPIST: I hear that you are so frustrated with your son's social media behavior and his bad decisions. You have continuously tried to talk with him and you're saying it doesn't seem to work, and as a result you got so angry that you threw and broke his phone. (Criterion 1) I am wondering if we can look more at how you are managing your emotions during these talks. There are different strategies that you could try in the moment when you feel yourself getting angry, like deep breathing and drinking very cold water, that may be helpful to use to reduce your frustration and may allow you to stay calm and not make choices you may regret, like throwing the phone. (Criterion 2) Would you be willing to give this a try, and do you think it would be helpful to discuss this further? (Criterion 3)

Example 3

CLIENT: [upset] It kills me to see Hector struggle in eighth grade. He tries so hard, but his learning disability makes it so tough for him. I often wonder if I did something wrong. I mean, I probably should have gotten him evaluated before sixth grade, but I didn't realize he was struggling until middle school. Other parents would have noticed.

THERAPIST: From how you are describing how you feel as it relates to Hector, it sounds like you are feeling so guilty and that you think it is your fault Hector is struggling in school. (Criterion 1) Pausing to label the emotion of guilt you are feeling can be helpful in managing your affect in the moment. It also sounds like you are having thoughts like "I should have gotten him evaluated earlier" and "It's my fault that Hector's struggling." These thoughts may also lead to negative feelings like guilt. Evidence suggests that if we are able to change our maladaptive thoughts to healthier thoughts, like "I did the best I could at the time and am trying my best right now," it can help decrease the intensity of our emotion. (Criterion 2) What do you think of working together to identify your emotion and come up with healthier thoughts related to your guilt? (Criterion 3)

INSTRUCTIONS FOR EXERCISE 10
Step 1: Role-Play and Feedback
• The client says the first beginner client statement. The therapist **improvises** a response based on the skill criteria.
• The trainer (or, if not available, the client) provides **brief** feedback based on the skill criteria.
• The client then repeats the same statement, and the therapist again improvises a response. The trainer (or client) again provides brief feedback.

INSTRUCTIONS FOR EXERCISE 10
Step 2: Repeat
• Repeat Step 1 for all the statements **in the current difficulty level** (beginner, intermediate, or advanced).
Step 3: Assess and Adjust Difficulty
• The therapist completes the Deliberate Practice Reaction Form (see Appendix A) and decides whether to make the exercise easier or harder or to repeat the same difficulty level.
Step 4: Repeat for Approximately 15 Minutes
• Repeat Steps 1 to 3 for at least 15 minutes.
• The trainees then switch therapist and client roles and start over.

> **Now it's your turn! Follow the exercise instructions.**

Remember: The goal of the role play is for trainees to practice improvising responses to the client statements in a manner that (a) uses the skill criteria and (b) feels authentic for the trainee. **Example therapist responses for each client statement are provided at the end of this exercise. Trainees should attempt to improvise their own responses before reading the examples.**

BEGINNER-LEVEL CLIENT STATEMENTS FOR EXERCISE 10
Beginner Client Statement 1
[Ashamed] Ziyad was playing Old Maid with his cousin. He's only 2 years older than his cousin, but 4 and 6 can be a big difference. They were playing so nicely at first, and next thing you know he starts hitting his cousin. It is all my fault that Ziyad does not know how to play nicely. I feel so guilty that I didn't play with him more when he was younger. I can't even believe what I started saying to him. . . . I raised my voice about the rules, but really I was just beating myself up for never teaching and giving him opportunities to learn how to play these games before. I am a terrible parent.
Beginner Client Statement 2
[Panicked] I had the longest morning at work and my phone rang, and guess who it was? Jacob's first-grade teacher. My heart just stopped. I froze. I was so worried something happened, and I became paralyzed. I just kept thinking "Jacob must have gotten seriously injured." I couldn't even move fast enough to pick up the phone in time. I missed the call. It took me 20 minutes to calm down after I heard everything was okay.
Beginner Client Statement 3
[Overwhelmed] Tommy had basketball practice at 4:45, Alex had karate at 5:00, Jenna had dance at 5:30. The kids have so many activities, and I'm just feeling so overwhelmed and stressed that I can't manage all of this. Like how I am supposed to get everyone to their activities on time and then cook dinner, keep the house clean, etc.? I just want to shut down and I really can't handle this.
Beginner Client Statement 4
[Frustrated] Gavin has just been so rude to me. I asked him to do the dishes after dinner, and he literally just looked at me and walked away. He is only 14 years old. I am still the adult! I was so angry, I threw my water bottle across the room and it broke. Why does it have to be this way with him?

BEGINNER-LEVEL CLIENT STATEMENTS FOR EXERCISE 10

Beginner Client Statement 5

[Upset] Josh's college applications are due next month. I was really hoping he was going to start working on them. I am just so sad that he will be leaving us this fall. I want to encourage him to apply to the schools that have the best engineering programs, but I will be depressed if he attends college more than an hour away. He keeps asking me why I am not excited for him to go to college and willing to help him review his applications. I really want to help him, but I am just so sad he is growing up. Gosh, this sounds so bad of me.

Assess and adjust the difficulty before moving to the next difficulty level (see Step 3 in the exercise instructions).

INTERMEDIATE-LEVEL CLIENT STATEMENTS FOR EXERCISE 10

Intermediate Client Statement 1

[Ashamed] Brett needs to be potty trained by next month before he starts preschool. I am so embarrassed to say that we haven't even started the process. Honestly, I just don't have the energy to chase after him. All the other parents found the time and potty trained their kids. This is so pathetic of me. Let's face it—I am an embarrassingly bad parent. He will definitely not be going to preschool because of this.

Intermediate Client Statement 2

[Exasperated] As you know, Max is 5 and is an absolute terror. Every time I try to bring him to a store he always knocks something over. I am done trying to bring him places. It is not worth it. I feel so stressed out. I just end up screaming at him, and then he starts to cry. It also takes me a long time to calm down afterward. It is so pointless to even try.

Intermediate Client Statement 3

[Overwhelmed] Jaimie is going to be a freshman this year. She had a really hard time in middle school and she's excited to be going to a new school. But I am so nervous about the transition to a new school. For the last 2 weeks, my mind has been racing with all these "what if" scenarios, and it impacts my sleep, which then impacts me the next day. I keep repeatedly asking her if she is nervous, and now I think that I'm *making* her nervous.

Intermediate Client Statement 4

[Stressed] Lucy is really into arts and crafts. I am happy she found something she loves, but she is making such a mess at home. I keep asking her to clean up and can just feel my blood boiling. She is 12; she knows how to clean up after herself. I know I should be praising her like you said, but only yelling works. I am just so angry that at 12, she cannot clean up after herself. I have come close to throwing out all her arts and crafts in a fit of anger. I haven't done that . . . yet!

Intermediate Client Statement 5

[Resignation] Millie asked to go to a concert on a school night. I said absolutely not because she failed her math test this week, not to mention she is only 13. She told me that I am the worst father in the world and that I should have never had kids. Honestly, I think she's right. I am a terrible father. I was better at handling the younger years, but middle school? I'm pretty bad and I feel so sad and down. I don't know what to do.

Assess and adjust the difficulty before moving to the next difficulty level (see Step 3 in the exercise instructions).

ADVANCED-LEVEL CLIENT STATEMENTS FOR EXERCISE 10

Advanced Client Statement 1

[Ashamed] Bonnie loves playing with blocks. I have been trying to stick to our schedule of special play time every day. It has been going well. Then on Tuesday, I became so busy at work, and I just could not fit it in. When I got home, she asked to play, and I snapped. I was so mean and yelled at her that it's not always about her and playtime. I am feeling so terrible right now. That is why I canceled our session yesterday, and I've been avoiding Bonnie all day.

Advanced Client Statement 2

[Overwhelmed] I overheard the other parents telling their kids to stay away from Madison. As you know, the beginning of second grade had been tough and she was aggressive, but she is doing better. I keep crying when I drop her off and see how the other parents look at me. Madison keeps asking me what's wrong. I snap at her and say "nothing." I can tell it's not the best way for us to start our day. These feelings stay with me all day and probably impact my work and definitely impact my parenting.

Advanced Client Statement 3

[Hopeless] Roger has a middle school dance on Friday. Based on his history, I keep having thoughts like "He will absolutely get in trouble." My stomach was so upset all night, and I could not focus on anything. My partner was excited for us to finally have date night, and I told him no. I even ended up texting Roger a few times during the dance to check in. What is wrong with me?

Advanced Client Statement 4

[Defeated] Kieran keeps forgetting his homework. I don't know what is wrong with him. He's 12! How hard can it be for him to pack his bag with his homework when he has visual reminders and me asking him if he did it? I know he is trying, but what's wrong with him? Yesterday when I got the email from the teacher telling me how many times over the past 2 weeks he's forgotten it, I just let him have it for a full 20 minutes on the car ride home, and then I pretty much ignored him the rest of the night. I am so done.

Advanced Client Statement 5

[Upset] Will told me he was going to his friend's house on Saturday to watch a movie. Typical activity for a 16-year-old. We are trying to let him be more independent since he has been doing so well in school, so we didn't ask too many questions. A week later, I found out he wasn't at his friend's house. I had no idea where he was. I just screamed and screamed and screamed. Something bad could have happened to him. I was upset and ended up grounding him for 3 months, which I know I cannot stick to.

Assess and adjust the difficulty here (see Step 3 in the exercise instructions). If appropriate, follow the instructions to make the exercise even more challenging (see Appendix A).

Example Therapist Responses: Providing Strategies for Parent Affect Management

Remember: Trainees should attempt to improvise their own responses before reading the examples. **Do not read the following responses verbatim unless you are having trouble coming up with your own!**

EXAMPLE RESPONSES TO BEGINNER-LEVEL CLIENT STATEMENTS FOR EXERCISE 10
Example Response to Beginner Client Statement 1
I am hearing that you are feeling guilty about never teaching Ziyad to play Old Maid and blaming yourself for him not playing nicely with his cousin. (Criterion 1) The moment you notice your guilt rise, I am wondering if it might be helpful for you to try to decrease the intensity of your own emotion. For example, in that moment could you take a deep breath while counting to five, pause, and then release your breath slowly for seven seconds? Managing your own emotions may help in your response to Ziyad. (Criterion 2) Do you think this could work, and would it be helpful to explore more strategies to manage your own emotions while parenting? (Criterion 3)
Example Response to Beginner Client Statement 2
It sounds like you became very worried seeing Jacob's school called. You were so worried that you were unable to pick up the phone. (Criterion 1) There are some strategies you may be able to use to help decrease the intensity of your worries, such as changing your catastrophic thoughts at that moment. For example, it could be helpful to think "Jacob's school is calling, and it may be about anything, not necessarily something horrific." By not thinking that the worst has happened, it may help when you experience paralysis in that moment. (Criterion 2) I am wondering if you think this could be helpful to you and is worth discussing more? (Criterion 3)
Example Response to Beginner Client Statement 3
It sounds like you are super overwhelmed trying to get the kids to all the after-school activities and get stressed to the point that you want to shut down. (Criterion 1) Sometimes when we try to do everything all at once, we can experience intense emotions, and it can be helpful to break down step by step what we need to accomplish. I am wondering if creating a schedule broken down into smaller time increments would be helpful. (Criterion 2) Is this something you've tried before, and would it be worth exploring further? (Criterion 3)
Example Response to Beginner Client Statement 4
I can completely understand feeling frustrated in this situation, but it sounds like, in this case, that frustration moved more toward anger. (Criterion 1) When you are angry, it may be helpful in the moment for you to use a strategy, like removing yourself from the situation for a minute or two when you feel your anger start to rise to that level. It may not help you feel happy in that moment, but evidence shows that if you decrease that anger to a possibly more adaptive emotional experience like frustration, it may help you not act on your impulses, like throwing the water bottle. (Criterion 2) Do you think focusing on strategies to decrease your anger may be helpful? (Criterion 3)

EXAMPLE RESPONSES TO BEGINNER-LEVEL CLIENT STATEMENTS FOR EXERCISE 10

Example Response to Beginner Client Statement 5

It sounds like you are sad about Josh growing up and possibly attending a college that is far away from your home. (Criterion 1) Our own feelings can affect how we react in a situation, like not helping Josh in the application process. In these moments when Josh is asking for help, it may actually be helpful to focus on a strategy to manage your own thoughts of sadness. It may be worthwhile to use a journal where you write down your feelings and thoughts so that in the moment, you can still be present with Josh and help him through this application process. (Criterion 2) What do you think of this strategy—would it help you manage your own emotions, and do you think it would be helpful to talk about this more? (Criterion 3)

EXAMPLE RESPONSES TO INTERMEDIATE-LEVEL CLIENT STATEMENTS FOR EXERCISE 10

Example Response to Intermediate Client Statement 1

It sounds like you are feeling embarrassed about this potty-training experience with Brett and like it may impact your motivation to continue to try. (Criterion 1) There are a couple of strategies you may want to try to help manage your own emotions during potty training that may be helpful. One strategy is for us to problem solve and work together to develop a specific schedule and plan to begin the potty-training process. Another strategy is to change your thoughts from "Brett isn't potty trained because I am embarrassingly a bad parent" to "This is hard but we will get through this." (Criterion 2) Do you think finding a strategy to manage your emotions could be helpful and is worth spending the rest of our session on, and then we can circle back to the toileting strategies? (Criterion 3)

Example Response to Intermediate Client Statement 2

Thank you for sharing your feelings of stress about bringing Max to the store. (Criterion 1) There are strategies that you can use to manage your own parenting emotions that may be helpful in changing how you respond to Max in these really tough moments. For example, taking a deep breath in and then exhaling nice and slow may be helpful in decreasing your frustration. Another strategy is to change your thoughts to healthier ones, like "This is hard, and I don't like it, but I can handle Max's tantrum. I have handled them before." Your frustration won't go away completely, but hopefully it will allow you to feel like you are more in control of your response. (Criterion 2) Do you think either of these strategies may help you, both to parent in these moments and to calm down faster afterward, and are they worth exploring further? (Criterion 3)

Example Response to Intermediate Client Statement 3

Thanks for sharing your worries about Jaimie going to high school. It is a big transition and those "what if" thoughts seem to be impacting your sleep as well as how and what you communicate to her. (Criterion 1) It may be helpful to write down your worries about Jaimie starting high school as an outlet and then to try and review these through a nonemotional lens. Taking a walk and exercising is another strategy that can be helpful in decreasing the intensity of worries. (Criterion 2) Would you consider trying either of these strategies, and could you see how they might help in your parenting responses? (Criterion 3)

EXAMPLE RESPONSES TO INTERMEDIATE-LEVEL CLIENT STATEMENTS FOR EXERCISE 10

Example Response to Intermediate Client Statement 4

It sounds like when you see and think about the mess Lucy makes while playing, you experience a lot of anger. (Criterion 1) When our emotions as parents take over, it can be hard to implement the new positive parenting strategies. There are a couple of strategies you can use in that moment to help manage your own emotions. For example, leave the room when you notice your blood boiling and then come back when you notice that the intensity of your anger has decreased. Another strategy may be to use imagery, such as a calming image, in that moment. (Criterion 2) Do you think this is worth discussing more and could be helpful to you with parenting Lucy? (Criterion 3)

Example Response to Intermediate Client Statement 5

I am hearing that you are very overwhelmed and feeling down and sad. (Criterion 1) When Millie says those hurtful comments to you, it may be best to try to manage your own emotional response at that moment. Changing your thoughts from "I am a terrible father" to "I am trying the best I can and it's okay to make mistakes" can be helpful in decreasing the intensity of your emotion and allow you to have time to think about how you want to respond in those moments. Also, thinking ahead about how you can respond to those comments can be helpful in reducing the emotional response you have. (Criterion 2) What do you think about discussing these strategies together and looking at your own emotions as a parent—do you think this could be helpful to you? (Criterion 3)

EXAMPLE RESPONSES TO ADVANCED-LEVEL CLIENT STATEMENTS FOR EXERCISE 10

Example Response to Advanced Client Statement 1

It sounds like you are feeling guilty about what happened with Bonnie, and *some* of that guilt makes sense. (Criterion 1) In those moments when you feel that guilt becoming so great that you are canceling appointments and avoiding Bonnie, it can be helpful to implement a strategy to decrease your own level of guilt. When noticing this level of guilt, it may be helpful to have a mantra you can say to yourself, like "I love Bonnie and I am not a perfect parent, but that is okay." Another strategy is to use progressive muscle relaxation, in which you tense different parts of your body and then relax those muscles before you interact with Bonnie. (Criterion 2) I am wondering if you have ever tried something like this to manage your emotions before you respond to her and if you think it would be helpful to focus on? (Criterion 3)

Example Response to Advanced Client Statement 2

It sounds like you are getting quite sad about the judgments from the other parents, and this impacts your behavior at work and as a parent. (Criterion 1) I am wondering if it's helpful to focus on ways to help you deal with your emotions so that you don't act on the impulse to snap at Madison? There are different strategies you can use, like writing down your thoughts and feelings about school mornings and then asking yourself if these thoughts are true and how helpful they are to you as a person and as a parent. Another strategy can be to problem solve the situation, like maybe finding a parent to connect with to have support at school. (Criterion 2) Managing our own emotions can help us change how we respond to our children, and I am wondering if you think it could be helpful to discuss further? (Criterion 3)

EXAMPLE RESPONSES TO ADVANCED-LEVEL CLIENT STATEMENTS FOR EXERCISE 10

Example Response to Advanced Client Statement 3

It sounds like you were very anxious about Roger attending the dance and were stressed to the point that you kept texting him. (Criterion 1) It can be tough to control our own impulses when our emotions about our kids are so heightened. If you were able to change your thoughts to more adaptive ones, like "I am hopeful Roger is going to enjoy the dance and follow the guidelines we discussed over the past few weeks; me getting stressed will not impact how he behaves," would that help decrease your worries? I am also curious if distracting yourself by going on the date would also help decrease, but not eliminate, your worries. (Criterion 2) Have you ever tried to manage your own anxiety and noticed if it had an impact on your parenting decisions? Would you want to spend part of the session today further exploring this? (Criterion 3)

Example Response to Advanced Client Statement 4

You sound very frustrated with Kieran regarding forgetting his homework so often, to the point that you let him have it and ignored him. I am guessing that in those moments, the frustration ends up becoming anger. (Criterion 1) When our emotions build up, it can impact how we respond to our kids in the moment. There are strategies you can use, like labeling your own emotion by saying "This is anger." Such a strategy may be helpful in decreasing the intensity of your emotion. Another strategy is to change your thoughts to more adaptive ones, like "He is struggling right now, and he is actively working on it." (Criterion 2) Do you think either of these strategies could be helpful to you? Would it be helpful to talk about other situations in which you notice your own emotions are heightened? (Criterion 3)

Example Response to Advanced Client Statement 5

You described being upset, and it sounds like you were angry that Will lied to you and were worried about what could have happened to him; that these feelings led to your yelling at him and grounding him for 3 months. (Criterion 1) Our own emotions can play a large role in how we respond to our children. Strategies like taking a deep breath in and slowly exhaling can be helpful to calm down. Also, finding a relaxing word and repeating it to ourselves can be helpful in reducing our anger in the moment. (Criterion 2) I am wondering if you have tried one of these strategies or would be willing to and whether you think it would be helpful to look at other parenting situations in which you notice your emotions heightened? (Criterion 3)

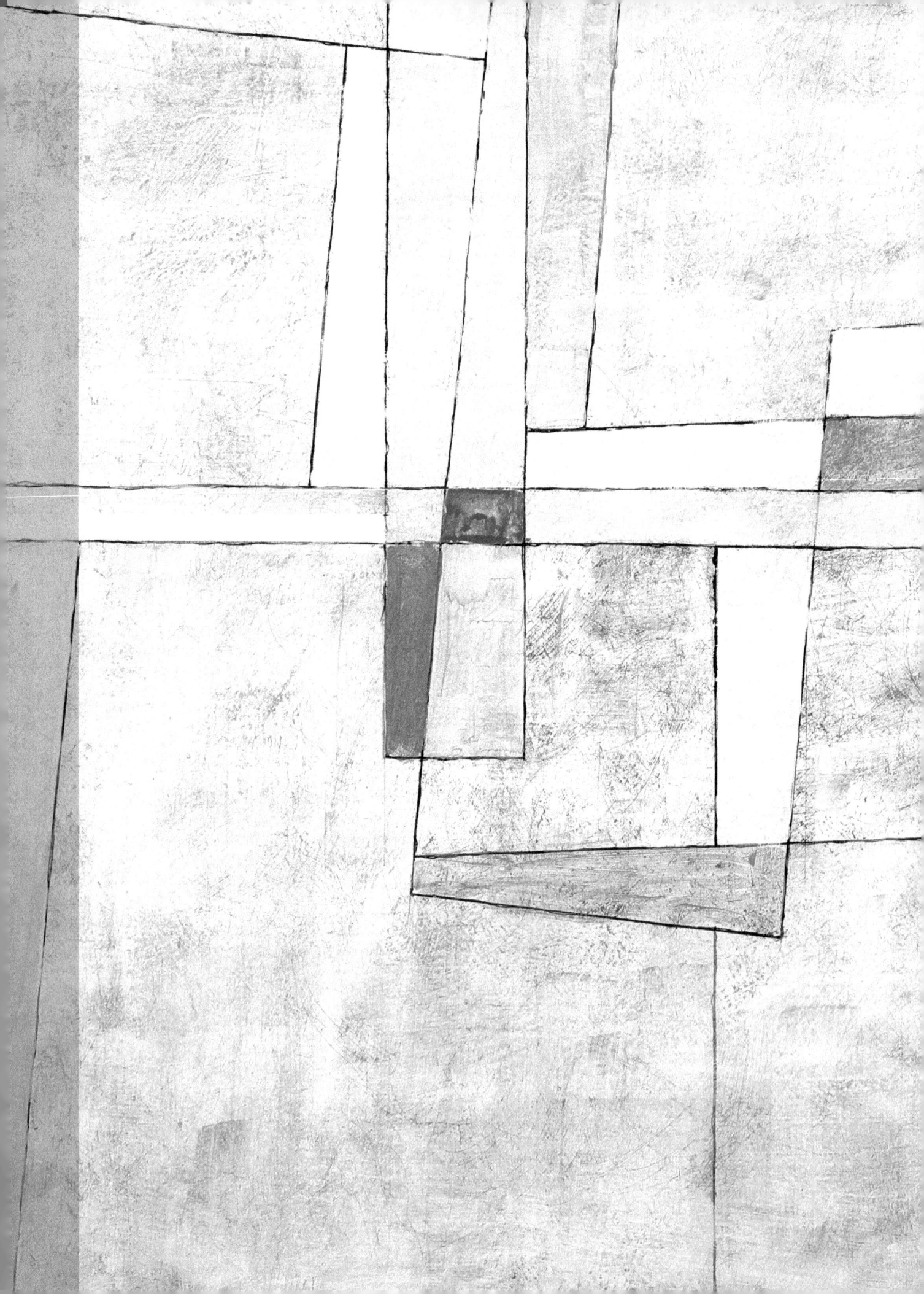

Teaching Parents About Managing Behavior in Public Settings

Preparations for Exercise 11

1. Read the instructions in Chapter 2.

2. Download the Deliberate Practice Reaction Form and the Deliberate Practice Diary Form at https://www.apa.org/pubs/books/deliberate-practice-behavioral-parent-training (see the "Resources" tab; also available in Appendixes A and B, respectively).

Skill Description

Skill Difficulty Level: Advanced

The purpose of this skill is for clinicians to work with parents on creating a plan for when their child misbehaves in a public setting. Often parents do not consider how their child will act in a public setting, like a grocery store (Barkley, 2013). For example, clinicians could ask parents to consider what they will do when their child wants a candy bar and starts to throw a tantrum in the middle of the grocery aisle. By preparing for this situation, parents will be able to have a plan in place that will allow them to cope better with the behavioral problem if it occurs. Knowing what to do and then doing it can be very challenging for parents. Implementing strategies learned throughout behavioral parent training (BPT) can become complicated because there are many other factors to consider in a public setting, including parent thoughts like "What are others thinking of me right now?" and parental feelings of shame and embarrassment. Therefore, anticipating behavioral challenges that might occur in public can be the key to managing one's child effectively (Barkley, 2013).

When creating a plan for a child's misbehavior in a public setting, all the skills previously discussed in this book can be used. Let's go back to our earlier example of a child having a tantrum in the grocery store aisle because they wanted a candy bar. During a

https://doi.org/10.1037/0000484-013

Deliberate Practice in Behavioral Parent Training, by M. D. Terjesen, H. B. Vidair, P. S. Ohr, O. A. Walsh, T. Rousmaniere, and A. Vaz

BPT session, you as the clinician would want to create a specific plan with the parent. First, the therapist should help the parent set expectations for the child (i.e., "We will not be buying any candy at the store"). If the child adheres to all rules, then a reward can be put into place (Exercise 8). Remind the parent to provide praise (Exercise 4) when the child is conducting themselves in an appropriate manner in the grocery store. Ignore any requests for the candy bar and any tantruming behavior (Exercise 6). In addition, it is important for the parent to be reminded to consider their own emotions if the child does have a tantrum and what strategies they can use to manage their own affect (Exercises 3 and 10).

As in previous exercises, examples of these skills in the statements that follow range in difficulty so that clinicians can practice initial mastery of this skill, as well as its use in more challenging interactions with parents. At the beginner difficulty level, the parent's prompt discusses effective tools used at home that can also be used in the public setting. At the intermediate level, no strategy is presented in the prompt, and the clinician has to choose a strategy to present to the parent to use in the public setting. Finally, at the advanced difficulty level, clinicians are asked to identify more than one strategy for the parents to use across settings.

SKILL CRITERIA FOR EXERCISE 11

1. Review/reflect the parent's current strategies across settings.

2. Provide psychoeducation on the skill(s) that may be applied in public settings. Examples of skills include (a) setting expectations and clear boundaries, (b) planned ignoring, (c) positive reinforcements (i.e., praise, rewards, privileges), (d) effective communication (i.e., commands), (e) use of consequence interventions, and (f) strategies for managing parent affect (e.g., cognitive restructuring, progressive muscle relaxation, deep breathing).

   - **Beginner and intermediate levels:** Identify one strategy for the parents to use across settings.

   - **Advanced level:** Identify more than one strategy.

3. Ask the parent if there are any barriers that may get in the way of using one of their skills.

Examples of Therapists Teaching Parents About Managing Behavior in Public Settings

Example 1

CLIENT: [*defeated*] We have decided to avoid any store where he is likely to have a meltdown. It's just too much to deal with when he screams and cries when he doesn't get what he wants. I would have predicted that by 9 years of age, he would have outgrown this. The challenge is that avoiding all stores with Johnny isn't really sustainable.

THERAPIST: It sounds like you're avoiding stores so that you don't have to deal with Johnny's meltdowns. Although it may be easier in the moment not to deal with his meltdown, it is probably not possible to avoid all stores, like never going to the grocery store again with Johnny. (Criterion 1) I am thinking that it may be helpful to think about this scenario and create a plan beforehand by setting expectations with Johnny and having clear guidelines. If he does have a meltdown, using your planned ignoring skill may be helpful. (Criterion 2) What do you think would get in the way of using these skills? (Criterion 3)

Example 2

CLIENT: [*resignation*] His cousin's birthday party is this weekend, and it's like we could write a script for how it's going to go. Over the course of the afternoon, Bobby will get more and more aggressive, and then someone will get hurt. My partner and I try to control him, but we can't watch him 100 percent of the time. We have to go, but honestly, I am dreading it.

THERAPIST: It sounds like you and your partner watch Bobby closely at birthday parties, hoping his behavior will not get too aggressive. Great thinking in trying to work together with your partner to manage Bobby's behaviors. (Criterion 1) I'm wondering if you have ever set expectations with Bobby before events like a birthday party. Setting expectations allows Bobby to understand clearly what behaviors you are specifically looking for. Then you may want to consider using rewards or privileges as an incentive for him engaging in these wanted behaviors. (Criterion 2) I can understand this may be challenging and would love to discuss any barriers that may get in the way of using these skills. (Criterion 3)

Example 3

CLIENT: [*ashamed*] Waiting his turn has always been a problem for Hayden. We are going to the town festival this weekend, and there will be rides, which he loves, but there will also be lines, which he hates. He will complain often and loudly and make it really unpleasant to be there. Every time he gets loud, I just find myself repeatedly saying that he needs to be quiet, and it gets quite embarrassing.

THERAPIST: It is great that you are already thinking ahead about what situations at the fair may be tough for Hayden. Thinking ahead allows you to create a plan. It sounds like now you're trying your best in the situation and find yourself telling him to be quiet. (Criterion 1) This makes me think about the planned ignoring skill and if Hayden is trying to get your attention inappropriately by whining or complaining. I am wondering if you can catch Hayden being good and give him lots of praise when he is standing nicely in line. As we know, giving him this attention through praise will encourage the behavior you are looking for. (Criterion 2) What challenges may come up with implementing some of these strategies? (Criterion 3)

INSTRUCTIONS FOR EXERCISE 11
Step 1: Role-Play and Feedback
• The client says the first beginner client statement. The therapist **improvises** a response based on the skill criteria.
• The trainer (or, if not available, the client) provides **brief** feedback based on the skill criteria.
• The client then repeats the same statement, and the therapist again improvises a response. The trainer (or client) again provides brief feedback.
Step 2: Repeat
• Repeat Step 1 for all the statements **in the current difficulty level** (beginner, intermediate, or advanced).

INSTRUCTIONS FOR EXERCISE 11
Step 3: Assess and Adjust Difficulty
• The therapist completes the Deliberate Practice Reaction Form (see Appendix A) and decides whether to make the exercise easier or harder or to repeat the same difficulty level.
Step 4: Repeat for Approximately 15 Minutes
• Repeat Steps 1 to 3 for at least 15 minutes. • The trainees then switch therapist and client roles and start over.

➡ **Now it's your turn! Follow the exercise instructions.**

Remember: The goal of the role play is for trainees to practice improvising responses to the client statements in a manner that (a) uses the skill criteria and (b) feels authentic for the trainee. **Example therapist responses for each client statement are provided at the end of this exercise. Trainees should attempt to improvise their own responses before reading the examples.**

BEGINNER-LEVEL CLIENT STATEMENTS FOR EXERCISE 11
Beginner Client Statement 1
[Ashamed] Marcus has been playing so nicely with his older sister Isabella. I really have been trying to give him the specific, labeled praise we talked about. However, at the park, it's a completely different story. There is another 5-year-old boy he likes to play with, but I constantly have to yell at him to stop hitting the boy. I saw his mom turn around and not come to the park yesterday when she saw us.
Beginner Client Statement 2
[Stressed] I am happy to report that Devon, at age 7, has finally stopped barging into my office and trying to dance on camera during my meetings on Tuesday afternoon. I really am proud of myself for sticking to the plan and ignoring him when he barges in. Now he finally has stopped coming in at all, so withholding the attention worked. I am really nervous, though, about how he is going to be at dinner with my friends this weekend. I just don't know what I am supposed to do if he gets up and starts dancing. You know what, now that I think about it, I am just going to cancel. It's easier.
Beginner Client Statement 3
[Nervous] When I first started coming here, I thought, "How am I going to get my 9-year-old to follow my directions?" Kai really has been doing an amazing job at cleaning up after himself. Using the direct commands has been really helpful in not giving him a choice. We are going to a new friend's house next week, and I already feel so nervous about it. What will I do if, when it's time to leave and clean up, Kai won't help? It will be so embarrassing, and then we won't be invited back again. I think it's better for me to just clean up and then I don't have to worry about anything.
Beginner Client Statement 4
[Panicked] During summer school, we have made such improvements in setting boundaries with completing his homework on time and, if he doesn't, having consequences in place like no video games. Tommy starts high school next week, and I'm really nervous about him asking me to go out with his friends after his soccer game this weekend. I don't want him not to be social, but I also don't want him to fall behind academically again. I know he is going to ask me in front of all the other parents. With Tommy, it is not as easy for me to just agree as it may be for the other parents. I think I will just figure it out after the game Saturday.

BEGINNER-LEVEL CLIENT STATEMENTS FOR EXERCISE 11

Beginner Client Statement 5

[Overwhelmed] Connie gets their ACT results on Saturday. I am so nervous—like, beyond nervous—for this. I know we discussed a lot about how my emotions can impact how I respond with Connie, and I have been working on using progressive muscle relaxation when I notice my anxiety go up. If Connie doesn't get the score they want, it just won't be good, and of course they have a basketball tournament the day the scores are released. I am thinking of just letting my partner handle it and not going to the game. It is better for me to just stay out of the way, but I know Connie will be mad at me for not going. Ugh— I just don't know how to handle this.

🛑 **Assess and adjust the difficulty before moving to the next difficulty level (see Step 3 in the exercise instructions).**

INTERMEDIATE-LEVEL CLIENT STATEMENTS FOR EXERCISE 11

Intermediate Client Statement 1

[Stressed] I know it sounds silly for a 4-year-old to be playing soccer, but it is what everyone in town does. I am very worried about Arnav being able to follow directions at soccer practice. The parents are very involved in the clinic, but I keep thinking about what will happen if he does not follow directions. It will be so embarrassing if we get kicked out, which, given his past behavior, is a possibility. I just don't know what I should be doing. I guess I will tell him that he will be punished if he doesn't listen.

Intermediate Client Statement 2

[Anxious] We haven't been to a restaurant as a family in over 2 years. With Jack's behavioral problems, we honestly have just avoided eating out at all costs. This weekend, we're going to a casual place, and my parents are joining us. I am very nervous about how it will go. If Jack starts throwing food because we are talking with my parents, I'm not really sure what I should do. I know I will want to yell at him, which is terrible of me.

Intermediate Client Statement 3

[Upset] Drew loves to dance. It is so nice for her to have a passion! But her behavior is so out of control. She literally told the dance teacher "no" to their face when she was told to get back in line. How embarrassing is that? She eventually stood in line, and I guess it was fine, but still. I screamed at her about this the whole way home, and now she won't go to dance. I feel terrible. I thought we were this behavior was behind us now that she's 10 years old. I know she loves dance, and I want this to be a fun experience.

Intermediate Client Statement 4

[Defeated] Gab has started to curse at me when I tell him he can't have a certain meal at a restaurant. I am so done with him. He is 15 years old and needs to understand he can't always order the most expensive meal on the menu. It is so embarrassing that I just have to give in or it's probably going to get worse. What else am I supposed to do?

Intermediate Client Statement 5

[Angry] Lynda has her license now. Can you believe that she is old enough to be driving on her own? After her basketball practice, she asks to go out with friends, and when I try to talk to her about curfews, she walks away from me every time. Then I just started threatening that I won't give her the keys, but of course I always do. It is so embarrassing to be having this argument in public. I don't know what to do.

🛑 **Assess and adjust the difficulty before moving to the next difficulty level (see Step 3 in the exercise instructions).**

ADVANCED-LEVEL CLIENT STATEMENTS FOR EXERCISE 11

Advanced Client Statement 1

[Frustrated] When I was 4, I knew that if I started crying at religious services, when I got home it would not be good. I would be screamed at and spanked. Raj is now 4 and is definitely old enough to be attending service with us. I just don't know what to do if he starts screaming. It's so quiet during service, and I just know he is going to yell. I am so overwhelmed and just don't know how I'm supposed to respond. I know I'm not supposed to use screaming or spanking, but what then?

Advanced Client Statement 2

[Upset] Mira is so excited for her sixth birthday party. We are having it at an arts and craft place where they get to paint pottery. If you remember, the last birthday party she went to was an absolute disaster. It ended with her having a tantrum in the middle of the party. I think she saw me helping another kid and got jealous. Then I ended up yelling at her, and it escalated from there. It was honestly traumatizing for everyone. I wish I was excited like how other parents are for their child's birthday, but I just can't wait for it to be over.

Advanced Client Statement 3

[Overwhelmed] We are visiting my brother's family tomorrow and he has two kids around Maya's age, 12. I have been sick to my stomach all week thinking about it. Last time we were all together, Maya ended up pushing Casey to the ground because she didn't want to wait her turn for the swing. The usual issue. Casey ended up hurting her wrist. I don't know if I can handle it. You know what? We shouldn't go.

Advanced Client Statement 4

[Anxious] The library has a really nice, kid-friendly book event on Saturdays. I am trying to take the kids to more events and was so excited when I saw it, but my wife said she can't go. I don't think it is a good idea for me to take George all by myself. I know he is 10 and is old enough to navigate an event, but I don't know what strategies I would use in this setting. I know he will have to use his quiet voice and not run around, but I'm not sure I can handle him. My wife is much better with these things than I am.

Advanced Client Statement 5

[Panicked] Since Sally just finished her junior year of high school, we have decided to take a road trip to visit colleges. Our first drive is about 6 hours and we go straight to a college tour. I am extremely anxious about this trip. At home, Sally and her brother have been in a good place and are fighting less, but what's going to happen on this tour after they are in a confined space for such a prolonged period? What do I do if a fight breaks out and we are in front of people from college admissions? I'm not sleeping lately because the thoughts about how this is a bad idea just keep racing through my mind. I know my yelling the entire trip and threatening punishment is not the best way to handle it.

✋ **Assess and adjust the difficulty here (see Step 3 in the exercise instructions). If appropriate, follow the instructions to make the exercise even more challenging (see Appendix A).**

Example Therapist Responses: Teaching Parents About Managing Behavior in Public Settings

Remember: Trainees should attempt to improvise their own responses before reading the examples. **Do not read the following responses verbatim unless you are having trouble coming up with your own!**

EXAMPLE RESPONSES TO BEGINNER-LEVEL CLIENT STATEMENTS FOR EXERCISE 11
Example Response to Beginner Client Statement 1
Great work in using the labeled praise skill for when Marcus plays with Isabella. It sounds like when Marcus is at the park, you are yelling at him to stop hitting the other kids. (Criterion 1) Specific, labeled praise can also be used with Marcus while he is at the park. When you notice him playing nicely and not being aggressive, that would be a great time to use this skill. (Criterion 2) Do you think there is anything that would get in the way of using labeled praise while at the park with Marcus? (Criterion 3)
Example Response to Beginner Client Statement 2
Great job implementing the planned ignoring skill we discussed. When thinking about dinner out with friends, it sounds like you want to avoid it all together. (Criterion 1) I am wondering if you considered using that same planned ignoring skill you just mentioned. When Devon starts dancing, we have established he is looking for attention. If you are able to ignore that behavior and not give him the attention at that moment, it will likely have the same effect of stopping the unwanted behavior. (Criterion 2) What do you think about this, and do you think it would be helpful to discuss anything that may get in the way of you using this planned ignoring skill at dinner? (Criterion 3)
Example Response to Beginner Client Statement 3
You have been doing such a great job using commands with Kai at home. It sounds like for this playdate, your current plan is just to clean up yourself. (Criterion 1) Giving commands is a great tool you can use in this setting too. Remember that when using commands, you want them to be direct, like "Kai, we are leaving in 15 minutes. Put the blocks back in the red container over there." You have success in using this skill at home, and it can be used in different settings. (Criterion 2) What could happen that may get in the way of using commands at his friend's house? (Criterion 3)
Example Response to Beginner Client Statement 4
I love how you are thinking ahead about what new issues may arise with Tommy starting high school and playing soccer. It seems like your plan is to wait until you have a possible problem. (Criterion 1) Tommy responded really nicely to having clear expectations and knowing the consequences of not completing his homework. Using this concept and having similar expectations and consequences for his social behavior is important as well. (Criterion 2) Are there any reasons why you might hesitate to set up expectations and consequences with Tommy on Friday, before the game, that would be helpful to discuss? (Criterion 3)
Example Response to Beginner Client Statement 5
Great job thinking about how your own emotions can impact how you react to Connie. It sounds like you are really nervous about having to be at the tournament when their scores get released and you are thinking of not going at all even though you want to. (Criterion 1) As we discussed, managing your emotions is critical, and I'm wondering, since you've have had success in progressive muscle relaxation, if it would be helpful to create a plan for yourself. You can have a script on your phone to use to help manage your own anxiety about Connie's scores. (Criterion 2) What do you think would get in the way of using this? (Criterion 3)

EXAMPLE RESPONSES TO INTERMEDIATE-LEVEL CLIENT STATEMENTS FOR EXERCISE 11

Example Response to Intermediate Client Statement 1

It is great that you are thinking ahead. Your plan right now is to tell him he will be punished if he doesn't listen. (Criterion 1) During the clinic, it will be important for you to use the praise skill for when Arnav is following directions—for example, "Great job picking up the soccer ball when the coach asked you!" This will encourage Arnav to continue those positive behaviors you are looking for. (Criterion 2) I think it will be helpful for us to discuss anything you think may get in the way of you using the praise skill at the clinic. (Criterion 3)

Example Response to Intermediate Client Statement 2

Wow—it sounds like your family has been avoiding eating out for a while. It is great you are already thinking about what behaviors may occur and what your impulse reaction may be, like yelling. (Criterion 1) If Jack starts to throw food, it may be helpful for you to ignore this negative behavior. Remember when we discussed ignoring attention-seeking behaviors, like food throwing, and how it is a great technique in decreasing them. (Criterion 2) I know this may be challenging and think it will be helpful to discuss any barriers that may get in the way of you using this strategy. (Criterion 3)

Example Response to Intermediate Client Statement 3

It sounds like you yelled at Drew for not listening during dance class. (Criterion 1) You also told me that Drew did end up listening and stood in line. Similar to what we encourage you to do at home, it is important for you to give Drew attention for the positive things she did during the dance class—for example, telling Drew, "Great job twirling in line when the teacher asked you to." We want to give attention to the positive behaviors and not the negative ones, like her telling the teacher "no." (Criterion 2) What would get in the way of you giving Drew this positive attention after the next dance class? (Criterion 3)

Example Response to Intermediate Client Statement 4

It has to be really tough when Gab is cursing at you at a restaurant, and I can understand how you want to just let him have the meal he wants. (Criterion 1) Thinking of this ahead of time will allow you to have a plan in place. Try giving a direct command on what he can order, like "Order a meal that costs $15 or less" to see if it is an effective strategy. Remember, if he does start to curse, do not shout back but use your normal tone of voice. (Criterion 2) What would get in the way of you being able to give Gab a direct command? (Criterion 3)

Example Response to Intermediate Client Statement 5

It sounds like when you talk to Lynda about driving after practice, it isn't productive and ends with her walking away and you yelling. (Criterion 1) You want to think ahead and talk with Lynda about the expectation for curfew before her asking after the game. It is best not to threaten to take away the keys but instead to have the consequences discussed and written out in advance. (Criterion 2) What do you think of this, and what may get in the way of having this conversation with Lynda? (Criterion 3)

EXAMPLE RESPONSES TO ADVANCED-LEVEL CLIENT STATEMENTS FOR EXERCISE 11

Example Response to Advanced Client Statement 1

It makes sense to feel concerned and be unsure how to react to Raj yelling at service. Great job in recognizing that spanking and screaming is not the best strategy. (Criterion 1) Evidence shows that using praise is more effective than spanking or yelling in getting our children to do what we expect. Remember, we want to be specific and use enthusiasm, like "Raj—great job reading the book quietly!" In addition, when it is time for Raj to do something, we want to use effective communication, like a direct command: "Raj, stand for the reading." (Criterion 2) When thinking about the service, what do you think could get in the way of using one of these strategies? (Criterion 3)

Example Response to Advanced Client Statement 2

It sounds like in the past when Mira would have a tantrum you would give her attention and yell at her. (Criterion 1) There are times when we intentionally want to not give our attention to a child's inappropriate behavior and use the planned ignoring skill we have discussed. It also could be helpful to combine this with giving Mira positive attention when she is demonstrating positive behavior—for example, saying "Mira, I love how nicely you are painting your pottery" and ignoring her when she is tantruming. (Criterion 2) What do you think could get in the way of you using one of these strategies at her birthday party? (Criterion 3)

Example Response to Advanced Client Statement 3

You are thinking of avoiding seeing your brother and his kids because you are nervous about how Maya will behave after she pushed Casey last time. (Criterion 1) It is important for you to talk with Maya about your expectations and rules before going to your brother's. Having a reward, like stopping for ice cream on the way home, is a good strategy to use. In addition, while you are at the party, don't forget to praise Maya for all her positive behavior. Remember, you want to be specific and enthusiastic. (Criterion 2) Do you think there is anything that may get in the way of you using these strategies? (Criterion 3)

Example Response to Advanced Client Statement 4

It's great you want to take George to the library event, and it sounds like you are having a hard time thinking about a strategy you can use to help George display appropriate library behaviors. (Criterion 1) Remember, you want to catch George doing good, so that would be him walking around the library and using his indoor voice. This can be achieved by giving George specific, labeled praise, like "I really like how you are using your quiet voice." Another strategy is to use a reward as an incentive for George to follow these desired behaviors. An example would be allowing him to check out a book after the event. (Criterion 2) After hearing these strategies, what do you think might get in the way of you using them? (Criterion 3)

Example Response to Advanced Client Statement 5

It sounds like you are feeling very anxious about this trip and questioning whether you will know how to handle your children's behaviors. It is great that you recognize that yelling the entire trip is not the most effective strategy. (Criterion 1) First, changing your thought from "this is a bad idea" to "I have the skills needed to handle any arguments that may arise" can be helpful in decreasing the intensity of your anxiety. Also, it's important to remember what behaviors you want to give attention to and what behaviors you want to ignore. When you see good behavior, even for a short period of time, we want you to make a big deal about it, even using your nonverbal cues! (Criterion 2) What could get in the way of using these strategies on the college tour? (Criterion 3)

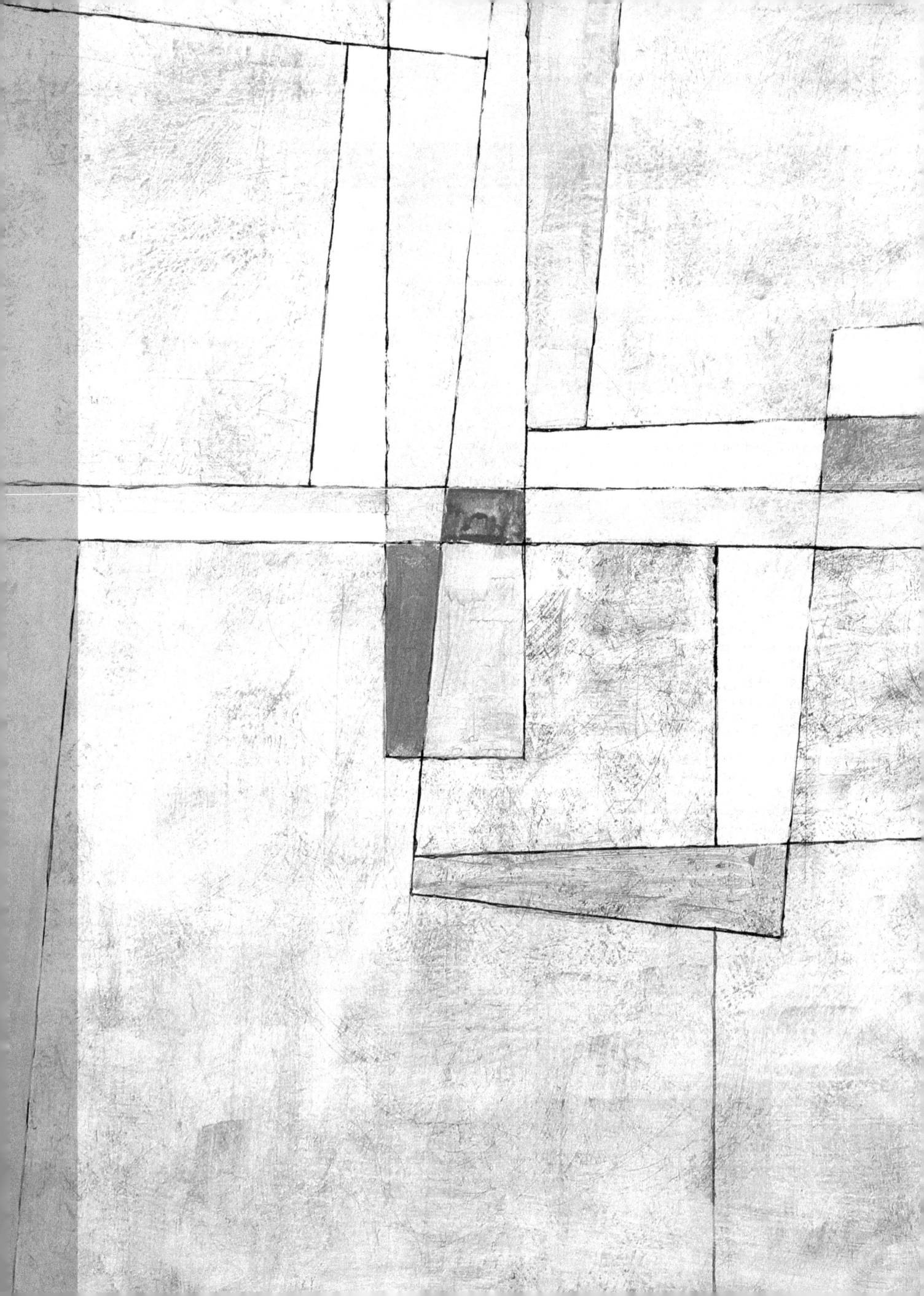

Development of Homework Assignments

Preparations for Exercise 12

1. Read the instructions in Chapter 2.

2. Download the Deliberate Practice Reaction Form and the Deliberate Practice Diary Form at https://www.apa.org/pubs/books/deliberate-practice-behavioral-parent-training (see the "Resources" tab; also available in Appendixes A and B, respectively).

Skill Description

Skill Difficulty Level: Advanced

The development and practice of skills in session are important, but ideally, we want to work with parents to have them effectively deliver these skills within the context of where the behavior occurs—that is, outside the clinician's office and in the home and community. To that end, the clinician provides between-session assignments that scaffold off of and are consistent with the content of the session. Homework is an active clinical component in cognitive behavior therapy for adults (Kazantzis et al., 2010; Mausbach et al., 2010), and some research has focused on homework within clinical work with youth with mixed outcomes (Jungbluth & Shirk, 2013). With parents, Danko and colleagues (2016) reported that in a sample of parents who completed a trial of PCIT, those parents who completed more homework typically completed treatment in fewer sessions and parents reported treatment satisfaction. Similarly, in a study of parents of preschoolers who completed a BPT protocol, Ros and colleagues (2017) reported a relationship among homework completion, negative parenting, and parenting skill self-efficacy. Homework completion was also related to session attendance. Nock and Kazdin (2005) described the effectiveness of a brief parent intervention that enhances treatment adherence (i.e., skill application) between sessions and proposed a model that promotes motivation to enhance clinical effectiveness. We agree with Chacko and colleagues (2013) that although homework is not often completed within BPT, it is an essential ingredient in its effectiveness.

https://doi.org/10.1037/0000484-014

Deliberate Practice in Behavioral Parent Training, by M. D. Terjesen, H. B. Vidair, P. S. Ohr, O. A. Walsh, T. Rousmaniere, and A. Vaz

Types of homework will vary depending on the stage of treatment and should be tailored to the behaviors described, as well as toward what the parents are capable of doing. As BPT clinicians work collaboratively with parents to develop homework, it is important for the parent to understand the rationale for the homework and how it is consistent with clinical goals (i.e., child behavior change). It also would be important for the clinician to review any barriers or obstacles (practical, emotional, or cognitive) that might prevent homework from being completed. Although there are many skills, even beyond those described in the previous 11 exercises, within BPT they will often involve assignment of in-between work (i.e., homework); here we chose five skills to provide an opportunity to differentiate assignments at different stages of BPT. These skills are functional behavior assessments (FBAs) related to function of child behavior (Exercise 2), use of praise (Exercise 4), positive attention (Exercise 5), planned ignoring (Exercise 6), and positive incentives (Exercise 8). Each of these skills is presented once at each difficulty level, and each difficulty level represents a different stage of treatment. The beginner statements occur in first or early treatment sessions. For the intermediate statements, parents have been engaged in BPT for a few sessions and are reporting some challenges. Advanced statements take place toward the end of treatment. The specific skills to be assigned as homework are identified before each client statement. Of note, we intentionally chose not to have homework assignments that involve consequence interventions. As discussed in Chapter 1 and in Exercise 9, although many parents want to focus on strategies to stop the negative behaviors, this does not get children to demonstrate the desired behaviors. In fact, sometimes consequence interventions may lead to further negative behaviors. Rather, we want homework to promote skills that will build desired or adaptive behaviors that will compete with negative behaviors.

Consistent with prior exercises and the discussion of treatment acceptability, we think it is also important for the clinician to ask parents if they believe that this homework assignment is acceptable to them—that is, asking parents one or more of the following: (a) if they believe that this would work, (b) if this is something that they would be willing to or think they could try, and (c) to identify any barriers toward implementing the homework. We recommend asking more acceptability questions at each difficulty level to demonstrate increasing competence with this criterion—that is, ask one accessibility question at the beginner level, ask two questions at the intermediate level, and ask three questions at the advanced level. The clinician can also ask an open-ended question such as "What are your thoughts?" as a summary of or transition into the other questions, but it shouldn't count toward the total number of questions per difficulty level.

SKILL CRITERIA FOR EXERCISE 12

1. Discuss creating a homework assignment that is focused on the underlined skill preceding the client statement.

2. Provide a rationale as to why this homework is important.

3. Assess the parent's beliefs as to the following: (a) the effectiveness of the intervention; (b) whether they could or are willing to carry it out; and (c) the presence of any practical, emotional, or cognitive obstacles that would make homework completion more challenging and less likely to be completed by the parent.

   - **Beginner level:** Ask one question about acceptability.
   - **Intermediate level:** Ask two questions about acceptability.
   - **Advanced level:** Ask three questions about acceptability.

Examples of Therapists Using Development of Homework Assignments

Example 1

Homework to assign: Functional behavioral assessment

CLIENT: [*exasperated*] Asking me why Charlie behaves this way is a question I have been asking for all 6 years of his life, and honestly I do not know.

THERAPIST: Understanding the "why" of child behavior can be tricky, and sometimes when we think we have figured it out, we then have to pivot and consider something else. To begin, I think it may be helpful for us to gather data on a daily basis as to his behavior and what immediately precedes it and then what immediately follows it. You can track this on your phone or just use an ABC sheet about behavior. (Criterion 1) This will allow us to look at any patterns of behavior and try and understand the "why" of his behavior. (Criterion 2) Is there anything that you think would get in the way of gathering this data to help us understand why? (Criterion 3)

Example 2

Homework to assign: Praise

CLIENT: [*defeated*] Sarah means well, but she also can . . . well . . . be mean, especially to her sister. Michelle is 9 so only 2 years younger, and Sarah tortures her almost daily. Not sure how I can praise her when so much of what she does is negative.

THERAPIST: That is often one of the challenges for many parents—how to praise when there are so many more negative behaviors. While it may be challenging, I think it would be great if you tried to identify two behaviors a day to praise when she is doing something desired. (Criterion 1) By praising the things we want to see, even if they are small behaviors, it increases the likelihood of those behaviors becoming stronger and occurring more often. (Criterion 2) What are your thoughts—do you think doing this is feasible for the week, and is there anything that may make it tough to do? (Criterion 3)

Example 3

Homework to assign: Positive incentives

CLIENT: [*annoyed*] For the life of me, I cannot get Grace to follow the limits we've put on screen use. I have caught her sneaking her devices into her room at night, and she lies to me about her use. I talk to some of the other high school mothers, and they share that their kids struggle as well. Not sure if I am trying to manage the unmanageable.

THERAPIST: I hear the frustration in your voice about getting Grace to follow the screen rules. We want to increase her following of these rules. What we know is that screens are highly rewarding for her. I think it may be helpful to use some incentives or a behavioral contract to increase her working toward your desired goals. I would suggest for this week that you sit with Grace, review expectations, and then talk about motivators or rewards for her meeting these expectations. (Criterion 1) Being clear about expectations and then allowing Grace to have a say in what the rewards would be for meeting these expectations may help set up a system for compliance. (Criterion 2) Do you think this would be a helpful first step, are you willing to do this, and is there anything you think may interfere with this? (Criterion 3)

INSTRUCTIONS FOR EXERCISE 12

Step 1: Role-Play and Feedback

- The client says the first beginner client statement. The therapist **improvises** a response based on the skill criteria.
- The trainer (or, if not available, the client) provides **brief** feedback based on the skill criteria.
- The client then repeats the same statement, and the therapist again improvises a response. The trainer (or client) again provides brief feedback.

Step 2: Repeat

- Repeat Step 1 for all the statements **in the current difficulty level** (beginner, intermediate, or advanced).

Step 3: Assess and Adjust Difficulty

- The therapist completes the Deliberate Practice Reaction Form (see Appendix A) and decides whether to make the exercise easier or harder or to repeat the same difficulty level.

Step 4: Repeat for Approximately 15 Minutes

- Repeat Steps 1 to 3 for at least 15 minutes.
- The trainees then switch therapist and client roles and start over.

> **Now it's your turn! Follow the exercise instructions.**

Remember: The goal of the role play is for trainees to practice improvising responses to the client statements in a manner that (a) uses the skill criteria and (b) feels authentic for the trainee. **Example therapist responses for each client statement are provided at the end of this exercise. Trainees should attempt to improvise their own responses before reading the examples.**

BEGINNER-LEVEL CLIENT STATEMENTS FOR EXERCISE 12

Beginner Client Statement 1

Homework to assign: Functional behavioral assessment

[Frustrated] It's good to know that I am not the core cause of Sierra's behavior, especially as she enters kindergarten, but even based on what you said, I'm struggling to try and figure out why she does these things.

Beginner Client Statement 2

Homework to assign: Praise

[Irritated] I understand what you said about the importance of using praise, but how can I do that when Josh really is only good maybe 10% of the time? Plus, he's 16 now. Shouldn't he know what he's supposed to do?

Beginner Client Statement 3

Homework to assign: Planned ignoring

[Embarrassed] You're probably right—Luna acts like this for attention like many middle schoolers do. But honestly, how and when can I ignore her when her behavior is so tough to ignore? I mean, she gets loud—really loud! I have to do something, and this week I yelled at her loudly to knock it off!

BEGINNER-LEVEL CLIENT STATEMENTS FOR EXERCISE 12

Beginner Client Statement 4

Homework to assign: Positive attention

[Annoyed] How tough is it to get out the door each morning? It's not like he has not done this before, but every morning Brady takes his time talking to me and doesn't seem to care if it impacts his younger sister making her miss her bus. I tell him at 13, he should be more responsible.

Beginner Client Statement 5

Homework to assign: Positive incentives

[Resignation] Rewards honestly do not work. Charlotte fought us on using them in middle school, and now as she enters her junior year, I have basically given up trying to get her to follow a schedule for schoolwork, gymnastics, and college-prep courses.

🛑 **Assess and adjust the difficulty before moving to the next difficulty level (see Step 3 in the exercise instructions).**

INTERMEDIATE-LEVEL CLIENT STATEMENTS FOR EXERCISE 12

Intermediate Client Statement 1

Homework to assign: Functional behavioral assessment

[Perplexed] I thought that we had determined that attention was why June kept acting that way, and I've tried to provide attention only when she does the desired behaviors, yet she continues to act this way. Is this normal for first graders? Now what?

Intermediate Client Statement 2

Homework to assign: Praise

[Annoyed] Praise works . . . but not always. As an example, I walk over as Jonah is working on his sixth-grade science presentation and I praise him by saying, "Nice job!" Five minutes later, he's back on his phone and off-task. I am close to giving up the praise approach and just taking away things he values each time I catch him off-task.

Intermediate Client Statement 3

Homework to assign: Planned ignoring

[Frustrated] I have now broken my "no screens at dinner" edict. I cannot seem to have a conversation with anyone at the table without Camille interrupting me . . . repeatedly. Like many teenagers, she wants to be on social media 24/7. I know it's wrong, but giving her the phone is the only way to get her to stop complaining about not having it—and frankly, the only way for me to get a moment's peace.

Intermediate Client Statement 4

Homework to assign: Positive attention

[Defeated] Frankie's absences keep piling up, and it's possible this impacts his high school graduation. I have tried working on his sleep schedule and validating that he doesn't see the need to take some of these courses, but he just argues and says I am overreacting to the point where, when I even mention going to school, he starts yelling and leaves the room. It has really been hurting our relationship. How can I get through to him when he won't listen?

INTERMEDIATE-LEVEL CLIENT STATEMENTS FOR EXERCISE 12

Intermediate Client Statement 5

Homework to assign: Positive incentives

[Stressed] The homework assigned to second graders is not that difficult, and I imagine it would only take Liliana 25 or 30 minutes of continuous effort. But this has become a daily fight, and it drags on to quite late in the evening. I try rewarding and praise Liliana when she does complete it, but that doesn't seem to change her effort. It's really quite stressful.

> ✋ **Assess and adjust the difficulty before moving to the next difficulty level (see Step 3 in the exercise instructions).**

ADVANCED-LEVEL CLIENT STATEMENTS FOR EXERCISE 12

Advanced Client Statement 1

Homework to assign: Functional behavioral assessment

[Exasperated] We gathered the data like we discussed, but I really cannot tell if Emma is acting this way for attention, for something tangible, or to get out of something. I have all these sheets, please tell me this wasn't a waste of time. Is it always this complicated when they begin kindergarten?

Advanced Client Statement 2

Homework to assign: Praise

[Embarrassed] Matthew is so disrespectful that it becomes tough to provide praise. He mostly acts this way in front of his fifth-grade basketball teammates, and it honestly is mortifying. I do the carpool each week for some of the players, and this past week he just imitated everything I said in a mocking way, with only a couple of moments where he responded appropriately. How am I supposed to praise that behavior?

Advanced Client Statement 3

Homework to assign: Planned ignoring

[Annoyed] Rose—and I say this jokingly because I love her—is not named appropriately as she is anything but a rose. As an example, just last night during our big Sunday dinner with her cousins, she got up from the dinner table and did a cartwheel, poured her drink to the top of the glass, and made inappropriate flatulence sounds. I mean, how do you ignore that? Her 13-year-old cousin is within 10 months of her age, and she doesn't act that way.

Advanced Client Statement 4

Homework to assign: Positive attention

[Angry] I am this close to being done with her. Ava does far more negative than positive things, with the positives being few and far between. She seems to care more about doing what she wants than following some simple household rules. She's 17, and some of these rules have been in place for years, yet she rarely, if ever, follows them, and never without a fight.

ADVANCED-LEVEL CLIENT STATEMENTS FOR EXERCISE 12
Advanced Client Statement 5
<u>Homework to assign: Positive incentives</u>
[Hopeless] I get it, rewards work, but honestly it seems like I am bribing my 8-year-old to do things that he should be able to do. Now whenever I ask Jeremy to do anything, he basically holds out his hand and asks, "What's in it for me?" Is that the message that I want him to learn? That he gets paid for every behavior?

> 🕐 **Assess and adjust the difficulty here (see Step 3 in the exercise instructions). If appropriate, follow the instructions to make the exercise even more challenging (see Appendix A).**

Example Therapist Responses: Development of Homework Assignments

Remember: Trainees should attempt to improvise their own responses before reading the examples. **Do not read the following responses verbatim unless you are having trouble coming up with your own!**

EXAMPLE RESPONSES TO BEGINNER-LEVEL CLIENT STATEMENTS FOR EXERCISE 12
Example Response to Beginner Client Statement 1
It can be a struggle to understand the function or the "why" of child behavior. While you and I can make some predictions as to why, it may be better for us to gather some information about specific behaviors that Sierra does that you find most challenging. Consider what comes immediately before it and then what happens after she does this behavior. These are the ABCs of behavior that we discussed. Remember that the behavior, or the B, has things that come before it that we call antecedents, or the A, which set the stage for the behavior and have consequences—the C—that follow the behavior and may maintain it going forward. I think it would be helpful if you tracked this daily for the next week. (Criterion 1) Then we can analyze the data and look at any patterns that precede and follow the behavior to truly ascertain the "why" of her behavior. (Criterion 2) What are your thoughts—is there anything that would stop this data from being gathered? (Criterion 3)
Example Response to Beginner Client Statement 2
I hear the challenges you are presenting that are associated with providing praise. You most likely are correct—Josh knows what is expected of him but still will not engage in those desired behaviors. Praise can be very powerful. Let's consider setting a goal of praising any of the behaviors you want, no matter how big or small. (Criterion 1) That praise sets the stage for future desired behaviors and may make these behaviors more likely to occur naturally. (Criterion 2) While the tendency may be to focus on the negatives, do you think that for this week you would be willing to make it your goal to praise him on a daily basis? (Criterion 3)

EXAMPLE RESPONSES TO BEGINNER-LEVEL CLIENT STATEMENTS FOR EXERCISE 12

Example Response to Beginner Client Statement 3

I can imagine that ignoring in those situations can be tough. As we discussed, parenting does not operate in a vacuum, and child behavior is often influenced by what follows it. From what you describe here, it sounds like attention. This week—and I know this may be tough—I would like you to pick a situation in which you know, based on history, that she tends to act up to get attention, then you will practice ignoring. (Criterion 1) When she sees that she can't get your attention, we can probably predict that initially her behavior may get worse, and eventually she will look for other ways to get your attention—hopefully by behaving. (Criterion 2) Is this something you think may be helpful in building your and her skills for the long term? (Criterion 3)

Example Response to Beginner Client Statement 4

Oftentimes, we focus mostly on the negative behaviors, and that makes sense because they are the ones that create challenges. I would like you to think about how you can look for any positive behaviors Brady does in the morning, even when tough to see, and give him attention for these by pointing out even 30 seconds where he is on-task and ignoring the times he is not. Can you try that each morning this week? (Criterion 1) Shifting your attention from his negative to his positive behaviors will strengthen the behaviors that we want to see him do. (Criterion 2) Is there anything that you can anticipate making this morning rewarding challenge more difficult for you to do? (Criterion 3)

Example Response to Beginner Client Statement 5

You may be correct that some rewards for Charlotte do not work, and she may not be so motivated to do the schedule you outlined. I imagine there are some things she does, in fact, find rewarding. Maybe we just need to have her be part of the planning. For this week, can you set a time to meet with Charlotte that is free of distractions and discuss what she finds rewarding, then pair them up with your expectations? (Criterion 1) While she may not want to do the things you described, when the right incentive is in place, it may increase her working toward these expectations. (Criterion 2) Are you willing to take this beginning step? (Criterion 3)

EXAMPLE RESPONSES TO INTERMEDIATE-LEVEL CLIENT STATEMENTS FOR EXERCISE 12

Example Response to Intermediate Client Statement 1

To begin, some of these behaviors may be typical for children her age, and each child may behave a certain way for a different reason. It is possible that attention is still a factor that influences June's behavior, but there may be other factors at play as well. I think it may be helpful for us to start a new round of daily data collection about her behavior and look again at what comes before that sets the stage—that's the antecedent, or A—and what comes after—the consequence, or C—that may maintain her behavior, the B. We can still use the same ABC worksheets. (Criterion 1) We can then look at the new data and see if there are any other functions, or "whys," of her behavior. (Criterion 2) What do you think, would you be willing to gather more information this week? Is there anything that would stop you from doing this? (Criterion 3)

EXAMPLE RESPONSES TO INTERMEDIATE-LEVEL CLIENT STATEMENTS FOR EXERCISE 12

Example Response to Intermediate Client Statement 2

The tendency to want to give up on a strategy when we don't see the results makes sense, but maybe don't give up on praising Jonah just yet. Praise works a good percentage of the time to increase desired behavior. I would suggest when giving praise that it would be good to be more specific as to what we are praising. Here, instead of "nice job," maybe say "I really like how hard you are working on your presentation." Specificity matters. I would like to propose we set a goal this week of two specific praises a day. (Criterion 1) By doing so, the praise makes these behaviors that are being reinforced more likely to occur going forward. (Criterion 2) What are your thoughts? Do you think that this is a strategy that would work and is this something you are willing to do? (Criterion 3)

Example Response to Intermediate Client Statement 3

It sounds like Camille makes many inappropriate efforts to get your attention, and then her behavior gets rewarded by getting her phone. Regrettably, it makes sense to me that she will continue to act this way as she gets what she wants. Further, you get what you want in the moment by getting some peace. In thinking about the "why" of her behavior, the attention from you is the first part of her behavior that gets rewarded and then the negative behaviors get rewarded by getting her phone. Let's plan for one dinner this week where, if she demands her phone and your attention, you practice that planned ignoring we discussed. (Criterion 1) The goal would be that by not giving her your attention and her not getting the phone, she will eventually change her behavior—basically, because her strategy is not working. (Criterion 2) What are your thoughts? Is this something you would be willing to do this week, and is there anything you can think of that will stop you from doing this? (Criterion 3)

Example Response to Intermediate Client Statement 4

Your concern here makes sense, and we want Frankie to graduate. Yet right now it is hard to even mention his attendance. How about we have you shift your attention to just spending time around him this week, without mentioning attendance? (Criterion 1) It is possible that focusing on having a positive interaction with him while temporarily avoiding discussion of his attendance could help improve things between you two and get him to a place where he is ready to listen. (Criterion 2) What are your thoughts about trying this? Do you think this will be helpful? Anything that may make this a challenge to do that we can plan for? (Criterion 3)

Example Response to Intermediate Client Statement 5

It sounds like the fights and arguments you have lead to a delay in completion of her homework and create stress for all. Having clear expectations can be helpful, so let's break down the homework into smaller units that we want to reinforce. Although rewarding her upon completion is good, maybe we want to reward the steps to completion. This week, can you take the entire process of homework completion and break it down into four or five smaller steps? For example, getting all her materials needed to complete the homework may be Step 1. (Criterion 1) Rewarding each step will help her move through them and strengthen the likelihood that she completes them. (Criterion 2) Is there anything that you can anticipate will make breaking down the homework and rewarding steps more challenging for you to complete? Do you think this would work with Liliana? (Criterion 3)

EXAMPLE RESPONSES TO ADVANCED-LEVEL CLIENT STATEMENTS FOR EXERCISE 12

Example Response to Advanced Client Statement 1

Great questions and thanks for gathering the data so far. Behavior can be more complicated for some children than others. I do not think gathering those sheets has been a waste of time, but maybe we need to review the examples of behavior gathered and the description of the antecedents and responses to the behavior. The antecedents are the As on the sheets, and the responses or consequences are the Cs; these are what precede and follow the behavior, the B. For this week, let's choose just two types of behavior and gather data on them. (Criterion 1) This will be more targeted and provide us an opportunity to look more closely at Emma's specific patterns of behavior and help narrow down the "why" of her behavior. (Criterion 2) You have done great in gathering data so far. Do you think it would be helpful to gather more data and are you willing to try and do this? Is there anything that you think would interfere with gathering this data to help us understand why? (Criterion 3)

Example Response to Advanced Client Statement 2

Yes, you definitely cannot praise his mocking behavior, and I hear how upsetting that is. As tough as it may be, when you see Matthew engaging in more appropriate behavior, we do want to praise that—ideally in the moment but also right after his friends leave the carpool. For the next carpool, have your focus be on looking for the positives and providing praise. (Criterion 1) Praising the specific behavior you want to see may make it more likely to occur naturally in future rides. (Criterion 2) What do you think? Is it possible during this week's carpool to look for opportunities to praise, even if it is the smallest of things? Do you think this praise would be helpful as we work on changing Matthew's behavior? Is there anything you think may make this homework a challenge to do? (Criterion 3)

Example Response to Advanced Client Statement 3

Although predictable, those behaviors Rose does can be frustrating. It sounds like your hypothesis is that she does these for attention, and you may be correct. While we won't ignore attention-seeking behaviors that put her safety at risk, we can ignore many of the other ones while also heaping praise on her cousin when she is behaving. Given the weekly family dinners, what are your thoughts about communicating to the adult family members your plan of ignoring these behaviors, providing them with a rationale for why you are doing this, and then ignoring her when she acts this way? (Criterion 1) By not giving your attention and giving it to her cousin, Rose may begin to seek your attention by changing her behavior. (Criterion 2) Would withholding attention from Rose work? Do you think this would be something you would be willing to try, and would anything interfere with doing this? (Criterion 3)

Example Response to Advanced Client Statement 4

It sounds like Ava's difficulties in following household rules create a lot of fighting. You said that she "rarely" follows them, but maybe this week, I would ask you to think of looking closely and acknowledging the rare times she does so, verbally and even with a thumbs up. Even if she breaks three other rules, let's make sure to ignore those for now. (Criterion 1) Focusing on the behaviors we want to see helps make them more likely and can help improve your relationship before we consider how to increase her following of the other rules. (Criterion 2) What are your thoughts? Do you think giving this positive attention would work with Ava? Although it's not easy to do in the face of some rule-breaking behavior, are you willing to try this and is there anything that you think would stop you from doing that this week? (Criterion 3)

EXAMPLE RESPONSES TO ADVANCED-LEVEL CLIENT STATEMENTS FOR EXERCISE 12

Example Response to Advanced Client Statement 5

I appreciate your questions about the use of rewards. The challenge is that, for whatever reason, he is not currently doing these behaviors. Our goal is eventually to fade out the use of most of these rewards, but only after we get him to do the behaviors. Let's try and build some early success this week by starting with two behaviors that we will make an effort to reward daily when performed, and we will be clear on what they are being rewarded for. (Criterion 1) By linking the behavior to the reward, this helps Jeremy understand what behaviors get rewarded, and then we hope to see a greater frequency of them. (Criterion 2) Do you think starting out with this approach may initially be a good way to increase his compliance, and are you willing to give it a shot? Is there anything you think could be a challenge in doing this? (Criterion 3)

Annotated Behavioral Parent Training Practice Session Transcript

Now you get a chance to put all the skills you have learned together! This exercise is a transcript of a session that is condensed to include aspects of each of the 12 skills you have learned. Each skill is labeled, providing an example of how therapists can include skills that are responsive to client needs.

Instructions

One trainee can play the therapist while the other plays the client, displaying a tone and affect congruent with the material. Both participants can read line-by-line from the transcript. As with all deliberate practice, after your first attempt, try it again! The purpose of this transcript is to provide you with an opportunity to experience how it feels to offer all the behavioral parent training (BPT) skills in the context of a session, albeit condensed, that mimics live therapy.

The focus of this book has been on BPT and 12 specific skills. That being said, we recognize that there are many other important clinical skills that may not fit neatly into these 12 skills. As an example, the research on common factors (e.g., therapeutic alliance, empathy, goal consensus, positive regard; Wampold, 2015) in psychotherapy as it relates to clinical outcomes is quite robust (Elliott et al., 2011; Horvath et al., 2011; Lambert & Shimokawa, 2011). Although the literature on these variables as it relates to BPT is sparse and the exact mechanism for how these factors work is debated (Cuijpers et al., 2019), we thought it important to recommend that clinicians consider these factors in their work with parents in the context of BPT. Some of these factors may be demonstrated within the skills and exercises, but we have not made them specific skills, which would be beyond the focus of a book specific to BPT. We believe that many of these common factors are addressed in the transcript.

In addition, as discussed in Chapter 1, we recommend that clinicians ask parents if their child is exhibiting behavioral problems in school. If so, the therapist can provide a rationale for contacting their child's teacher(s), school psychologist, and/or guidance

https://doi.org/10.1037/0000484-015

Deliberate Practice in Behavioral Parent Training, by M. D. Terjesen, H. B. Vidair, P. S. Ohr, O. A. Walsh, T. Rousmaniere, and A. Vaz

counselor and coordinating a plan across home and school (e.g., daily report card on a few targeted child behaviors from a teacher, incentives provided by parents at home for teacher report of positive behaviors in school; Barkley, 2013). A plan across home and school settings is more typical with younger children, although this can be helpful at any age.

Note to Therapists

Remember to be aware of your vocal quality. Match your tone to the client's presentation. Thus, if clients present vulnerable, soft emotions behind their words, soften your tone to be soothing and calm. If, on the other hand, clients are aggressive and angry, match your tone to be firm and solid.

Annotated Behavioral Parent Training Transcript

CLIENT 1: Thanks for meeting with me. I start a new job in 2 weeks where I have to commute to the city 3 days a week and work from home 2 days. The fall sports and extracurricular schedule for my kids is rough, but my main concerns are about my 10-year-old going on 16, Adam. Adam has really become difficult. His behavior is so challenging to deal with, and he just doesn't listen. Rarely, if ever, does he do what I ask. He blames me for everything and is so disrespectful in how he talks to me. I am worried that he will be really difficult on the days that I have to work from home and interrupt me constantly, like he typically does. I try to praise him, I offer rewards, I take away his phone, yet nothing seems to change his behavior. I'm at my wit's end.

THERAPIST 1: Thanks for sharing. From what you have described, it sounds like your biggest concern is Adam's behavior and, more specifically, his noncompliance, tendency to interrupt you, disrespectful behavior, lying, and not doing what you expect of him. A research-based approach that I recommend and think may be helpful is called behavioral parent training, or BPT. In doing BPT, we work together to change some of your own behaviors to set up systems to hopefully lead to the kind of behavioral change that you want that will make the home function better. This often will involve looking at Adam's pattern of behavior, as well as how you respond to it. If those responses aren't working, we then want to set up rewards for appropriate behavior and, when necessary, set up consequences for these problematic behaviors. From what you have described, I do think BPT could be effective in addressing Adam's behavior. Is this something you would like to consider and explore further? (Skill 1: Psychoeducation About Behavioral Parent Training)

CLIENT 2: Yes, I am looking for anything that might help. As I said, I am losing it and find I yell more than I thought I ever would as a parent. Yet still, it doesn't work. I try to plan and predict and just when things seem to be going well, they don't. I just don't understand why he does some of these things. Some of his behaviors are so embarrassing, and I often question what I'm doing wrong.

THERAPIST 2: I definitely hear the frustration as you describe Adam's behaviors, your efforts to manage them, as well as how you struggle to understand why he does these things (Skill 3: Identifying and Validating Parent Affect). Earlier you described his disrespectful and noncompliant behavior and both preventative strategies—offering rewards—and consequential strategies—punishments—that unfortunately don't seem to be changing his behavior. Within BPT, we make efforts to try and understand the purpose or the function as to why he behaves this way. Then we look more closely at the strategies you are using and see if we can work together to develop more effective, consistent parenting responses to his behaviors that will hopefully increase more positive behaviors in Adam. Is that something that you'd like to explore as an approach to help address this? (Skill 2: Psychoeducation About the Functions of Child Behaviors)

CLIENT 3: Sure, that makes sense, but the "why" of his behavior escapes me. How do we do that?

THERAPIST 3: Well, to begin, we would want to track his behavior and specifically what comes before as well as what follows this behavior. This is called an ABC sheet and stands for A, the antecedent, or what comes before; B, the behavior; and C, the consequence, or what comes after the behavior is performed. I will give you a sheet at the end of the session and ask you to gather data on this over the course of the week. For today, maybe you could give me a specific example, and we can try and understand the function of why. (Skill 2: Psychoeducation About the Functions of Child Behaviors)

CLIENT 4: Sure, where do I start? Well, how about the big screaming match we had on Sunday night. I knew he had that global studies project for school due on Monday and I reminded him maybe four or five times over the week. And I did it in a nice way, saying, "Adam, you may want to think about starting your global project." He kept saying he was working on it. Finally, Sunday comes around and I asked to see it, and he hadn't even started it yet! I honestly lost it. He lied to me. Repeatedly! I looked at his screen use, and he was on his screens all weekend, when he was supposedly working on it. He got it done, but we were both up until 11 p.m. I barely spoke to him on the ride to school on Monday. I hate that this is the kind of parent I've become.

THERAPIST 4: Recognizing how you feel and think about Adam and your responses will be an important part of this process, and we will make sure that we address this today. To begin, based on what you've described, let's try and look at both his behavior and yours. When he tells you he was working on it, basically not telling you the truth, I assume you left him alone. He avoided it because presumably there was something else more enjoyable to do—screens—and he lied because telling you he was working on it got rewarded by you leaving him alone. Does that make sense? Also, even though you didn't like doing it, the fact that he eventually did it after yelling makes you more likely to yell in the future. Does this make sense? (Skill 2: Psychoeducation About the Functions of Child Behaviors)

CLIENT 5: Yes, that makes sense. Don't do what you are supposed to do, do something fun instead. And lie about it! It's so infuriating. So what should I have done?

THERAPIST 5: We will discuss strategies in a moment, but one area we might start with is communication. In this example, despite your reminders to start this, he didn't do it, and you describe yelling at him. Maybe we start with teaching you effective commands. The types of commands you give are important, and we want to give direct commands. Direct commands make it clear to Adam that he is being told, not asked, to start his global studies project. Effective commands are specific, singular, and delivered in a positive and respectful way, usually with a reason. In the situation with the global studies project, when telling Adam to start the project, you could tell rather than ask and use a calm, neutral tone of voice. Perhaps say, "Please start the project now." When Adam complies, remember to give a positive statement, such as "Great job starting the project." Is this something you can do? (Skill 7: Teaching Parents About Effective Communication)

CLIENT 6: Yes, I could do that. In thinking about it, I also don't check his assignments or check in with his teachers nearly enough about the quality of his work due to my frustration here.

THERAPIST 6: Given this, I do think it would be helpful for you to speak to the school about your concerns regarding his behavior and see if they have anything to report. This would be important for us as we begin to change behavior in the home to see how any changes here may also be related to or impact his behavior in school.

CLIENT 7: OK, yes, I will try and do that when I'm not super frustrated. Honestly, all of this is so infuriating. He's not doing what he is supposed to do while also lying to me. It is really upsetting, and it's tough to calm down. If he were my employee, I would have fired him. I hate that I think that way as a father. Also, I am dreading this new job! I have to work from home, and I can see that he will constantly interrupt me. It just doesn't look good professionally to be allowed to work from home and then have your kid interrupt you constantly. He's old enough, and it's about dumb things!

THERAPIST 7: A few times now I have heard you describe being upset, and mostly angry, about Adam's behavior, especially the noncompliance, disrespectful behavior, and lying. I also hear some worry about starting this new job and how he will interrupt you. Noticing your anger and your worries and how these emotions may impact your parenting behaviors is important. Our emotions can impact how we parent and vice versa. Have you noticed that your anger and worries impact your parenting, and would you want to explore this? (Skill 3: Identifying and Validating Parent Affect)

CLIENT 8: Of the two, I think I get angry more than most and do think sometimes it impacts my parenting, but if he was just honest and did what he is supposed to, I wouldn't get angry. How do I get him to change?

THERAPIST 8: I appreciate your awareness of the role of anger and also hear that to start, you would prefer to work on strategies to change his behavior. If time allows, maybe we can circle back to your emotions, but for now, let's discuss strategies to change Adam's behavior. To start, you mentioned earlier that you praise Adam. Could you maybe describe how and when you use praise?

CLIENT 9: Sure, I think I praise him when he does what I want and will say "nice job" and hug him at the end of the day and say, "I'm proud of you." Sometimes I give him his favorite treat or candy, but he really should be doing these things without the praise or a reward. These are his responsibilities! The world doesn't praise you every time you do what's expected of you.

THERAPIST 9: To start, I do like that you are praising him at certain points. While you may be right about how the world operates, research shows that when you want behaviors to be performed consistently, praising is actually quite strategic initially because providing praise will increase the likelihood of Adam complying. Based on what you said, one change I'd suggest is to try and be more immediate when giving praise rather than waiting until the end of the day. In addition, we want Adam to know specifically what he is being praised for, so be more specific about what behavior your praise is for. For example, if you tell him to put away his lacrosse equipment and he does so, you could say, "Nice job putting your equipment away!" or "I'm so proud of you for putting your equipment away when I told you to!" What are your thoughts? Do you think you can try this? (Skill 4: Teaching Parents How to Provide Praise)

CLIENT 10: Yes, I can try that. It makes sense, reward what you want to see. But what do I do about the fact that he needs attention from me 24 hours a day, 7 days a week? It never ends. He will interrupt me for the smallest thing, and it often seems to happen when I'm doing something I enjoy, like reading a book or, lately, when I am trying to finish a project for work. He gets more attention from me than my other kids, and they probably actually need the attention more because they are younger than him. I give him plenty of one-on-one attention, whether good or bad, but I must be doing something wrong.

THERAPIST 10: That's a great observation on your part, and I am not sure you are doing anything incorrectly. He may be a child who needs more attention than others, but a goal we may want to try to focus on is to move your attention away from any of Adam's negative behaviors, like interrupting, to more of those positive behaviors that you want to see, like waiting patiently. Now to be fair, it can be a challenge when in a sea of negative behaviors I am asking you to look for the positives, which may be less common. Ideally, we want to focus on these positive behaviors and avoid commenting on the negative ones because this makes it likely his positive behaviors will increase. I would suggest an experiment where you give Adam an activity to do when you are doing something that you want to do, like reading, and when you see him occupying himself, give him a thumbs up, and say something like, "I love how you're playing while I read right now!" Give attention to those behaviors and make efforts not to comment on moments he interrupts you. Do you think you may be able to try this? (Skill 5: Teaching Parents to Provide Positive Attention)

CLIENT 11: Yes, I can do that. It won't be easy, but I will try. I imagine you are going to tell me punishment doesn't work, but how do I change his negative behaviors?

THERAPIST 11: Well, we will discuss consequences, but to start, I would rather hear how you reward behaviors that you want to see. We discussed verbal praise earlier, but do you ever offer any other types of rewards?

CLIENT 12: I knew you were going to suggest that. I struggle with this. All he wants is gift cards for lacrosse or for his gaming system. They are both expensive, and I really don't want to buy those, but at this point I don't know what else to do. I just need him to do what he is supposed to do.

THERAPIST 12: What rewards or incentives you offer are up to you, but strategically we have a better chance of getting Adam to behave the way you want if we offer an incentive, or something he really wants to receive. We can work together on a plan where if he does what is expected, then he earns a reward. For example, you could say that if he completes sections of a project on 4 out of 5 days this week, you would reward him with a gift card for lacrosse equipment. I imagine you do not want to do this long term, but what are your thoughts about starting this to begin to see the behaviors you want? (Skill 8: Teaching Parents How to Implement Positive Incentives to Bring About Behavioral Change)

CLIENT 13: Yes, I can start that way, but you have to promise me that my plan is not to bribe him to do what he is supposed to do for the rest of my life.

THERAPIST 13: Yes, we first want to introduce a reward system to see the behaviors that we want to see and then we will collaboratively work on this to make it more sustainable and use more natural reinforcers like activities. Does that make sense?

CLIENT 14: Yes, I understand. That may work to get him to do the things I want, but what do I do when he screams and yells at me or even curses me out in front of family members or parents of his teammates? It's humiliating and sometimes I just give in and give him what he wants.

THERAPIST 14: It sounds like part of the reason why or, as we said earlier, the function of Adam's screaming and disrespect is to get what he wants or possibly to upset or embarrass you to the point that you end up giving him what he wants. On those occasions when you do give in, this may only serve to reinforce or strengthen his behavior. By changing your response to his demands, you are altering the reinforcers at play that impact his behavior. As tough as it may be, I would suggest that you try planned ignoring. This means that you intentionally remove any attention to inappropriate behaviors when he is doing them either to gain something such as parental attention, or to get something he wants, such as an object or participating in an activity, like gaming. So, in this example, I think removing your attention from Adam's inappropriate behavior immediately and returning your attention only when he is no longer behaving inappropriately could be helpful. The key here is to give him positive attention, such as praise, for the change in his behavior. I would suggest that in a calm moment, you explain to Adam that you will remove your attention when he is engaging in those disruptive and disrespectful behaviors but will give him attention when he behaves appropriately. While at first I would predict some pushback from Adam in the moment, if you are consistent with both the ignoring and acknowledgment of his respectful behavior, you will start seeing decreased screaming and disrespect. Do you think planned ignoring would be a strategy you would be willing to use? (Skill 6: Teaching Planned Ignoring With Positive Attention)

CLIENT 15: Yes, I can try to ignore the bad and pay attention to the good behaviors, but what do I do when he clearly violates a household rule, like screen time? The house rule is that all devices are shut off at 7:45 p.m. This is a fight every night for us, and sometimes I let him win. He just doesn't listen, and I don't have the energy.

THERAPIST 15: Adam has learned to ignore your house rules because it doesn't sound like there are any consequences for it. Further, it sounds like he also gets a lot of attention for this and sometimes gets what he wants, like later screen time. Earlier you had asked about punishment. Response cost is the loss of something rewarding or desired upon performance of a negative behavior, like breaking the screen time rule. Response cost, although it may not teach children what you want them to do, often leads to a decrease in problem behaviors. In the described situation, tell Adam he loses a privilege for noncompliance with the screen time house rule. Explain what privilege he'll lose, such as 15 minutes of video gaming the next day. Tell Adam that he will not lose game time for a clearly defined, positive opposite behavior, like shutting off devices at the agreed-upon time. Should he misbehave, remind him about his choice. If he continues, tell Adam he's lost his privilege. I would suggest you try not to engage in arguments about this because it means giving him more attention. Also, even if it's been a rough day, it is important that you stick to the plan and not allow video-game playing, or you'll be reinforcing his problematic behaviors. But if he does comply with the rule, praise him for this. How does that sound? (Skill 9: Teaching Parents About Consequence Interventions)

CLIENT 16: That sounds fine about how to respond to violation of house rules, but how am I supposed to handle it out of the house? As an example, next Saturday we have his cousin's birthday party. He and his cousin usually get along, but his cousin will logically be the center of attention. I predict that to redirect some of that attention toward himself, Adam will start misbehaving. Even further, I predict he will start being rude and obnoxious to me in front of my family. I can predict this, but it is still infuriating. I have debated not going, but this is my sister's kid and my nephew.

THERAPIST 16: It sounds like you know your son well and are probably pretty accurate in making predictions about his behavior. While canceling may be easier to avoid dealing with this, it doesn't sound like the best option because you really want to be there for your nephew and your sister. I am thinking that creating a plan beforehand with Adam that has clear expectations would be helpful. Tell him what he earns if he meets these expectations, and I would encourage you to praise him throughout the party when he is meeting them. If he starts misbehaving and behaving disrespectfully toward you, the planned ignoring skill may be helpful. What do you think would get in the way of using these skills? (Skill 11: Teaching Parents About Managing Behavior in Public Settings)

CLIENT 17: Outside of my stress, nothing. I think I can do this. But honestly, I get so anxious and worried thinking about his behavior. Want to hear another prediction? I won't sleep the night before and will not enjoy the party because I will be worried the whole time. That is my fear about working from home, that even if he doesn't interrupt me—and he will—I won't be able to concentrate and get my work done because I will be worried that he will interrupt me.

THERAPIST 17: I can understand you feeling nervous about his behavior at the party and what sounds like probable behavior he will do when you are working from home. These worries will interfere with your enjoying the party and being productive while working. Earlier, you also mentioned some anger about his behaviors and how at points these built-up emotions lead you to not making the best decisions. While our focus will be on changing Adam's behavior through changing how you respond to him, it may also be helpful for us to look at your emotional responses and see if we can work on healthier ways to manage your feelings and think during those moments when you experience worry and anger. If we are able to change some of the thoughts that lead to the worry and anger, that may allow you to enjoy the party more, get work done from home, and not make parenting decisions when you are angry. Do you think this is something that would be helpful and worth giving a try? (Skill 10: Providing Strategies for Parent Affect Management)

CLIENT 18: Yes, I recognize my role in this and recognize that I am not the best parent I can be when upset. Right now, I would like to focus more on what I can do to change him, but I do think it's important that we come back to my parenting emotions at a later point. I just want him to listen and behave. Of all the things we discussed, I think the disrespectful language and the not doing what I ask are the two biggest issues for me. So what do I do now?

THERAPIST 18: That's a great question. BPT is a process with many different skills, as we discussed today. To begin, I would like you to complete one of these ABC worksheets that track his behavior this week. This will assist us in understanding the "why" of some of the things he does. Second, and I recognize that this may be challenging, I think it would be great if you tried each day to identify two of Adam's behaviors to praise when he is doing something desired upon your directives. This will increase the likelihood of those behaviors becoming stronger and occurring more often. I also think that, given the party is this weekend, it will be a good opportunity for you to set expectations with Adam and choose rewards for when he meets those expectations. Here, too, I would encourage you to praise him when he is doing well and meeting expectations at multiple points throughout the party. Do you think this may be a good beginning step, and is there anything you think may interfere with this? Also, please continue to be mindful of your parenting emotions. Next week we can spend more time developing these skills. (Skill 12: Development of Homework Assignments)

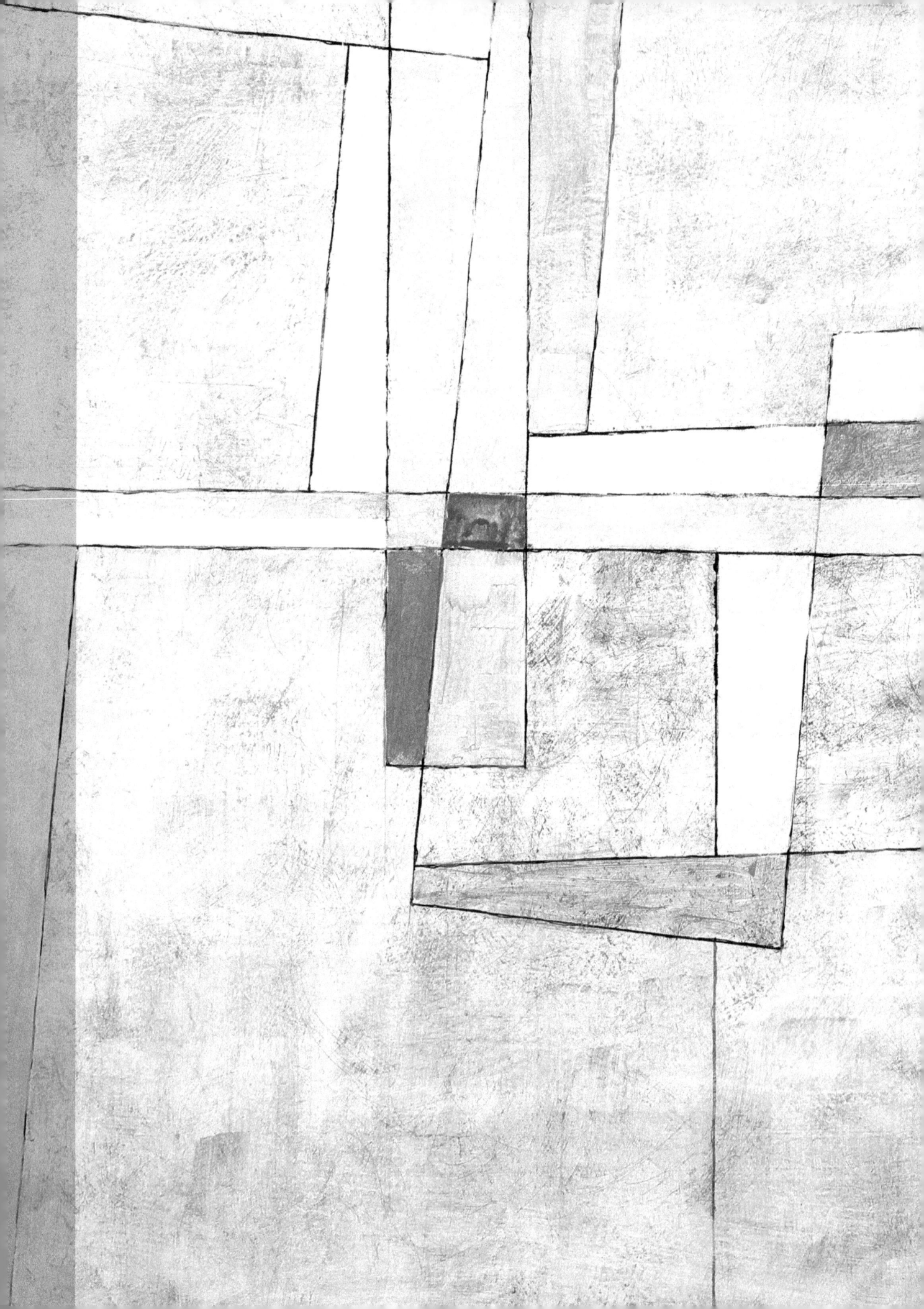

Mock Behavioral Parent Training Sessions

In contrast to highly structured and repetitive deliberate practice exercises, a mock behavioral parent training (BPT) session is an unstructured and improvised role-play therapy session. Like a jazz rehearsal, mock sessions let you practice the art and science of *appropriate responsiveness* (Hatcher, 2015; Stiles & Horvath, 2017), putting your therapy skills together in a way that is helpful to the mock parent. This exercise outlines the procedure for conducting a mock BPT session. Given that the child is typically considered the client while the parent is the one who primarily or solely attends therapy sessions, the mock sessions that follow offer different parent profiles you may choose to adopt when role-playing the parent.

Mock sessions are an opportunity for trainees to practice the following:

- using BPT skills responsively;
- navigating challenging choice points in therapy;
- choosing which BPT interventions to use;
- guiding treatment in the context of the parent's preferences and child's developmental stage;
- determining realistic goals for therapy in the context of the parent and child's capacities;
- knowing how to proceed when the therapist is unsure, lost, or confused;
- recognizing and recovering from therapeutic errors;
- discovering your personal BPT style; and
- building endurance for working with real parents.

Mock Behavioral Parent Training Session Overview

For the mock session, **you will perform a role play of an initial therapy session.** As is true with the exercises to build individual skills, the role play involves three people: One trainee role-plays the therapist, another trainee role-plays the parent, and a trainer

https://doi.org/10.1037/0000484-016

Deliberate Practice in Behavioral Parent Training, by M. D. Terjesen, H. B. Vidair, P. S. Ohr, O. A. Walsh, T. Rousmaniere, and A. Vaz

(a professor or a supervisor) observes and provides feedback. This is an open-ended role play, as is commonly done in training. However, this differs in two important ways from the role plays used in more traditional training. First, the therapist will use their hand to indicate how difficult the role play feels. Second, the parent will attempt to make the role play easier or harder to ensure the therapist is practicing at the right difficulty level.

Preparation

1. Download the Deliberate Practice Reaction Form and Diary Form from the "Resources" tab at https://www.apa.org/pubs/books/deliberate-practice-behavioral-parent-training (also available in Appendixes A and B). Every student will need their own copy of the Deliberate Practice Reaction Form on a separate piece of paper so they can access it quickly.

2. Designate one student to role-play the therapist and one student to role-play the parent. The trainer will observe and provide corrective feedback.

Mock Behavioral Parent Training Session Procedure

1. The trainees will role-play an initial (first) therapy session. The trainee role-playing the client selects a parent profile from the end of this exercise.

2. Before beginning the role play, the therapist raises their hand to their side, at the level of their chair seat (see Figure E14.1). They will use this hand throughout the whole

FIGURE E14.1. Ongoing Difficulty Assessment Through Hand Level

Note. Left: Start of role play. Right: Role play is too difficult. From *Deliberate Practice in Emotion-Focused Therapy* (p. 156), by R. N. Goldman, A. Vaz, and T. Rousmaniere, 2021, American Psychological Association (https://doi.org/10.1037/0000227-000). Copyright 2021 by the American Psychological Association.

role play to indicate how challenging it feels to them to help the parent. Their starting hand level (chair seat) indicates that the role play feels easy. By raising their hand, the therapist indicates that the difficulty is rising. If their hand rises above their neck level, it indicates that the role play is too difficult.

3. The therapist begins the role play. The therapist and parent should engage in the role play in an improvised manner, as they would engage in a real therapy session. The therapist keeps their hand out at their side throughout this process. (This may feel strange at first!)

4. Whenever the therapist feels that the difficulty of the role play has changed significantly, they should move their hand up if it feels more difficult and down if it feels easier. If the therapist's hand drops below the seat of their chair, the parent should make the role play more challenging; if the therapist's hand rises above their neck level, the parent should make the role play easier. Instructions for adjusting the difficulty of the role play are described in the "Varying the Level of Challenge" section.

> **Note to Therapists**
>
> Remember to be aware of your vocal quality. Match your tone to the parent's presentation. Thus, if the parent presents as vulnerable, with soft emotions behind their words, soften your tone to be soothing and calm. If, on the other hand, a parent is aggressive and angry, change your tone to be firm and solid.

5. The role play continues for at least 15 minutes. The trainer may provide corrective feedback during this process if the therapist gets significantly off-track. However, trainers should exercise restraint and keep feedback as short and tight as possible because this will reduce the therapist's opportunity for experiential training.

6. After the role play is finished, the therapist and parent switch roles and begin a new mock session.

7. After both trainees have completed the mock session as a therapist, the trainees and the trainer discuss the experience.

Varying the Level of Challenge

If the therapist indicates that the mock session is too easy, the person enacting the role of the parent can use the following modifications to make it more challenging (see also Appendix A):

-   The parent can improvise with topics that are more evocative or make the therapist uncomfortable, such as expressing currently held strong feelings or beliefs about parenting (see Figure A.2).

-   The parent can use a distressed voice (angry, sad, sarcastic, etc.) or unpleasant facial expression. This increases the emotional tone.

-   Blend complex mixtures of opposing feelings (e.g., love and rage) and thoughts about their child's behavior as well as their role as parents.

- Become confrontational, questioning the purpose of parent training or the therapist's fitness for the role.

  If the therapist indicates that the mock session is too hard, try the following:

- The parent can be guided by Figure A.2 to
  - present topics that are less evocative,
  - present material on any topic but without expressing feelings, or
  - present material concerning the future or the past or events outside therapy.

- The parent can ask the questions in a soft voice or with a smile. This softens the emotional stimulus.

- The therapist can take short breaks during the role play.

- The trainer can expand the "feedback phase" by discussing BPT and the theory behind it and how child maladaptive behaviors develop and get maintained.

Mock Session Parent Profiles

Following are six parent profiles for trainees to use during mock sessions, presented in order of difficulty. The choice of parent profile may be determined by the trainee playing the therapist, the trainee playing the parent, or assigned by the trainer.

The most important aspect of role plays is for trainees to convey both the concerns reflected as well as, where appropriate, the emotional tone indicated by the parent profile (e.g., "angry" or "sad"). While the child behavior problem as described by the parent and the age of the child are important to consider in the role play, the other demographics of the child (e.g., gender) and specific content of the parent profiles are not important. Thus, trainees should adjust the parent profile to be most comfortable and easy for the trainee to role-play. For example, a trainee may change the parent profile from female to male, from 45 to 22 years old, and so on.

Beginner Profile: Managing Frustration Regarding School-Age Child Behavior With a Receptive Parent

Frances is a 40-year-old Latinx waitress who has been having considerable challenges managing her own frustration at the behavior of her 6- and 9-year-old girls, Ella and Gracie. She is a single parent and has limited support from extended family, and the father's involvement is inconsistent and not particularly helpful. She reports that the girls are "always fighting" and "never listen," and she is emotionally triggered quite easily. She then resorts to yelling and screaming, and then she reports feeling bad about this and has a negative view of herself as a parent. Frances wants to learn how to parent better to help manage them, especially during transitions (i.e., getting ready for school; bedtime), as well as how to manage her own emotions.

- **Child behaviors:** Arguing and noncompliance
- **Parent reactions:** Yelling and screaming, anger/frustration, and guilt
- **Parent's goals for therapy:** Frances wants to improve her ability to manage her children's behaviors, as well as her own complex feelings about parenting.
- **Parent's attitude toward therapy:** Frances has never been in therapy but is open-minded about BPT being able to assist her with her children.
- **Parent's strengths:** Frances is very motivated for therapy and willingly shares with the therapist.

Beginner Profile: Addressing Child Behavior in Public Settings With an Engaged Parent

Robin is a 33-year-old African American physician who coparents her 5-year-old son Stephon with her husband, who is also a physician. She describes Stephon as a "holy terror" in public when he does not get his way. She thinks he is missing the "embarrassment gene" because he does not seem to care if his meltdowns are just with both of them at a restaurant or in front of all of his friends at a birthday party. He will reportedly yell, complain, scream, and throw himself on the floor until he gets what he wants. Robin reports that his teacher describes his behavior as quite the opposite, stating that he is polite, respectful, and handles being told "no" appropriately. She reports that they have started to skip certain events and order takeout for dinner more often because they do not want to deal with the predictable meltdowns and the stress that they feel as parents, which makes them enjoy going out less and often leads them to give in to his behavior.

- **Child behaviors:** Yelling, complaining, screaming, and throwing himself on the floor in public with his parents, yet polite and respectful in school with the teacher

- **Parent reactions:** Stress and challenges in handling the son's behavior in public and avoidance of events

- **Parent's goals for therapy:** Robin wants to learn strategies to manage her child's behaviors consistently and tolerate the stress that goes along with them.

- **Parent's attitude toward therapy:** Robin has had positive experiences in therapy before but none that have addressed her parenting skills. She is optimistic that this therapy will help as well.

- **Parent's strengths:** Robin is motivated to engage in the therapy tasks and learn new skills and is open to sharing her personal challenges in parenting.

Intermediate Profile: Troubleshooting Rewards and Consequences for a Middle Schooler With an Exhausted Parent

Richard is a 45-year-old White gym teacher who has been struggling with his 12-year-old daughter, Penelope. Penelope is constantly on her phone after school. It distracts her from getting her homework done, although she says she needs it because she and her classmates work on their homework together over text and this really helps her. She also stays up late at night on her phone. Richard and his wife, who is a teacher herself, have tried using check marks that lead to a reward, but he says they find Penelope loses interest. They have also gotten into arguments when she needs to go to sleep and have taken away her phone for the weekend, although they either end up giving it back to stop her crying about it or endure great distress, as she will continue crying for what feels like the entire weekend. Richard said he and his wife are exhausted by all the conflict around the phone. He constantly gets out of bed to tell Penelope to turn it off, and between this and her crying if it is taken away, he ends up losing sleep whether she has her phone or not.

- **Child behaviors:** Distracted by her phone, not going to be on time, and continuously crying when punished

- **Parent reactions:** Vacillating between rewards and punishment, feeling ineffective, and giving in or enduring great distress including loss of sleep

- **Parent's goals for therapy:** Richard wants to figure out how to decrease Penelope's phone use without putting effort into ineffective reward plans or consequences that feel like punishments for him and his wife.

- **Parent's attitude toward therapy:** Richard is skeptical that BPT can be of help but feels desperate to find something that works so he can get more sleep at night.

- **Parents' strengths:** Richard and his wife work well together as a team.

Intermediate Profile: Helping a Parent Adjust Their Parenting Style When Their Child Begins Middle School

Angelina is a 32-year-old White mother of Joey, an 11-year-old boy who recently started middle school. Angelina and Joey's stepfather suddenly feel confused about how to interact with him because he no longer wants to play games with them and would rather spend time on the weekends playing with his friends after basketball practice. She has made several suggestions for things they can all play together, but Joey snaps at her that her ideas are stupid and babyish. Angelina also used to assist Joey with his homework, but now he has assignments for multiple classes and insists he can handle it himself. Unfortunately, however, he recently missed submitting some assignments and even failed a test. She offered to review his homework after he finishes it or help him study, but he keeps turning down her offers to help. When she drives him and his friends some place, he will make disrespectful comments to her, even cursing at times when she yells at him for speaking to her that way. She used to punish him with time-outs but feels he is too big for this and, because all their interactions are so negative, that punishing him will only make things worse.

- **Child behaviors:** Spending less time with his mother and stepfather and more time with friends, disrespectful to his mother, cursing, not completing homework, and grades declining

- **Parent reactions:** Confused about how to adjust her parenting style now that her son is older and wants to be more social and independent

- **Parent's goals for therapy:** Angelina wants to learn how to increase positive times with Joey, decrease his disrespectful behavior toward her as well as his cursing, and decrease her yelling. She also wants to find a way to help him keep up with his homework that he will agree to.

- **Attitude toward therapy:** Angelina is open to hearing what the therapist suggests yet is skeptical that anything will help because she has tried talking to Joey several times to no avail, and he is willing to be disrespectful to her in front of his friends.

- **Parent's strengths:** Angelina feels motivated to improve the situation and is open to hearing any parenting strategies she has not tried.

Advanced Profile: Helping a Parent Abused as a Child With Her Teen Son Who Is Being Bullied

Jennifer is a 37-year-old White woman who is in her second year of law school, after being a full-time parent since her son was born 14 years ago. She is the single mother of Kyle, a mixed-race teen who is being bullied at school, including being cornered in the school bathroom at least once a week by older boys who shout racial insults and threaten to molest him if he tells anyone. Kyle shared this with his mother but threatened to run away if she reported this to the school. At home Kyle deals with his strong emotions by isolating himself in his room. When Jennifer tries to talk to Kyle, he is verbally and physically aggressive, including pushing her, cursing, and threatening to hurt her. To avoid this interaction, Jennifer lets him stay in his room, even letting him eat there. Jennifer has told Kyle she will take away his electronics if he keeps being disrespectful, which provokes a full-blown tantrum with Kyle destroying objects, such as furniture. Jennifer is scared of Kyle when he is so dysregulated and wonders if she should call the police, but she doesn't want him put in jail or taken away from her. Jennifer believes she is a failure as a mother because of her upbringing. As a child she was repeatedly sexually molested by her father and witnessed her father's physical abuse of her mother. She feels guilty about not protecting her son and helpless because she knows she needs to tell the school to protect him or the police to protect herself but does not want to lose Kyle.

- **Child behaviors:** Isolating himself in his room and verbally and physically aggressive behavior including cursing, pushing, and threatening to hurt his mother, as well as destroying objects. Threatening to run away.

- **Parent reactions:** Guilt about not protecting son. Anger toward her parents and feeling like a failure as a parent because of them. Fearful of her son and of losing her son. Accommodates her son's anger and threatening behavior by letting him isolate himself and not sharing concerns with school or police.

- **Parent's goals for therapy:** Jennifer wants to learn communication and problem-solving skills so that she and Kyle can effectively address the bullying in school. She also wants to learn how to manage her son's verbal and physical aggression.

- **Parent's attitude toward therapy:** Jennifer went to therapy for 2 years while in college to address trauma related to the sexual and physical abuse she experienced as a child. Jennifer no longer experiences several symptoms related to the childhood abuse and believes therapy helped.

- **Parent's strengths:** Jennifer is very intelligent; she is motivated to improve her relationship with her son and provide an environment that is safe for both herself and Kyle.

Advanced Profile: Helping a Mother–Daughter Dyad With Mood Lability

Janelle is a 32-year-old African American architect who is having problems in her relationship with her daughter, Raina. Janelle was 16 years old when Raina was born, the same age that Raina is now. Janelle and Raina's father never married, and Janelle was single until a year earlier. At that time, she began dating and reports that she sometimes feels deeply in love with her boyfriend, then hates and breaks up with him, only to welcome him back later. This behavior is impacting her relationship with her daughter as well because Raina has a good relationship with her mother's boyfriend. When Janelle is in conflict with her daughter, she gets angry and depressed, thinking that Raina will abandon her and she will have no one. She reacts to conflict with Raina by threatening her with unreasonable consequences, such as being grounded for a month. Janelle noticed that Raina similarly fluctuates between liking her school friends and then feeling betrayed and hurt should they reject her. Raina's moods have become unpredictable, and Janelle feels she is "walking on ice" as Raina may react to a simple "hello" with a vulgar curse and other expressions of anger, such as pinching Janelle, or she may burst into tears and run into her room crying and saying that her mother doesn't love her and is going to leave her.

- **Child's behaviors:** Mood lability, verbal and physical aggression, and interpersonal conflict

- **Parent reactions:** Mood lability, parent–child conflict, and fears of abandonment

- **Parent's goals for therapy:** Janelle wants to learn the best way to react to Raina's mood fluctuations and their conflicts because she realizes her consequences are not working. She would also like to learn how to manage her daughter's mood fluctuations as well as understand how her own cyclical behaviors intersect with her daughter's.

- **Parent's attitude toward therapy:** Janelle has never been in therapy before, although she has wondered if she needed to be because she has always gone through such highs and lows. Despite her hesitation to be in her own therapy, Janelle said she would like to engage in BPT to improve her relationship with Raina.

- **Parent's strengths:** Janelle is an intelligent woman who is very open to what the therapist says. She is self-reflective and wants to understand her daughter's perspective.

Strategies for Enhancing the Deliberate Practice Exercises

Part III consists of one chapter, Chapter 3, that provides additional advice and instructions for trainers and trainees so that they can reap more benefits from the deliberate practice exercises in Part II. Chapter 3 offers six key points for getting the most out of deliberate practice, guidelines for practicing appropriately responsive treatment, evaluation strategies, methods for ensuring trainee well-being and respecting their privacy, and advice for monitoring the trainer–trainee relationship.

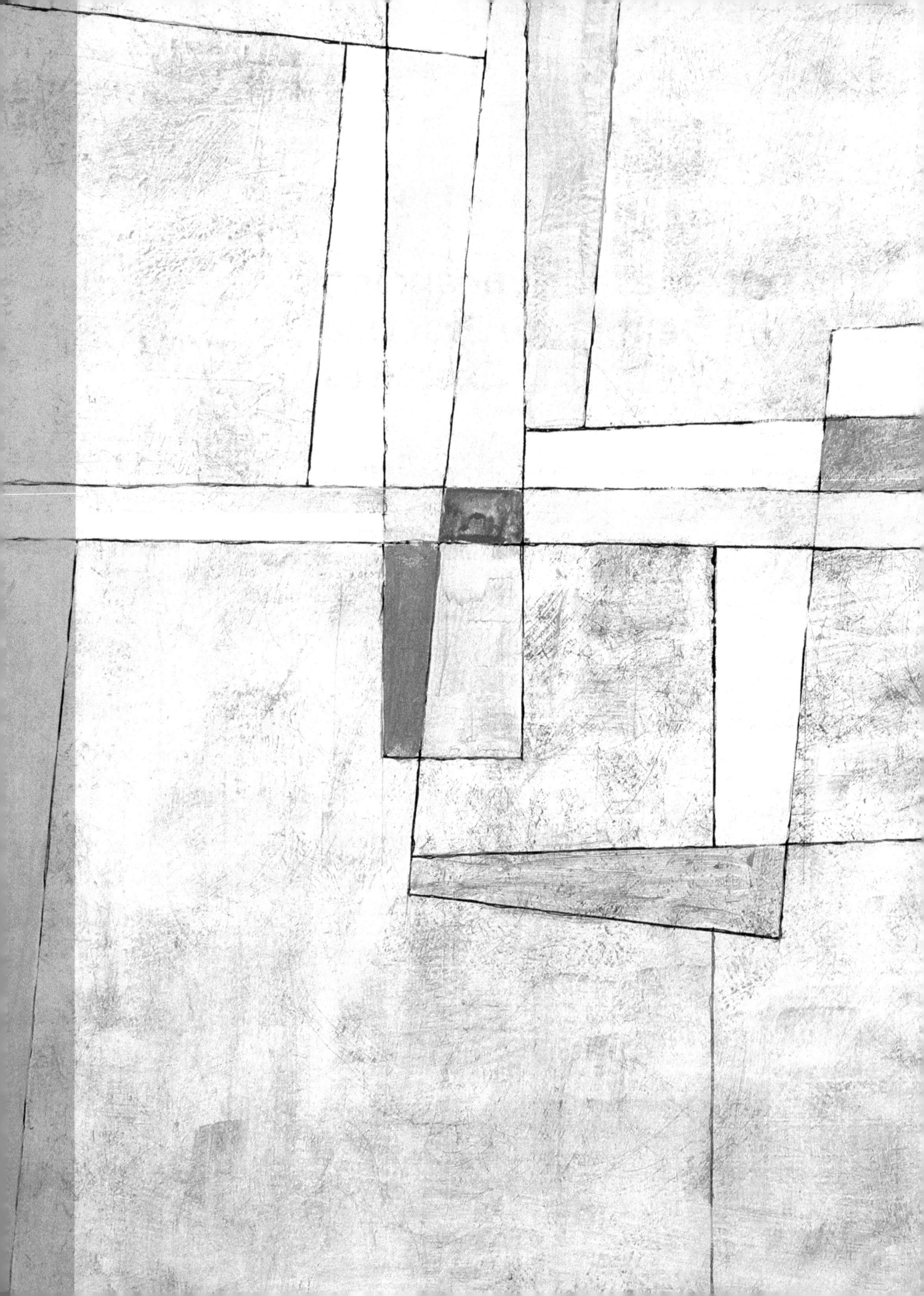

How to Get the Most Out of Deliberate Practice: Additional Guidance for Trainers and Trainees

In Chapter 2 and in the exercises themselves, we have provided instructions for completing the deliberate practice exercises. This chapter provides guidance on big-picture topics that trainers will need to integrate deliberate practice successfully into their training program. This guidance is based on relevant research and the experiences and feedback from trainers at more than a dozen psychotherapy training programs who volunteered to test the deliberate practice exercises in this book. We cover topics including evaluation, getting the most from deliberate practice, trainee well-being, respecting trainee privacy, trainer self-evaluation, responsive treatment, and the trainee–trainer alliance.

Six Key Points for Getting the Most From Deliberate Practice

Following are six key points of advice for trainers and trainees to get the most benefit from the behavioral parent training (BPT) deliberate practice exercises. The following advice is gleaned from experiences vetting and practicing the exercises, sometimes in different languages, with many trainees, across many countries.

Key Point 1: Create Realistic Emotional Stimuli

A key component of deliberate practice is using stimuli that provoke similar reactions to challenging real-life work settings. For example, pilots train with flight simulators that present mechanical failures and dangerous weather conditions; surgeons practice with surgical simulators that present medical complications with only seconds to respond. Training with challenging stimuli will increase trainees' capacity to perform therapy effectively under stress, for example with clients they find challenging. The stimuli used for BPT deliberate practice exercises are role plays of challenging client statements in therapy. **It is important that the trainee who is role-playing the client perform the**

https://doi.org/10.1037/0000484-017

Deliberate Practice in Behavioral Parent Training, by M. D. Terjesen, H. B. Vidair, P. S. Ohr, O. A. Walsh, T. Rousmaniere, and A. Vaz

script with appropriate emotional expression and maintain eye contact with the therapist. For example, if the client statement calls for sad emotion, the trainee should try to express sadness eye-to-eye with the therapist. We offer these suggestions regarding emotional expressiveness:

1. The emotional tone of the role-play matters more than the exact words of each script. Trainees role-playing the client should feel free to improvise and change the words if it will help them be more emotionally expressive. Trainees do not need to stick 100% exactly to the script. In fact, to read off the script during the exercise can sound flat and prohibit eye contact. Rather, trainees in the client role should first read the client statement silently to themselves, then, when ready, say it in an emotional manner while looking directly at the trainee playing the therapist. This will help the experience feel more real and engaging for the therapist.

2. Trainees whose first language isn't English may particularly benefit from reviewing and changing the words in the client statement script before each role play so that they can find words that feel congruent and facilitate emotional expression.

3. Trainees role-playing the client should try to use tonal and nonverbal expressions of feelings. For example, if a script calls for anger, the trainee can speak with an angry voice and make fists with their hands; if a script calls for shame or guilt, the trainee could hunch over and wince; if a script calls for sadness, the trainee could speak in a soft or deflated voice.

4. If trainees are having persistent difficulties acting believably when following a particular script in the role of client, it may help to first do a "demo round" by reading directly from paper, and then, immediately after, dropping the paper to make eye contact and repeating the same client statement from memory. Some trainees reported this helped them "become available as real clients" and made the role play feel less artificial. Some trainees did three or four "demo rounds" to get fully into their role as a client.

Key Point 2: Customize the Exercises to Fit Your Unique Training Circumstances

Deliberate practice is less about adhering to specific rules than it is about using training principles. Every trainer has their own individual teaching style and every trainee their own learning process. Thus, the exercises in this book are designed to be flexibly customized by trainers across different training contexts within different cultures. Trainees and trainers are encouraged to adjust exercises continually to optimize their practice. The most effective training will occur when deliberate practice exercises are customized to fit the learning needs of each trainee and culture of each training site. In our experience with numerous trainers and trainees across many countries, we found that everyone spontaneously customized the exercises for their unique training circumstances. No two trainers followed the exact same procedure. Here are a few examples.

- One supervisor used the exercises with a trainee who found all the client statements to be too hard, including the "beginner" stimuli. This trainee had multiple reactions in the "too hard" category, including nausea, severe shame, and self-doubt. The trainee disclosed to the supervisor that she had experienced extremely harsh learning environments earlier in her life and found the role plays to be highly evocative. To help, the supervisor followed the suggestions offered in Appendix A to make the stimuli progressively easier until the trainee reported feeling "good challenge" on the Deliberate Practice Reaction Form. Over many weeks of practice, the trainee developed a sense of safety and was able to practice with more difficult client statements. (Note that if the supervisor had proceeded with the too hard difficulty level, the trainee might have complied while hiding her negative reactions, becoming emotionally flooded and overwhelmed, leading to withdrawal and thus prohibiting her skill development and risking dropout from training.)

- Supervisors of trainees for whom English was not their first language adjusted the client statements to their own primary language.

- One supervisor used the exercises with a trainee who found all the stimuli to be too easy, including the advanced client statements. This supervisor quickly moved to improvising more challenging client statements from scratch by following the instructions in Appendix A on how to make client statements more challenging.

Key Point 3: Discover Your Own Unique Personal Therapeutic Style

Deliberate practice in psychotherapy can be likened to the process of learning to play jazz music. Every jazz musician prides themselves on their skillful improvisations, and the process of "finding your own voice" is a prerequisite for expertise in jazz musicianship. Yet improvisations are not a collection of random notes but the culmination of extensive deliberate practice over time. Indeed, the ability to improvise is built on many hours of dedicated practice of scales, melodies, harmonies, and so on. Much in the same way, psychotherapy trainees are encouraged to experience the scripted interventions in this book not as ends in themselves but as a means to promote skill in a systematic fashion. Over time, effective therapeutic creativity can be aided, instead of constrained, by dedicated practice in these therapeutic "melodies."

Key Point 4: Engage in a Sufficient Amount of Rehearsal

Deliberate practice uses rehearsal to move skills into procedural memory, which helps trainees maintain access to skills even when working with challenging clients. This only works if trainees engage in many repetitions of the exercises. Think of a challenging sport or musical instrument you learned: How many rehearsals would a professional need to feel confident performing a new skill? Psychotherapy is no easier than those other fields!

Key Point 5: Continually Adjust Difficulty

A crucial element of deliberate practice is training at an optimal difficulty level: neither too easy nor too hard. To achieve this, do difficulty assessments and adjustments with the Deliberate Practice Reaction Form in Appendix A. **Do not skip this step!** If trainees don't feel any of the "good challenge" reactions at the bottom of the Deliberate Practice Reaction Form, then the exercise is probably too easy; if they feel any of the "too hard" reactions then the exercise could be too difficult for the trainee to benefit. Advanced trainees and therapists may find all the client statements too easy. If so, they should follow the instructions in Appendix A on making client statements harder to make the role-plays sufficiently challenging.

Key Point 6: Putting It All Together With the Practice Transcript and Mock Therapy Sessions

Some trainees may seek greater contextualization of the individual therapy responses associated with each skill, feeling the need to integrate the disparate pieces of their training in a more coherent manner with a simulation that mimics a real therapy session.

The annotated transcript in Exercise 13 and the mock therapy sessions in Exercise 14 give trainees this opportunity, allowing them to practice delivering different responses sequentially in a more realistic therapeutic encounter.

Responsive Treatment

The exercises in this book are designed not only to help trainees acquire specific skills of BPT, but to use them in ways that are responsive to each individual client. Across the psychotherapy literature, this stance has been referred to as *appropriate responsiveness*, in which the therapists exercise flexible judgment, based in their perception of the client's emotional state, needs, and goals, and integrate techniques and other interpersonal skills in pursuit of optimal client outcomes (Hatcher, 2015; Stiles et al., 1998). The effective therapist is responsive to the emerging context. As Stiles and Horvath (2017) argued, therapists are effective because they are appropriately responsive. Doing the "right thing" may be different each time and means providing each client with an individually tailored response.

Appropriate responsiveness counters a misconception that deliberate practice rehearsal is designed to promote robotic repetition of therapy techniques. Psychotherapy researchers have shown that overadherence to a particular model while neglecting client preferences reduces therapy effectiveness (e.g., Castonguay et al., 1996; Henry et al., 1993; Owen & Hilsenroth, 2014). Therapist flexibility, on the other hand, has been shown to improve outcomes (e.g., Bugatti & Boswell, 2016; Kendall & Beidas, 2007; Kendall & Frank, 2018). It is important, therefore, that trainees practice their newly learned skills in a manner that is flexible and responsive to the unique needs of a diverse range of clients (Hatcher, 2015; Hill & Knox, 2013). It is thus of paramount importance for trainees to develop the necessary perceptual skills to be able to attune to what the client is experiencing in the moment and form their response based on the client moment-by-moment context (Greenberg & Goldman, 1988).

The supervisor must help the supervisee to attune themselves specifically to the unique and specific interpersonal needs of the clients during sessions. By enacting responsiveness with the supervisee, the supervisor can demonstrate its value and make it more explicit. In these ways, attention can be given to the larger picture of appropriate responsiveness. Here the trainee and supervisor can work together to help the trainee master not just the techniques but how therapists can use their judgment to put the techniques together to foster positive change. Helping trainees keep this overarching goal in mind while reviewing the therapy process is a valuable feature of supervision that is difficult to obtain otherwise (Hatcher, 2015).

It is also important that deliberate practice occurs within a context of wider BPT learning. As noted in Chapter 1, training should be combined with supervision of actual therapy recordings, theoretical learning, observation of competent BPT clinicians/psychotherapists, as well as personal therapeutic work. When the trainer or trainee determines that the trainee is having difficulty acquiring BPT skills, it is important to assess carefully what is missing or needed. Assessment should then lead to the appropriate remedy, as the trainer and trainee collaboratively determine what is needed.

Being Mindful of Trainee Well-Being

Although negative effects that some clients experience in psychotherapy have been well documented (Barlow, 2010), negative effects of training and supervision on trainees have received less attention (Ellis et al., 2014). To support strong self-efficacy, trainers must ensure that trainees are practicing at a correct difficulty level. The exercises in this book feature guidance for frequently assessing and adjusting the difficulty level so that trainees can rehearse at a level that precisely targets their personal skill threshold. Trainers and supervisors must be mindful to provide an appropriate challenge. One risk to trainees that is particularly pertinent to this book occurs when using role-plays that are too difficult. The Deliberate Practice Reaction Form in Appendix A is provided to help trainers ensure that role plays are done at an appropriate challenge level. Trainers or trainees may be tempted to skip the difficulty assessments and adjustments, out of their motivation to focus on rehearsal to make fast progress and quickly acquire skills. But across all our test sites, we found that skipping the difficulty assessments and adjustments caused more problems and hindered skill acquisition more than any other error. Thus, trainers are advised to remember that **one of their most important responsibilities is to remind trainees to do the difficulty assessments and adjustments.**

Additionally, the Deliberate Practice Reaction Form serves a dual purpose of helping trainees develop the important skills of self-monitoring and self-awareness (Bennett-Levy, 2019). This will help trainees adopt a positive and empowered stance regarding their own self-care and should facilitate career-long professional development.

Respecting Trainee Privacy

The deliberate practice exercises in this book may stir up complex or uncomfortable personal reactions within trainees, including for example memories of past traumas. Exploring psychological and emotional reactions may make some trainees feel vulnerable. Therapists of every career stage, from trainees to seasoned therapists with decades of experience, commonly experience shame, embarrassment, and self-doubt in this process. Although these experiences can be valuable for building trainees' self-awareness, it is important that training remain focused on professional skill development and not blur into personal therapy (e.g., Ellis et al., 2014). Therefore, one trainer role is to remind trainees to maintain appropriate boundaries.

Trainees must have the final say about what to disclose or not disclose to their trainer. Trainees should keep in mind that the goal is for the trainee to expand their own self-awareness and psychological capacity to stay active and helpful while experiencing uncomfortable reactions. The trainer does not need to know the specific details about the trainee's inner world for this to happen.

Trainees should be instructed to disclose only personal information that they feel comfortable sharing. The Deliberate Practice Reaction Form and difficulty assessment process is designed to help trainees build their self-awareness while retaining control over their privacy. Trainees can be reminded that the goal is for them to learn about their own inner world. They do not necessarily have to share that information with trainers or peers (Bennett-Levy & Finlay-Jones, 2018). Likewise, trainees should be instructed to respect the confidentiality of their peers.

Trainer Self-Evaluation

The exercises in this book were tested at a wide range of training sites around the world, including graduate courses, practicum sites, and private practice offices. Although trainers reported that the exercises were highly effective for training, some also said that they felt disoriented by how different deliberate practice feels when compared to their traditional methods of clinical education. Many felt comfortable evaluating their trainees' performance but were less sure about their own performance as trainers.

The most common concern we heard from trainers was, "My trainees are doing great, but I'm not sure if I am doing this correctly!" To address this concern, we recommend trainers perform periodic self-evaluations along the following five criteria:

1. Observe trainees' work performance.
2. Provide continual corrective feedback.
3. Ensure rehearsal of specific skills is just beyond the trainees' current ability.
4. Ensure that the trainee is practicing at the right difficulty level (neither too easy nor too challenging).
5. Continuously assess trainee performance with real clients.

Criterion 1: Observe Trainees' Work Performance

Determining how well we are doing as trainers means first having valid information about how well trainees are responding to training. This requires that we directly observe trainees practicing skills to provide corrective feedback and evaluation. One risk of deliberate practice is that trainees gain competence in performing therapy skills in role plays, but those skills do not transfer to trainees' work with real clients. Thus, trainers will ideally also have the opportunity to observe samples of trainees' work with real clients, either live or via recorded video. Supervisors and consultants rely heavily—and, too often, exclusively—on supervisees' and consultees' narrative accounts of their work with clients (Goodyear & Nelson, 1997). Haggerty and Hilsenroth (2011) described this challenge as follows:

> Suppose a loved one has to undergo surgery and you need to choose between two surgeons, one of whom has never been directly observed by an experienced surgeon while performing any surgery. He or she would perform the surgery and return to his or her attending physician and try to recall, sometimes incompletely or inaccurately, the intricate steps of the surgery they just performed. It is hard to imagine that anyone, given a choice, would prefer this over a professional who has been routinely observed in the practice of their craft. (p. 193)

Criterion 2: Provide Continual Corrective Feedback

Trainees need corrective feedback to learn what they are doing well, doing poorly, and how to improve their skills. Feedback should be as specific and incremental as possible. The following are examples of specific feedback: "Your voice sounds rushed. Try slowing down by pausing for a few seconds between your statements to the client" and "You're doing an excellent job at making eye contact with the client." Examples of vague and nonspecific feedback are "Try to build better rapport with the client" and "Try to be more open to the client's feelings."

Criterion 3: Specific Skill Rehearsal Just Beyond the Trainees' Current Ability (Zone of Proximal Development)

Deliberate practice emphasizes skill acquisition via behavioral rehearsal. Trainers should endeavor not to get caught up in client conceptualization at the expense of focusing on skills. For many trainers, this requires significant discipline and self-restraint. It is simply more enjoyable to talk about psychotherapy theory (e.g., case conceptualization, treatment planning, nuances of psychotherapy models, similar cases the supervisor has had) than watch trainees rehearse skills. Trainees have many questions and supervisors have an abundance of experience; the allotted supervision time can easily be filled by sharing knowledge. The supervisor gets to sound smart, while the trainee doesn't have to struggle with acquiring skills at their learning edge. Although answering questions is important, trainees' intellectual knowledge about psychotherapy can quickly surpass their procedural ability to perform psychotherapy, particularly with clients they find challenging. Here's a simple rule of thumb: The trainer provides the knowledge, but the behavioral rehearsal provides the skill (Rousmaniere, 2019).

Criterion 4: Practice at the Right Difficulty Level (Neither Too Easy nor Too Challenging)

Deliberate practice involves *optimal strain*: practicing skills just beyond the trainee's current skill threshold so that they can learn incrementally without becoming overwhelmed (Ericsson, 2006).

Trainers should use difficulty assessments and adjustments throughout deliberate practice to ensure that trainees are practicing at the right difficulty level. Note that some trainees are surprised by their unpleasant reactions to exercises (e.g., dissociation, nausea, blanking out), and may be tempted to "push through" exercises that are too hard. This can happen out of fear of failing a course, fear of being judged as incompetent, or negative self-impressions by the trainee (e.g., "This shouldn't be so hard"). Trainers should normalize the fact that there will be wide variation in perceived difficulty of the exercises and encourage trainees to respect their own personal training process.

Criterion 5: Continuously Assess Trainee Performance With Real Clients

The goal of deliberately practicing psychotherapy skills is to improve trainees' effectiveness at helping real clients. One of the risks in deliberate practice training is that the benefits will not generalize: Trainees' acquired competence in specific skills may not translate into work with real clients. Thus, it is important that trainers assess the impact of deliberate practice on trainees' work with real clients. Ideally, this is done through triangulation of multiple data points:

- Client data (verbal self-report and routine outcome monitoring data)
- Supervisor's report
- Trainee's self-report

If the trainee's effectiveness with real clients is not improving after deliberate practice, the trainer should do a careful assessment of the difficulty. If the supervisor or trainer feels it is a skill acquisition issue, they may want to consider adjusting the deliberate practice routine to better suit the trainee's learning needs or style.

Therapists have traditionally been evaluated from a lens of *process accountability* (Markman & Tetlock, 2000; see also Goodyear, 2015), which focuses on demonstrating specific behaviors (e.g., fidelity to a treatment model) without regard to the impact on clients. We propose that clinical effectiveness is better assessed through a lens tightly focused on client outcomes and that learning objectives shift from performing behaviors that experts have decided are effective (i.e., the competence model) to highly individualized behavioral goals tailored to each trainee's zone of proximal development and performance feedback. This model of assessment has been termed *outcome accountability*

(Goodyear, 2015), which focuses on client changes rather than therapist competence, independent of how the therapist might be performing expected tasks.

Guidance for Trainees

The central theme of this book has been that skill rehearsal is not automatically helpful. Deliberate practice must be done well for trainees to benefit (Ericsson & Pool, 2016). In this chapter and in the exercises, we offer guidance for effective deliberate practice. We would also like to provide additional advice specifically for trainees. That advice is drawn from what we have learned at our volunteer deliberate practice test sites around the world. We cover how to discover your own training process, active effort, playfulness and taking breaks during deliberate practice, your right to control your self-disclosure to trainers, monitoring training results, monitoring complex reactions toward the trainer, and your own personal therapy.

Individualized Training in Behavioral Parent Training: Finding Your Zone of Proximal Development

Deliberate practice works best when training targets each trainee's personal skill thresholds. Also termed the *zone of proximal development*, a term first coined by Vygotsky in reference to developmental learning theory (Zaretskii, 2009), this is the area just beyond the trainee's current ability that is possible to reach with the assistance of a teacher or coach (Wass & Golding, 2014). **If a deliberate practice exercise is either too easy or too hard, the trainee will not benefit.** To maximize training productivity, elite performers follow a "challenging but not overwhelming" principle: Tasks that are too far beyond their capacity will prove ineffective and even harmful, it is equally true that mindlessly repeating what they already can do confidently will prove equally fruitless. Because of this, deliberate practice requires ongoing assessment of the trainee's current skill and concurrent difficulty adjustment to target a "good enough" challenge consistently. Thus, if you are practicing Exercise 5: Teaching Parents to Provide Positive Attention, and it just feels too difficult, consider moving back to a more comfortable skill such as Exercise 4: Teaching Parents How to Provide Praise or Exercise 3: Identifying and Validating Parent Affect that you may feel you have already mastered.

Active Effort

It is important for trainees to maintain an active and sustained effort while doing the deliberate practice exercises in this book. Deliberate practice really helps when trainees push themselves up to and past their current ability. This is best achieved when trainees take ownership of their own practice by guiding their training partners to adjust role plays to be as high on the difficulty scale as possible without hurting themselves. This will look different for every trainee. Although it can feel uncomfortable or even frightening, this is the zone of proximal development where the most gains can be made. Simply reading and repeating the written scripts will provide little or no benefit. Trainees are advised to remember that their effort from training should lead to more confidence and comfort in session with real clients.

Stay the Course: Effort Versus Flow

Deliberate practice only works if trainees push themselves hard enough to break out of their old patterns of performance, which then permits growth of new skills (Ericsson &

Pool, 2016). Because deliberate practice constantly focuses on the current edge of one's performance capacity, it is inevitably a straining endeavor. Indeed, professionals are unlikely to make lasting performance improvements unless there is sufficient engagement in tasks that are just at the edge of their current capacity (Ericsson, 2003, 2006). From athletics or fitness training, many of us are familiar with this process of being pushed out of our comfort zones followed by adaptation. The same process applies to our mental and emotional abilities.

Many trainees may be surprised to discover that deliberate practice for BPT feels harder than psychotherapy with a real client. This may be because when working with a real client a therapist can get into a state of *flow* (Csikszentmihalyi, 1997), where work feels effortless. As young BPT therapists in training, clinicians are instructed to maintain the conceptual focus on interpersonal aspects of clients' presentations. Specifically, when asking questions or making clarifications, BPT clinicians are asked to focus on interpersonal functioning to further expand clients' interpersonal awareness. This might be challenging to maintain throughout the session because for some clinicians this might be a new way to look at the content and process in therapy. Sometimes clinicians who are new to BPT might find it difficult to continue to hold conceptual focus on interpersonal distress. In such cases, therapists may want to move back to offering response formats with which they are more familiar and feel more proficient in, and try those for a short time, in part to increase a sense of confidence and mastery.

Discover Your Own Training Process

The effectiveness of deliberate practice is directly related to the effort and ownership trainees exert while doing the exercises. Trainers can provide guidance, but it is important for trainees to learn about their own idiosyncratic training processes over time. This will let them become masters of their own training and prepare for a career-long process of professional development. The following are a few examples of personal training processes trainees discovered while engaging in deliberate practice:

- One trainee noticed that she needed to master and understand, more than other clinicians, the initial examples in each exercise before she was to be able to move on and start practicing an exercise on her own.

- One trainee noticed that she needed to go back to Chapter 1 and other resources to catch the "therapeutic stance and spirit" of BPT before she could start practicing exercises.

- One trainee noticed that she was good at persisting when an exercise was challenging but also that she required more rehearsal than other trainees to feel comfortable with a new skill. This trainee focused on developing patience with her own pace of progress.

- One trainee noticed that he could acquire new skills rather quickly, with only a few repetitions. However, he also noticed that his reactions to evocative client statements could jump very quickly and unpredictably from the "good challenge" to the "too hard" categories, so he needed to attend carefully to the reactions listed on the Deliberate Practice Reaction Form.

- One trainee described herself as "perfectionistic" and felt a strong urge to "push through" an exercise even when she had anxiety reactions, such as nausea and dissociation, in the "too hard" category. This caused the trainee not to benefit from the exercises and risk becoming demoralized. This trainee focused on going slower, developing self-compassion regarding her anxiety reactions, and asking her training partners to make role plays less challenging.

Trainees are encouraged to reflect deeply on their own experiences using the exercises to learn the most about themselves and their personal learning processes.

Playfulness and Taking Breaks

Psychotherapy is serious work that often involves painful feelings. However, practicing psychotherapy can be playful and fun (Scott Miller, personal communication, 2017). Trainees should remember that one of the main goals of deliberate practice is to experiment with different approaches and styles of therapy. If deliberate practice ever feels rote, boring, or routine, it probably isn't going to help advance trainees' skill. In this case, trainees should try to liven it up. A good way to do this is to introduce an atmosphere of playfulness. For example, trainees can try the following:

- Use different vocal tones, speech pacing, body gestures, or other languages. This can expand trainees' communication range.

- Practice while simulating being blind (with a blindfold). This can increase sensitivity of the other senses.

- Practice while standing up or walking around outside. This can help trainees get new perspectives on the process of therapy.

The supervisor can also ask trainees if they would like to take a 5- to 10-minute break between questions, particularly if the trainees are dealing with difficult emotions and are feeling stressed.

Additional Deliberate Practice Opportunities

This book focuses on deliberate practice methods that involve active, live engagement between trainees and a supervisor. Importantly, deliberate practice can extend beyond these focused training sessions and be used for homework. For example, a trainee might read the client stimuli quietly or aloud and practice their responses independently between sessions with a supervisor. In such cases, it is important for the trainee to say their therapist responses aloud, rather than rehearse silently in their head. Alternatively, two trainees can practice as a pair, without the supervisor. Although the absence of a supervisor limits one source of feedback, the peer trainee who is playing the client can serve this role, as they can when a supervisor is present.

To optimize the quality of deliberate practice when conducted independently or without a supervisor, we have developed a Deliberate Practice Diary Form that can be found in Appendix B or downloaded from https://www.apa.org/pubs/books/deliberate-practice-behavioral-parent-training (see the "Resources" tab). This form provides a template for the trainee to record their experience of the deliberate practice activity, and, ideally, it will aid in the consolidation of learning. This form can be used as part of the evaluation process with the supervisor but is not necessarily intended for that purpose, and trainees are certainly welcome to bring their experience with the independent practice into the next meeting with the supervisor.

Monitoring Training Results

While trainers will evaluate trainees using a competency-focused model, trainees are also encouraged to take ownership of their own training process and look for results of deliberate practice themselves. Trainees should experience the results of deliberate practice within a few training sessions. A lack of results can be demoralizing for trainees and can result in their applying less effort and focus in deliberate practice. Trainees who are not seeing results should openly discuss this problem with their trainer and experiment with adjusting their deliberate practice process. Results can include improved client outcomes and improving the trainee's own work as a therapist, their personal development, and their overall training.

Client Outcomes

The most important result of deliberate practice is an improvement in trainees' client outcomes. This can be assessed via routine outcome measurement (Lambert, 2010; Prescott et al., 2017), qualitative data (McLeod, 2017), and informal discussions with clients. However, trainees should note that an improvement in client outcome due to deliberate practice can sometimes be challenging to achieve quickly, given that the largest amount of variance in client outcome is due to client variables (Bohart & Wade, 2013). For example, a client with severe chronic symptoms may not respond quickly to any treatment, regardless of how effectively a trainee practices. For some clients, an increase in patience and self-compassion regarding their symptoms may be a sign of progress, rather than an immediate decrease in symptoms. Thus, trainees are advised to keep their expectations for client change realistic in the context of their client's symptoms, history, and presentation. It is important that trainees do not try to force their clients to improve in therapy for the trainees to feel like they are making progress in their training (Rousmaniere, 2016).

Trainee's Work as a Therapist

One important result of deliberate practice is change within the trainee regarding their work with clients. For example, trainees at test sites reported feeling more comfortable sitting with evocative clients, more confident addressing uncomfortable topics in therapy, and more responsive to a broader range of clients.

Trainee's Personal Development

Another important result of deliberate practice is personal growth within the trainee. For example, trainees at test sites reported becoming more in touch with their own feelings, increased self-compassion, and enhanced motivation to work with a broader range of clients.

Trainee's Training Process

Another valuable result of deliberate practice is improvement in the trainee's training process. For example, trainees at test sites reported becoming more aware of their personal training style, preferences, strengths, and challenges. Over time, trainees should grow to feel more ownership of their training process. Also, training to be a psychotherapist is a complex process that occurs over many years. Experienced, expert therapists still report continuing to grow well beyond their graduate school years (Orlinsky & Ronnestad, 2005). Furthermore, training is not a linear process. Some clinicians reported feeling "good enough mastery" of the BPT approach after implementing BPT with about two or three clients, from the beginning to the very end of treatment.

The Trainee–Trainer Alliance: Monitoring Complex Reactions Toward the Trainer

Trainees who engage in difficult deliberate practice often report experiencing complex feelings toward their trainer. For example, one trainee said, "I know this is helping, but I also don't look forward to it!" Another trainee reported feeling both appreciation and frustration toward her trainer simultaneously. Trainees are advised to remember intensive training they have done in other fields, such as athletics or music. When a coach pushes a trainee to the edge of their ability, it is common for the trainee to have complex reactions toward them.

This does not necessarily mean that the trainer is doing anything wrong. In fact, intensive training inevitably stirs up reactions toward the trainer, such as frustration, annoyance, disappointment, or anger that coexist with the appreciations they feel. In fact, if trainees do not experience complex reactions, it is worth considering if the deliberate practice is sufficiently challenging. But what we asserted earlier about rights to privacy apply here as well. Because professional mental health training is hierarchical and evaluative, trainers should not require or even expect trainees to share complex reactions they may be experiencing toward them. Trainers should stay open to their sharing, but the choice always remains with the trainee.

Trainee's Own Therapy

When engaging in deliberate practice, many trainees discover aspects of their inner world that may benefit from attending their own psychotherapy. For example, one trainee discovered that her clients' anger stirred up her own painful memories of abuse, another trainee found himself disassociating while practicing empathy skills, and another trainee experienced overwhelming shame and self-judgment when she couldn't master skills after just a few repetitions.

Although these discoveries were unnerving at first, they were ultimately very beneficial because they motivated the trainees to seek out their own therapy. Many therapists attend their own therapy. In fact, Norcross and Guy (2005) found in their review of 17 studies that about 75% of the more than 8,000 therapist participants have attended their own therapy. Orlinsky and Ronnestad (2005) found that more than 90% of therapists who attended their own therapy reported it to be helpful.

QUESTIONS FOR TRAINEES

1. Are you balancing the effort to improve your skills with patience and self-compassion for your learning process?
2. Are you attending to any shame or self-judgment arising from training?
3. Are you being mindful of your personal boundaries and also respecting any complex feelings you may have toward your trainers?

Difficulty Assessments and Adjustments

Deliberate practice works best if the exercises are performed at a "good challenge" level that is neither too hard nor too easy. To ensure that they are practicing at the correct difficulty, trainees should do a difficulty assessment and adjustment after each level of client statement is completed (beginner, intermediate, and advanced). To do this, use the following instructions and the Deliberate Practice Reaction Form (Figure A.1), which is also available in the "Resources" tab at https://www.apa.org/pubs/books/deliberate-practice-behavioral-parent-training. **Do not skip this process!**

How to Assess Difficulty

The therapist completes the reaction form (Figure A.1). If they

- rate the difficulty of the exercise above an 8 or had any of the reactions in the "Too Hard" column, follow the instructions to make the exercise easier;

- rate the difficulty of the exercise below a 4 or didn't have any of the reactions in the "Good Challenge" column, proceed to the next level of harder client statements or follow the instructions to make exercise harder; or

- rate the difficulty of the exercise between 4 and 8 and have at least one reaction in the "Good Challenge" column, do not proceed to the harder client statements but rather repeat the same level.

Making Client Statements Easier

If the therapist ever rates the difficulty of the exercise above an 8 or has any of the reactions in the "Too Hard" column, use the previous level client statements (e.g., if you were using advanced client statements, switch to intermediate). But if you already were using beginner client statements, use the following methods to make the client statements even easier:

- The person playing the client can use the same beginner client statements but this time in a softer, calmer voice and with a smile. This softens the emotional tone.

FIGURE A.1. Deliberate Practice Reaction Form

Question 1: How challenging was it to fulfill the skill criteria for this exercise?

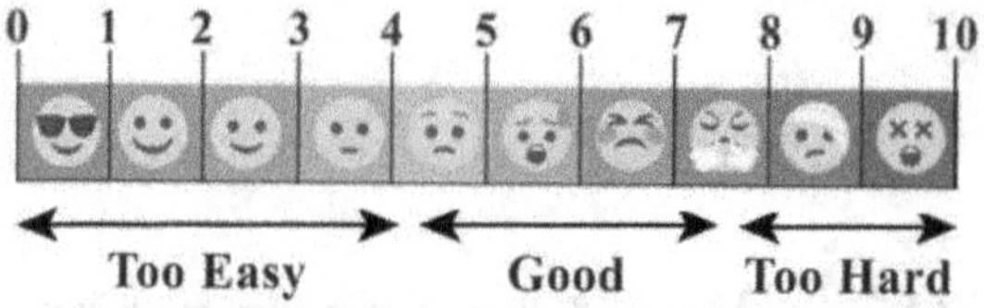

Question 2: Did you have any reactions in "good challenge" or "too hard" categories? (yes/no)					
Good Challenge			**Too Hard**		
Emotions and Thoughts	Body Reactions	Urges	Emotions and Thoughts	Body Reactions	Urges
Manageable shame, self-judgment, irritation, anger, sadness, etc.	Body tension, sighs, shallow breathing, increased heart rate, warmth, dry mouth	Looking away, withdrawing, changing focus	Severe or overwhelming shame, self-judgment, rage, grief, guilt, etc.	Migraines, dizziness, foggy thinking, diarrhea, disassociation, numbness, blanking out, nausea, etc.	Shutting down, giving up

Too Easy ⬇ **Proceed to next difficulty level**	**Good Challenge** ⬇ **Repeat the same difficulty level**	**Too Hard** ⬇ **Go back to previous difficulty level**

Note. From *Deliberate Practice in Emotion-Focused Therapy* (p. 180), by R. N. Goldman, A. Vaz, and T. Rousmaniere, 2021, American Psychological Association (https://doi.org/10.1037/0000227-000). Copyright 2021 by the American Psychological Association.

- The client can improvise with topics that are less evocative or make the therapist more comfortable, such as talking about topics without expressing feelings, the future or past (avoiding the here and now), or any topic outside therapy (see Figure A.2)

- The therapist can take a short break (5–10 minutes) between questions.

- The trainer can expand the "feedback phase" by discussing behavioral parent training or psychotherapy theory and research. This should shift the trainees' focus toward more detached or intellectual topics and reduce the emotional intensity.

Making Client Statements Harder

If the therapist rates the difficulty of the exercise below a 4 or didn't have any of the reactions in the "Good Challenge" column, proceed to next level client statements. If you were already using the advanced client statements, the client should make the exercise even harder, using the following guidelines:

FIGURE A.2. How to Make Client Statements Easier or Harder in Role Plays

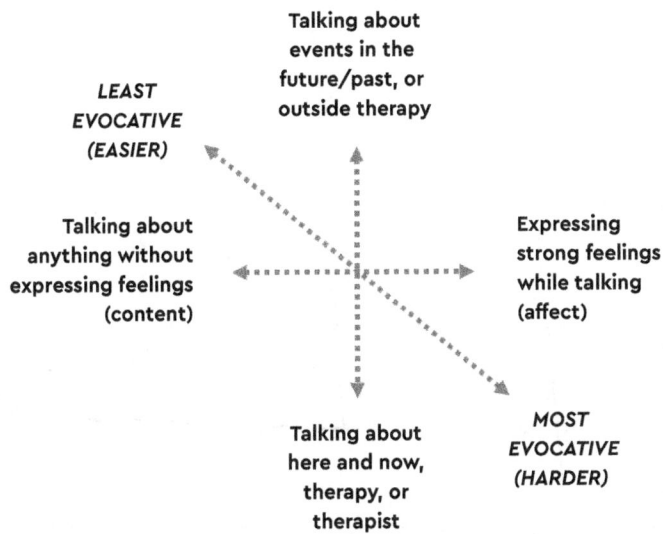

Note. Figure created by Jason Whipple, PhD.

- The person playing the client can use the advanced client statements again with a more distressed voice (very angry, sad, sarcastic, etc.) or unpleasant facial expression. This should increase the emotional tone.

- The client can improvise new client statements with topics that are more evocative or make the therapist uncomfortable, such as expressing strong feelings or talking about the here and now, therapy, or the therapist (see Figure A.2).

> *Note.* The purpose of a deliberate practice session is not to get through all the client statements and therapist responses, but rather to spend as much time as possible practicing at the correct difficulty level. This may mean that trainees repeat the same statements and responses many times, which is okay as long as the difficulty remains at the "good challenge" level.

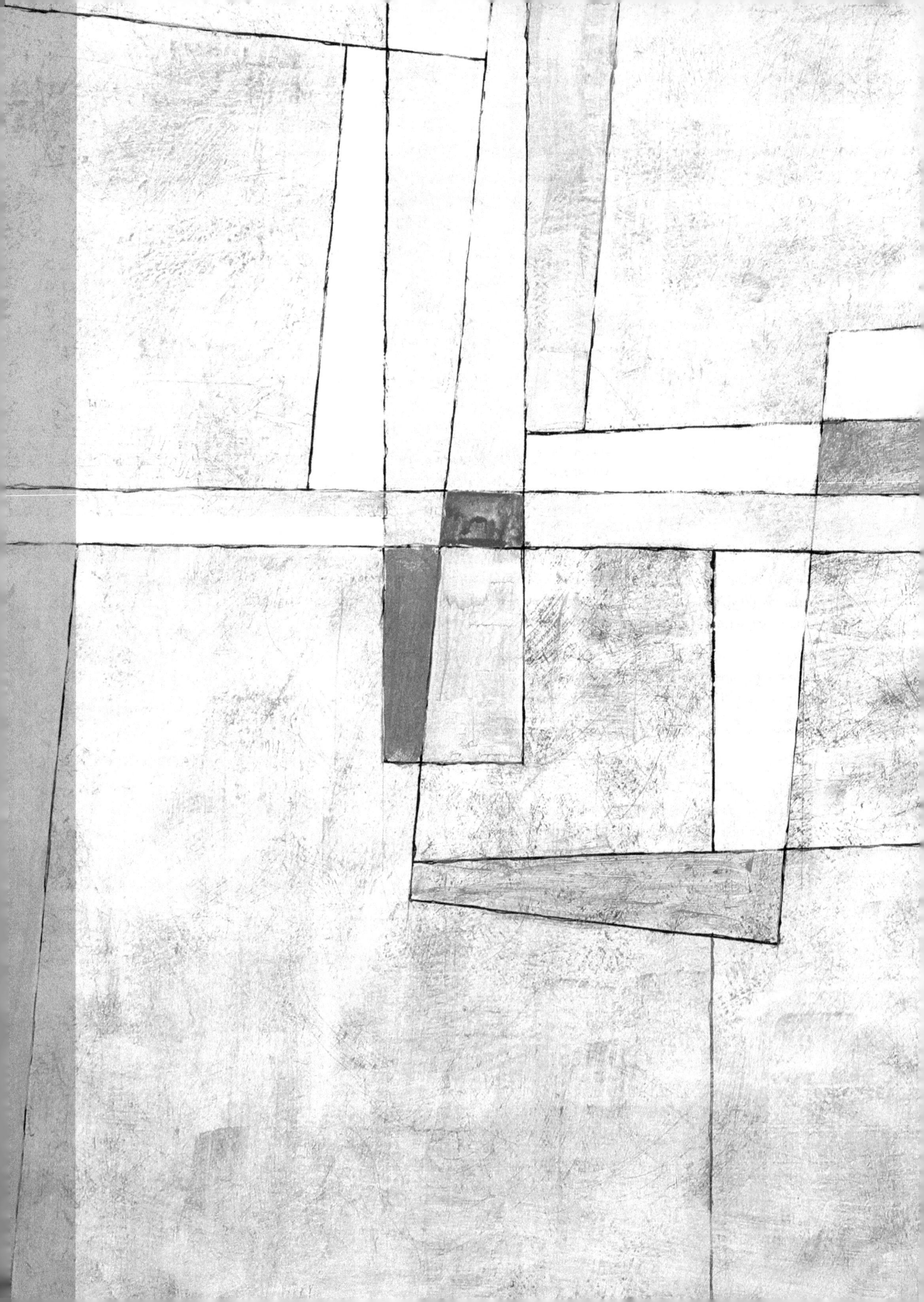

Deliberate Practice Diary Form

This book focuses on deliberate practice methods that involve active, live engagement between trainees and a supervisor. Importantly, deliberate practice can extend beyond these focused training sessions. For example, a trainee might read the client stimuli quietly or aloud and practice their responses independently between sessions with a supervisor. In such cases, it is important for the trainee to speak aloud rather than rehearse silently in their head. Alternatively, two trainees can practice without the supervisor. Although the absence of a supervisor limits one source of feedback, the peer trainee who is playing the client can serve this role, as they can when a supervisor is present. Importantly, these additional deliberate practice opportunities are intended to take place between focused training sessions with a supervisor. To optimize the quality of the deliberate practice when conducted independently or without a supervisor, we have developed a Deliberate Practice Diary Form that can also be downloaded from the "Resources" tab online (https://www.apa.org/pubs/books/deliberate-practice-behavioral-parent-training). This form provides a template for the trainee to record their experience of the deliberate practice activity and, ideally, will aid in the consolidation of learning. This form can also be used as part of the evaluation process with the supervisor but is not necessarily intended for that purpose, and trainees are certainly welcome to bring their experience with the independent practice into the next meeting with the supervisor.

Deliberate Practice Diary Form

Use this form to consolidate learnings from the deliberate practice exercises. Please protect your personal boundaries by only sharing information that you are comfortable disclosing.

Name: _____ Date: _____

Exercise: _____

Question 1. What was helpful or worked well this deliberate practice session? In what way?

Question 2. What was unhelpful or didn't go well this deliberate practice session? In what way?

Question 3. What did you learn about yourself, your current skills, and skills you'd like to keep improving? Feel free to share any details, but only those you are comfortable disclosing.

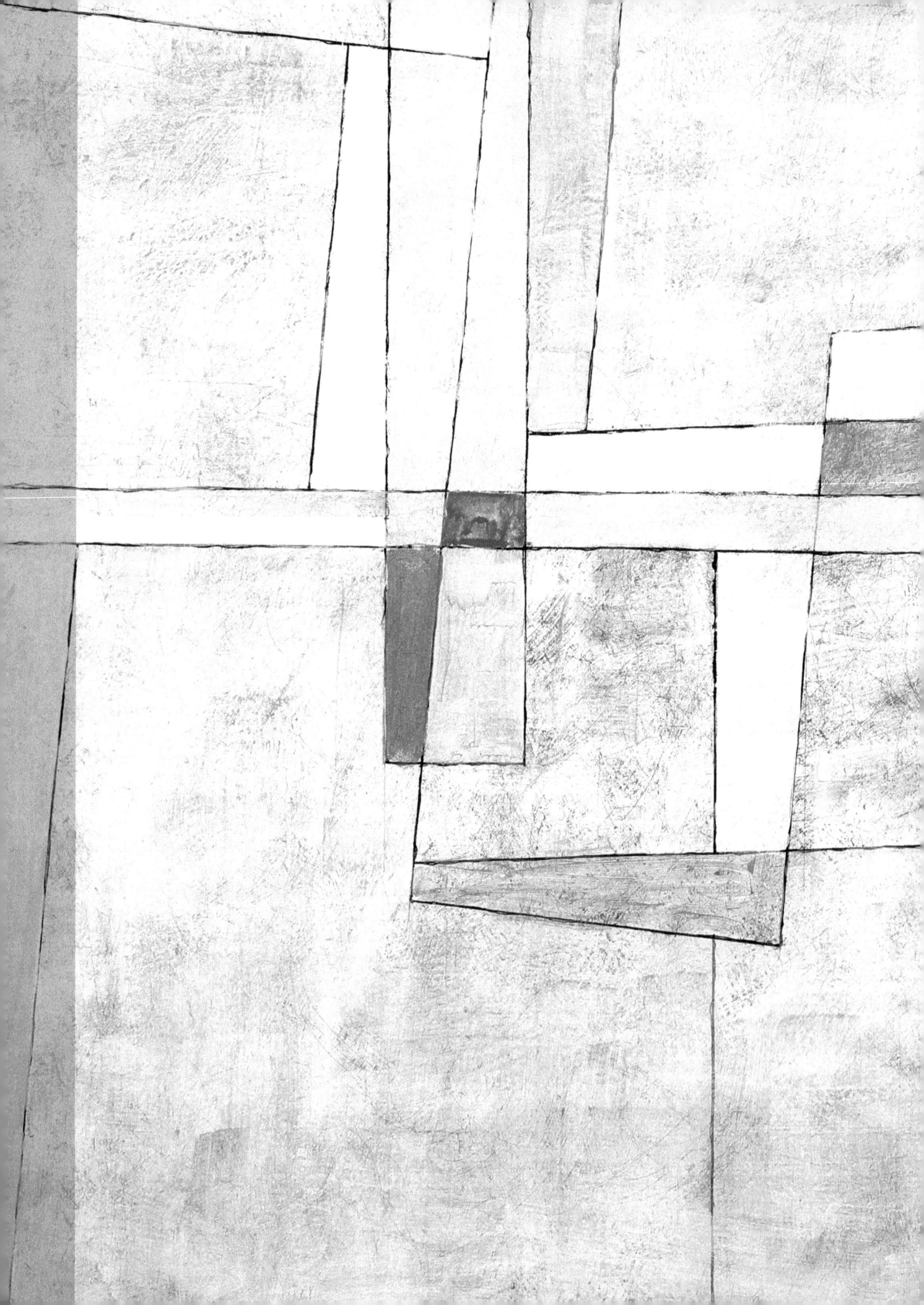

Sample Behavioral Parent Training Syllabus With Embedded Deliberate Practice Exercises

This appendix provides a sample one-semester, three-unit course dedicated to teaching behavioral parent training (BPT). This course is appropriate for graduate students (master's and doctoral students) at all levels of training, including first-year students who have not yet worked with clients. If a limited BPT course is offered, or the content of BPT is integrated within another course, aspects of the syllabus and associated exercises can be adapted for use in such a course, in a practicum, in didactic training events at externships and internships, in workshops, and in a continuing education program for postgraduate therapists.

Course Title: Behavioral Parent Training: Theory, Clinical Activities, and Deliberate Practice

Course Description

This course teaches beginning practitioners the theory, principles, and core clinical skills of behavioral parent training (BPT). This course has both didactic and practical elements; it reviews the theory and research on BPT to formulate and understand client problems and employs the deliberate practice approach to guide students to acquire 12 key BPT skills.

Course Objectives

Students who complete this course will be able to

1. describe the core theory and clinical skills of BPT,
2. apply the principles of deliberate practice for career-long clinical skill development in BPT,
3. demonstrate key BPT skills,
4. evaluate how practitioners can use BPT skills in their work with clients' presenting with several clinical presentations, and
5. employ BPT with clients from a diverse range of cultural backgrounds.

215

Date	Lecture and Discussion	Skills Lab	Readings
Week 1	Introduction to behavioral parent training (BPT): History, theory, and research	Exercise 1: Psychoeducation About Behavioral Parent Training	Eyberg et al. (2008) Forehand et al. (2014) Kaehler et al. (2016) Kaminski & Claussen (2017) Patterson (1982) Reitman & McMahon (2013) Wierson & Forehand (1994)
Week 2	Common, shared, and unique aspects of BPT; psychoeducation about functions of child behaviors for parents	Exercise 2: Psychoeducation About the Functions of Child Behaviors	Barnhill (2005) Chronis et al. (2004) Fettig & Barton (2014) Miller & Lee (2013)
Week 3	The role of emotion in BPT; introduction to principles and advantages of deliberate practice	Exercise 3: Identifying and Validating Parent Affect	Collard & O'Kelly (2011) Rathus & Miller (2015) Rousmaniere (2016) Rousmaniere et al. (2017) Rueger et al. (2011) Tracey et al. (2014)
Week 4	Teaching parents how to use praise effectively within BPT: Specificity matters!	Exercise 4: Teaching Parents How to Provide Praise	Barkley (2013) Kazdin (2005) McNeil & Hembree-Kigin (2010)
Week 5	The role of attention in BPT; teaching parents about positive and negative attention	Exercise 5: Teaching Parents to Provide Positive Attention	Barkley (2013) McNeil & Hembree-Kigin (2010)
Week 6	Why, how, and where to use extinction and planned ignoring within BPT	Exercise 6: Teaching Planned Ignoring With Positive Attention	Kazdin (2005) Kazdin (2017)
Week 7	Parent communication strategies to increase positive behavior	Exercise 7: Teaching Parents About Effective Communication	Barkley & Robin (2014) Greene & Ablon (2006) McNeil & Hembree-Kigin (2010)
Week 8	Midterm paper due Self-evaluation and skill feedback	Mock BPT sessions (beginner profiles)	Not applicable
Week 9	Incentivizing change: Changing behavior through rewards	Exercise 8: Teaching Parents How to Implement Positive Incentives to Bring About Behavioral Change	Barkley (2013) Barkley & Robin (2014)
Week 10	Teaching parents how to deliver consequential interventions when needed	Exercise 9: Teaching Parents About Consequence Interventions	Kazdin (2005) Kazdin (2008) Lieneman & McNeil (2023) Michelson et al. (2013)
Week 11	Teaching parents to manage their own thoughts, emotions, and behaviors	Exercise 10: Providing Strategies for Parent Affect Management	Hajal & Paley (2020) Leahy (2017) Morris et al. (2017) Rueger et al. (2011) Zimmer-Gembeck et al. (2022)
Week 12	Anticipating and managing challenges outside of the home	Exercise 11: Teaching Parents About Managing Behavior in Public Settings	Barkley (2013)
Week 13	Where change happens: The work between sessions	Exercise 12: Development of Homework Assignments	Chacko et al. (2009) Chacko et al. (2013) Danko et al. (2016) Nock & Kazdin (2005) Ros et al. (2017)
Week 14	Organizing the skills into a whole session	Mock BPT sessions (intermediate and advanced profiles)	Not applicable
Week 15	Final paper due Final exam Self-evaluation and skill feedback	Exam	Exercise 13: Annotated Behavioral Parent Training Practice Session Transcript

Format of Class

Classes are 3 hours long. Course time is split evenly between learning BPT theory (lecture/discussion) and acquiring and practicing BPT skills.

Lecture/Discussion Class: Each week, class focuses on one lecture/discussion topic for 1.5 hours explaining an aspect of BPT theory and intervention activities.

BPT Skills Lab: Each week there will be one BPT Skills Lab for 1.5 hours, during which students will rehearse the BPT skill being covered that week across several clinical problems typically presented by clients seeking psychotherapy. The Skills Labs primarily focus on practicing BPT skills using the exercises in this BPT deliberate practice book. The exercises use therapy simulations (role-plays), which are designed to accomplish the following goals:

1. Build trainees' skill and confidence for using BPT skills with real client problems.
2. Provide students the opportunity to engage in highly structured and repetitive deliberate practice exercises that rehearse the BPT skills.
3. Provide a safe space for experimenting with different therapeutic skills and interventions, without fear of criticism or making mistakes.
4. Provide opportunities for beginning therapists to explore different styles of therapy so that they can discover their own personal, unique therapy style.

Mock Sessions: Twice in the semester (Weeks 8 and 14), trainees will do a psychotherapy mock session using the skills taught in the BPT Skills Lab. The psychotherapy mock sessions are unstructured role-played therapy sessions. Mock sessions allow trainees to

1. practice using BPT skills accurately,
2. experiment with clinical decision making concerning which skill to employ in an unscripted context,
3. discover their personal therapeutic style, and
4. build self-efficacy for working with real clients.

Homework

Homework will be assigned each week and will include reading, 1 hour of skills practice with an assigned practice partner, and occasional writing assignments. For the skills practice homework, trainees will repeat the exercise they did for that week's BPT Skills Lab. Because the instructor will not be present to evaluate performance, trainees should complete the Deliberate Practice Reaction Form and the Deliberate Practice Diary Form as self-evaluations.

Writing Assignments

Students are to write two papers: one due at midterm and one due on the last day of class. The first paper will explore one aspect of BPT theory or the empirical literature on BPT. The second paper will involve the completion of a BPT case formulation.

Multicultural Orientation

This course is taught in a multicultural context, defined as "how the cultural worldviews, values, and beliefs of the client and therapist interact and influence one another to co-create a relational experience that is in the spirit of healing" (Davis et al., 2018,

p. 3). Core features of the multicultural orientation include cultural comfort, humility, and responding to cultural opportunities (or previously missed opportunities). Throughout this course, students are encouraged to reflect on their own cultural identity and improve their ability to attune with their clients' cultural identities (Hook et al., 2017). For further guidance on this topic and deliberate practice exercises to improve multicultural skills, see the book *Deliberate Practice in Multicultural Therapy* (Harris et al., 2024).

Vulnerability, Privacy, and Boundaries

In accordance with the *Ethical Principles of Psychologists and Code of Conduct* (American Psychological Association, 2017), students are **not required to disclose personal information.** Because this class is about developing both interpersonal and BPT competence, following are some important points so that students are fully informed as they make choices to self-disclose:

- Students choose how much, when, and what to disclose. Students are not penalized for the choice not to share personal information.

- The learning environment is susceptible to group dynamics much like any other group space, and therefore students may be asked to share their observations and experiences of the class environment with the singular goal of fostering a more inclusive and productive learning environment.

Confidentiality

To create a safe learning environment that is respectful of client and therapist information and diversity and to foster open and vulnerable conversation in class, students are required to agree to strict confidentiality within and outside of the instruction setting.

Evaluation

Self-Evaluation: At the end of the semester (Week 15), trainees will perform a self-evaluation. This will help trainees track their progress and identify areas for further development. The Guidance for Trainees section in Chapter 3 of this book highlights potential areas of focus for self-evaluation.

Grading Criteria

Students will be evaluated on the level and quality of their performance in

- the lecture/discussion,
- the skills lab (exercises and mock sessions),
- weekly homework assignments,
- midterm and final papers, and
- a final exam.

Recommended and Required Readings

Arnold, L. E., Hodgkins, P., Kahle, J., Madhoo, M., & Kewley, G. (2020). Long-term outcomes of ADHD: academic achievement and performance. *Journal of Attention Disorders*, 24(1), 73–85. https://doi.org/10.1177/1087054714566076

Baggio, S., Fructuoso, A., Guimaraes, M., Heller, P., Perroud, N., Young, S., & Delessert, D. (2018). Prevalence of attention deficit hyperactivity disorder in detention settings: A systematic review and meta-analysis. *Frontiers in Psychiatry, 9*, Article 359070. https://doi.org/10.3389/fpsyt.2018.00331

Barkley, R. A. (2013). *Defiant children: A clinician's manual for assessment and parent training* (3rd ed.). The Guilford Press.

Barkley, R. A., & Robin, A. L. (2014). *Defiant teens: A clinician's manual for assessment and family intervention* (2nd ed.). The Guilford Press.

Barnhill, G. P. (2005). Functional behavioral assessment in schools. *Intervention in School and Clinic, 40*(3), 131–143. https://doi.org/10.1177/10534512050400030101

Brennan, L. M., Shaw, D. S., Dishion, T. J., & Wilson, M. N. (2015). The predictive utility of early childhood disruptive behaviors for school-age social functioning. *Journal of Abnormal Child Psychology, 43*(6), 1187–1199. https://doi.org/10.1007/s10802-014-9967-5

Burke, J. D., Pardini, D. A., & Loeber, R. (2008). Reciprocal relationships between parenting behavior and disruptive psychopathology from childhood through adolescence. *Journal of Abnormal Child Psychology, 36*(5), 679–692. https://doi.org/10.1007/s10802-008-9219-7

Bussing, R., Zima, B. T., Mason, D. M., Meyer, J. M., White, K., & Garvan, C. W. (2012). ADHD knowledge, perceptions, and information sources: Perspectives from a community sample of adolescents and their parents. *Journal of Adolescent Health, 51*(6), 593–600. https://doi.org/10.1016/j.jadohealth.2012.03.004

Chacko, A., Anderson, L., Wymbs, B. T., & Wymbs, F. A. (2013). Parent-endorsed reasons for not completing homework in group-based behavioural parent training for high-risk families of youth with ADHD. *Behaviour Change, 30*(4), 262–272. https://doi.org/10.1017/bec.2013.25

Chacko, A., Wymbs, B. T., Arnold, F. W., Pelham, W. E., Swanger-Gagne, M., Girio, E. L., Pirvics, L., Herbst, L., Guzzo, J., Phillips, C., & O'Connor, B. (2009). Enhancing traditional behavioral parent training for single-mothers of children with ADHD. *Journal of Clinical Child and Adolescent Psychology, 38*(2), 206–218. https://doi.org/10.1080/15374410802698388

Chronis, A. M., Chacko, A., Fabiano, G. A., Wymbs, B. T., & Pelham, W. E. (2004). Enhancements to the behavioral parent training paradigm for families of children with ADHD: Review and future directions. *Clinical Child and Family Psychology Review, 7*(1), 1–27. https://doi.org/10.1023/b:ccfp.0000020190.60808.a4

Colalillo, S., & Johnston, C. (2016). Parenting cognition and affective outcomes following parent management training: A systematic review. *Clinical Child and Family Psychology Review, 19*(3), 216–235. https://doi.org/10.1007/s10567-016-0208-z

Collard, J., & O'Kelly, M. (2011). Rational emotive behaviour therapy: A positive perspective. *Journal of Rational-Emotive & Cognitive-Behavior Therapy, 29*(4), 248–256. https://doi.org/10.1007/s10942-011-0146-0

Cuijpers, P., Reijnders, M., & Huibers, M. J. (2019). The role of common factors in psychotherapy outcomes. *Annual Review of Clinical Psychology, 15*(1), 207–231. https://doi.org/10.1146/annurev-clinpsy-050718-095424

Danko, C. M., Brown, T., Van Schoick, L., & Budd, K. S. (2016, June). Predictors and correlates of homework completion and treatment outcomes in parent–child interaction therapy. *Child and Youth Care Forum, 45*(3), 467–485. https://doi.org/10.1007/s10566-015-9339-5

Elliott, R., Bohart, A. C., Watson, J. C., & Greenberg, L. S. (2011). Empathy. In J. Norcross (Ed.), *Psychotherapy relationships that work* (2nd ed., pp. 132–152). Oxford University Press. https://doi.org/10.1093/acprof:oso/9780199737208.003.0006

Evans, S. W., Owens, J. S., & Bunford, N. (2014). Evidence-based psychosocial treatments for children and adolescents with attention-deficit/hyperactivity disorder. *Journal of Clinical Child and Adolescent Psychology, 43*(4), 527–551. https://doi.org/10.1080/15374416.2013.850700

Eyberg, S. M., Nelson, M. M., & Boggs, S. R. (2008). Evidence-based psychosocial treatments for children and adolescents with disruptive behavior. *Journal of Clinical Child & Adolescent Psychology, 37*(1), 215–237. https://doi.org/10.1080/15374410701820117

Fettig, A., & Barton, E. E. (2014). Parent implementation of function-based intervention to reduce children's challenging behavior: A literature review. *Topics in Early Childhood Special Education, 34*(1), 49–61. https://doi.org/10.1177/0271121413513037

Forehand, R., Lafko, N., Parent, J., & Burt, K. B. (2014). Is parenting the mediator of change in behavioral parent training for externalizing problems of youth? *Clinical Psychology Review, 34*(8), 608–619. https://doi.org/10.1016/j.cpr.2014.10.001

Gardner, F., Burton, J., & Klimes, I. (2006). Randomised controlled trial of a parenting intervention in the voluntary sector for reducing child conduct problems: Outcomes and mechanisms of change. *Journal of Child Psychology and Psychiatry, and Allied Disciplines, 47*(11), 1123–1132. https://doi.org/10.1111/j.1469-7610.2006.01668.x

Ghandour, R. M., Sherman, L. J., Vladutiu, C. J., Ali, M. M., Lynch, S. E., Bitsko, R. H., & Blumberg, S. J. (2019). Prevalence and treatment of depression, anxiety, and conduct problems in US children. *The Journal of Pediatrics, 206,* 256–267.e3. https://doi.org/10.1016/j.jpeds.2018.09.021

Graf, F. A., Grumm, M., Hein, S., & Fingerle, M. (2014). Improving parental competencies: Subjectively perceived usefulness of a parent training matters. *Journal of Child and Family Studies, 23*(1), 20–28. https://doi.org/10.1007/s10826-012-9682-1

Greene, R. W., & Ablon, J. S. (2006). *Treating explosive kids: The collaborative problem-solving approach.* The Guilford Press.

Hajal, N. J., & Paley, B. (2020). Parental emotion and emotion regulation: A critical target of study for research and intervention to promote child emotion socialization. *Developmental Psychology, 56*(3), 403–417. https://doi.org/10.1037/dev0000864

Hawes, M. T., Carlson, G. A., Finsaas, M. C., Olino, T. M., Seely, J. R., & Klein, D. N. (2020). Dimensions of irritability in adolescents: Longitudinal associations with psychopathology in adulthood. *Psychological Medicine, 50*(16), 2759–2767. https://doi.org/10.1017/S0033291719002903

Horvath, A. O., Del Re, A. C., Flückiger, C., & Symonds. D. (2011). Alliance in individual psychotherapy. *Psychotherapy 48*(1), 9–16. https://doi.org/10.1037/a0022186

Howard, A. L., Kennedy, T. M., Mitchell, J. T., Sibley, M. H., Hinshaw, S. P., Arnold, L. E., Roy, A., Stehli, A., Swanson, J. M., & Molina, B. S. (2020). Early substance use in the pathway from childhood attention-deficit/hyperactivity disorder (ADHD) to young adult substance use: Evidence of statistical mediation and substance specificity. *Psychology of Addictive Behaviors, 34*(2), 281–292. https://doi.org/10.1037/adb0000542

Johnson, A. M., Hawes, D. J., Eisenberg, N., Kohlhoff, J., & Dudeney, J. (2017). Emotion socialization and child conduct problems: A comprehensive review and meta-analysis. *Clinical Psychology Review, 54,* 65–80. https://doi.org/10.1016/j.cpr.2017.04.001

Johnston, C., & Chronis-Tuscano, A. (2015). Families and ADHD. In R. A. Barkley (Ed.), *Attention-deficit/hyperactivity disorder: A handbook for diagnosis and treatment* (4th ed., pp. 191–209). The Guilford Press.

Jungbluth, N. J., & Shirk, S. R. (2013). Promoting homework adherence in cognitive-behavioral therapy for adolescent depression. *Journal of Clinical Child & Adolescent Psychology, 42*(4), 545–553. https://doi.org/10.1080/15374416.2012.743105

Kaehler, L. A., Jacobs, M., & Jones, D. J. (2016). Distilling common history and practice elements to inform dissemination: Hanf-model BPT programs as an example. *Clinical Child and Family Psychology Review, 19*(3), 236–258. https://doi.org/10.1007/s10567-016-0210-5

Kaminski, J. W., & Claussen, A. H. (2017). Evidence base update for psychosocial treatments for disruptive behaviors in children. *Journal of Clinical Child & Adolescent Psychology, 46*(4), 477–499. https://doi.org/10.1080/15374416.2017.1310044

Kaminski, J. W., Valle, L. A., Filene, J. H., & Boyle, C. L. (2008). A meta-analytic review of components associated with parent training program effectiveness. *Journal of Abnormal Child Psychology, 36*(4), 567–589. https://doi.org/10.1007/s10802-007-9201-9

Kazantzis, N., Whittington, C., & Dattilio, F. (2010). Meta-analysis of homework effects in cognitive and behavioral therapy: A replication and extension. *Clinical Psychology: Science and Practice, 17*(2), 144–156. https://doi.org/10.1111/j.1468-2850.2010.01204.x

Kazdin, A. E. (2000). Perceived barriers to treatment participation and treatment acceptability among antisocial children and their families. *Journal of Child and Family Studies, 9*(2), 157–174. https://doi.org/10.1023/A:1009414904228

Kazdin, A. E. (2005). *Parent management training: Treatment for oppositional, aggressive, and antisocial behavior in children and adolescents.* Oxford University Press.

Kazdin, A. E. (2008). *The Kazdin method for parenting the defiant child*. Houghton Mifflin.

Kazdin, A. E. (2017). Parent management training and problem-solving skills training for child and adolescent conduct problems. In J. R. Weisz & A. E. Kazdin (Eds.), *Evidence-based psychotherapies for children and adolescents* (3rd ed., pp. 142–158). The Guilford Press.

Kazdin, A. E., Holland, L., & Crowley, M. (1997). Family experience of barriers to treatment and premature termination from child therapy. *Journal of Consulting and Clinical Psychology, 65*(3), 453–463.

Lambert, M. J., & Shimokawa, K. (2011). Collecting client feedback. *Psychotherapy, 48*(1), 72–79. https://doi.org/10.1037/a0022238

Leahy, R. L. (2017). *Cognitive therapy techniques: A practitioner's guide*. The Guilford Press.

Lieneman, C. C., & McNeil, C. B. (2023). *Time-out in child behavior management*. Hogrefe Publishing Corporation.

Liu, C. Y., Huang, W. L., Kao, W. C., & Gau, S. S. F. (2017). Influence of disruptive behavior disorders on academic performance and school functions of youths with attention-deficit/hyperactivity disorder. *Child Psychiatry & Human Development, 48*(6), 870–880. https://doi.org/10.1007/s10578-017-0710-7

Lunkenheimer, E., Sturge-Apple, M. L., & Kelm, M. R. (2023). The importance of parent self-regulation and parent–child coregulation in research on parental discipline. *Child Development Perspectives, 17*(1), 25–31. https://doi.org/10.1111/cdep.12470

Mackler, J. S., Kelleher, R. T., Shanahan, L., Calkins, S. D., Keane, S. P., & O'Brien, M. (2015). Parenting stress, parental reactions, and externalizing behavior from ages 4 to 10. *Journal of Marriage and Family, 77*(2), 388–406. https://doi.org/10.1111/jomf.12163

Martin, G., & Pear, J. J. (2019). *Behavior modification: What it is and how to do it*. Routledge.

Mausbach, B. T., Moore, R., Roesch, S., Cardenas, V., & Patterson, T. L. (2010). The relationship between homework compliance and therapy outcomes: An updated meta-analysis. *Cognitive Therapy and Research, 34*(5), 429–438. https://doi.org/10.1007/s10608-010-9297-z

McMahon, R. J., & Forehand, R. L. (2005). *Helping the noncompliant child: Family-based treatment for oppositional behavior* (2nd ed.). The Guilford Press.

McMahon, R. J., & Forehand, R. L. (2019). *Helping the noncompliant child*. Springer International Publishing.

McNeil, C. B., & Hembree-Kigin, T. L. (2010). *Parent–child interaction therapy* (2nd ed.). Springer Science + Business Media. https://doi.org/10.1007/978-0-387-88639-8

Michelson, D., Davenport, C., Dretzke, J., Barlow, J., & Day, C. (2013). Do evidence-based interventions work when tested in the "real world?" A systematic review and meta-analysis of parent management training for the treatment of child disruptive behavior. *Clinical Child and Family Psychology Review, 16*(1),18–34. https://doi.org/10.1007/s10567-013-0128-0

Miller, F. G., & Lee, D. L. (2013). Do functional behavioral assessments improve intervention effectiveness for students diagnosed with ADHD? A single-subject meta-analysis. *Journal of Behavioral Education, 22*(3), 253–282. https://doi.org/10.1007/s10864-013-9174-4

Montoya, A., Colom, F., & Ferrin, M. (2011). Is psychoeducation for parents and teachers of children and adolescents with ADHD efficacious? A systematic literature review. *European Psychiatry, 26*(3), 166–175. https://doi.org/10.1016/j.eurpsy.2010.10.005

Morris, A. S., Criss, M. M., Silk, J. S., & Houltberg, B. J. (2017). The impact of parenting on emotion regulation during childhood and adolescence. *Child Development Perspectives, 11*(4), 233–238. https://doi.org/10.1111/cdep.12238

Nock, M. K., & Kazdin, A. E. (2005). Randomized controlled trial of a brief intervention for increasing participation in parent management training. *Journal of Consulting and Clinical Psychology, 73*(5), 872–879. https://doi.org/10.1037/0022-006X.73.5.872

Patterson, G. R. (1982). *Coercive family process*. Castalia Publishing Company.

Rathus, J. H., & Miller, A. L. (2015). *DBT skills manual for adolescents*. The Guilford Press.

Reitman, D., & McMahon, R. J. (2013). Constance "Connie" Hanf (1917–2002): The mentor and the model. *Cognitive and Behavioral Practice, 20*(1), 106–116. https://doi.org/10.1016/j.cbpra.2012.02.005

Retz, W., Ginsberg, Y., Turner, D., Barra, S., Retz-Junginger, P., Larsson, H., & Asherson, P. (2021). Attention-deficit/hyperactivity disorder (ADHD), antisociality and delinquent behavior over the lifespan. *Neuroscience & Biobehavioral Reviews, 120*, 236–248. https://doi.org/10.1016/j.neubiorev.2020.11.025

Ros, R., Graziano, P. A., & Hart, K. C. (2017). Parental homework completion and treatment knowledge during group parent–child interaction therapy. *Journal of Early Intervention, 39*(4), 299–320.

Rousmaniere, T. G. (2016). *Deliberate practice for psychotherapists: A guide to improving clinical effectiveness.* Routledge Press/Taylor & Francis. https://doi.org/10.4324/9781315472256

Rousmaniere, T. G., Goodyear, R., Miller, S. D., & Wampold, B. E. (Eds.). (2017). *The cycle of excellence: Using deliberate practice to improve supervision and training.* John Wiley & Sons. https://doi.org/10.1002/9781119165590

Rueger, S. Y., Katz, R. L., Risser, H. J., & Lovejoy, M. C. (2011). Relations between parental affect and parenting behaviors: A meta-analytic review. *Parenting: Science and Practice, 11*(1), 1–33. https://doi.org/10.1080/15295192.2011.539503

Sanders, M. R., Bor, W., & Morawska, A. (2007). Maintenance of treatment gains: A comparison of enhanced, standard, and self-directed Triple P-Positive Parenting Program. *Journal of Abnormal Child Psychology, 35*(6), 983–998. http://doi.org/10.1007/s10802-007-9148-x

Sanders, M. R., Kirby, J. N., Tellegen, C. L., & Day, J. J. (2014). The Triple P-Positive Parenting Program: A systematic review and meta-analysis of a multi-level system of parenting support. *Clinical Psychology Review, 34*(4), 337–357. https://doi.org/10.1016/j.cpr.2014.04.003

Thomas, R., Abell, B., Webb, H. J., Avdagic, E., & Zimmer-Gembeck, M. J. (2017). Parent–child interaction therapy: A meta-analysis. *Pediatrics, 140*(3), Article e20170352. https://doi.org/10.1542/peds.2017-0352

Tracey, T. J. G., Wampold, B. E., Lichtenberg, J. W., & Goodyear, R. K. (2014). Expertise in psychotherapy: An elusive goal? *American Psychologist, 69*(3), 218–229. https://doi.org/10.1037/a0035099

Wampold, B. E. (2015). How important are the common factors in psychotherapy? An update. *World Psychiatry, 14*(3), 270–277. https://doi.org/10.1002/wps.20238

Webster-Stratton, C. (1998). Preventing conduct problems in Head Start children: Strengthening parenting competencies. *Journal of Consulting and Clinical Psychology, 66*(5), 715–730. https://doi.org/10.1037//0022-006x.66.5.715

Webster-Stratton, C. (2012). *Collaborating with parents to reduce children's behavior problems: A book for therapists using the Incredible Years.* Incredible Years.

Wierson, M., & Forehand, R. (1994). Parent behavioral training for child noncompliance: Rationale, concepts, and effectiveness. *Current Directions in Psychological Science, 3*(5), 146–150. https://doi.org/10.1111/1467-8721.ep10770643

Wojciechowski, T. W. (2021). The role of ADHD in predicting the development of violent behavior among juvenile offenders: Participation versus frequency. *Journal of Interpersonal Violence, 36*(1–2), NP625–NP642. https://doi.org/10.1177/0886260517734225

Zalewski, M., Maliken, A. C., Lengua, L. J., Martin, C. G., Roos, L. E., & Everett, Y. (2023). Integrating dialectical behavior therapy with child and parent training interventions: A narrative and theoretical review. *Clinical Psychology: Science and Practice, 30*(4), 365–376. https://doi.org/10.1111/cpsp.12363

Zimmer-Gembeck, M. J., Rudolph, J., Kerin, J., & Bohadana-Brown, G. (2022). Parent emotional regulation: A meta-analytic review of its association with parenting and child adjustment. *International Journal of Behavioral Development, 46*(1), 63–82. https://doi.org/10.1177/01650254211051086

Zitzmann, J., Rombold-George, L., Rosenbach, C., & Renneberg, B. (2024). Emotion regulation, parenting, and psychopathology: A systematic review. *Clinical Child and Family Psychology Review, 27*(1), 1–22. https://doi.org/10.1007/s10567-023-00452-5

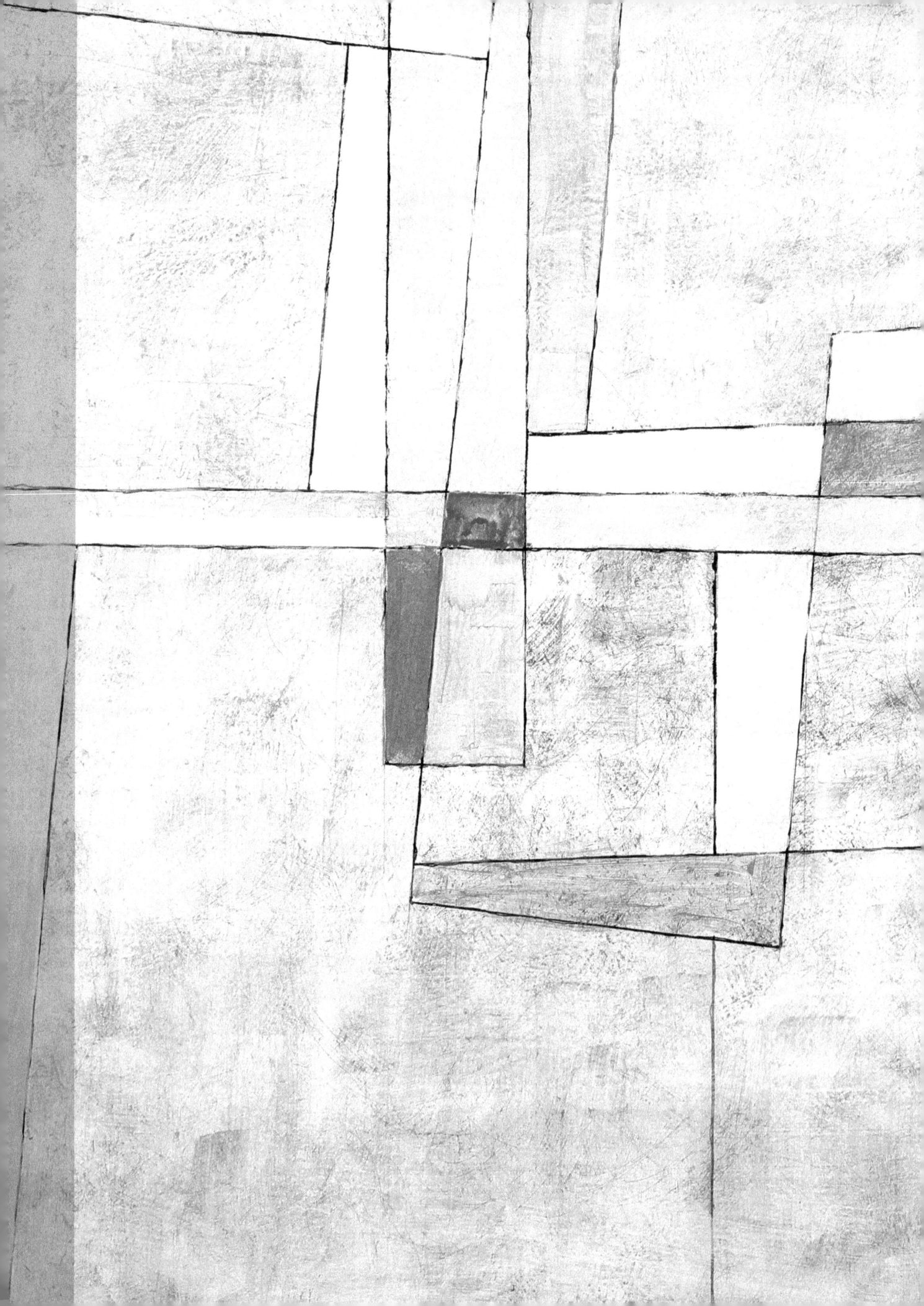

References

American Psychological Association. (2017). *Ethical principles of psychologists and code of conduct* (2002, Amended June 1, 2010, and January 1, 2017). http://www.apa.org/ethics/code/index.aspx

Anderson, T., Ogles, B. M., Patterson, C. L., Lambert, M. J., & Vermeersch, D. A. (2009). Therapist effects: Facilitative interpersonal skills as a predictor of therapist success. *Journal of Clinical Psychology, 65*(7), 755–768. https://doi.org/10.1002/jclp.20583

Arnold, L. E., Hodgkins, P., Kahle, J., Madhoo, M., & Kewley, G. (2020). Long-term outcomes of ADHD: Academic achievement and performance. *Journal of Attention Disorders, 24*(1), 73–85. https://doi.org/10.1177/1087054714566076

Baggio, S., Fructuoso, A., Guimaraes, M., Fois, E., Golay, D., Heller, P., Perroud, N., Aubry, C., Young, S., Delessert, D., Gétaz, L., Tran, N. T., & Wolff, H. (2018). Prevalence of attention deficit hyperactivity disorder in detention settings: A systematic review and meta-analysis. *Frontiers in Psychiatry, 9*, Article 331. https://doi.org/10.3389/fpsyt.2018.00331

Bailey, R. J., & Ogles, B. M. (2019, August 1). Common factors as a therapeutic approach: What is required? *Practice Innovations, 4*(4), 241–254. https://doi.org/10.1037/pri0000100

Barkley, R. A. (2013). *Defiant children: A clinician's manual for assessment and parent training* (3rd ed.). The Guilford Press.

Barkley, R. A., & Robin, A. L. (2014). *Defiant teens: A clinician's manual for assessment and family intervention* (2nd ed.). The Guilford Press.

Barlow, D. H. (2010). Negative effects from psychological treatments: A perspective. *American Psychologist, 65*(1), 13–20. https://doi.org/10.1037/a0015643

Barnhill, G. P. (2005). Functional behavioral assessment in schools. *Intervention in School and Clinic, 40*(3), 131–143. https://doi.org/10.1177/10534512050400030101

Bennett-Levy, J. (2019). Why therapists should walk the talk: The theoretical and empirical case for personal practice in therapist training and professional development. *Journal of Behavior Therapy and Experimental Psychiatry, 62*, 133–145. https://doi.org/10.1016/j.jbtep.2018.08.004

Bennett-Levy, J., & Finlay-Jones, A. (2018). The role of personal practice in therapist skill development: A model to guide therapists, educators, supervisors and researchers. *Cognitive Behaviour Therapy, 47*(3), 185–205. https://doi.org/10.1080/16506073.2018.1434678

Bohart, A. C., & Wade, A. G. (2013). The client in psychotherapy. In M. J. Lambert (Ed.), *Bergin and Garfield's handbook of psychotherapy and behavior change* (6th ed., pp. 219–257). John Wiley & Sons.

Brennan, L. M., Shaw, D. S., Dishion, T. J., & Wilson, M. N. (2015). The predictive utility of early childhood disruptive behaviors for school-age social functioning. *Journal of Abnormal Child Psychology, 43*(6), 1187–1199. https://doi.org/10.1007/s10802-014-9967-5

Bugatti, M., & Boswell, J. F. (2016). Clinical errors as a lack of context responsiveness. *Psychotherapy: Theory, Research, & Practice, 53*(3), 262–267. https://doi.org/10.1037/pst0000080

Burke, J. D., Pardini, D. A., & Loeber, R. (2008). Reciprocal relationships between parenting behavior and disruptive psychopathology from childhood through adolescence. *Journal of Abnormal Child Psychology, 36*(5), 679–692. https://doi.org/10.1007/s10802-008-9219-7

Bussing, R., Zima, B. T., Mason, D. M., Meyer, J. M., White, K., & Garvan, C. W. (2012). ADHD knowledge, perceptions, and information sources: Perspectives from a community sample of adolescents and their parents. *The Journal of Adolescent Health, 51*(6), 593–600. https://doi.org/10.1016/j.jadohealth.2012.03.004

Castonguay, L. G., Goldfried, M. R., Wiser, S., Raue, P. J., & Hayes, A. M. (1996). Predicting the effect of cognitive therapy for depression: A study of unique and common factors. *Journal of Consulting and Clinical Psychology, 64*(3), 497–504. https://doi.org/10.1037/0022-006X.64.3.497

Chacko, A., Anderson, L., Wymbs, B. T., & Wymbs, F. A. (2013). Parent-endorsed reasons for not completing homework in group-based behavioural parent training for high-risk families of youth with ADHD. *Behaviour Change, 30*(4), 262–272. https://doi.org/10.1017/bec.2013.25

Chacko, A., Wymbs, B. T., Wymbs, F. A., Pelham, W. E., Swanger-Gagne, M. S., Girio, E., Pirvics, L., Herbst, L., Guzzo, J., Phillips, C., & O'Connor, B. (2009). Enhancing traditional behavioral parent training for single mothers of children with ADHD. *Journal of Clinical Child and Adolescent Psychology, 38*(2), 206–218. https://doi.org/10.1080/15374410802698388

Chronis, A. M., Chacko, A., Fabiano, G. A., Wymbs, B. T., & Pelham, W. E., Jr. (2004). Enhancements to the behavioral parent training paradigm for families of children with ADHD: Review and future directions. *Clinical Child and Family Psychology Review, 7*(1), 1–27. https://doi.org/10.1023/B:CCFP.0000020190.60808.a4

Coker, J. (1990). *How to practice jazz.* Jamey Aebersold.

Colalillo, S., & Johnston, C. (2016). Parenting cognition and affective outcomes following parent management training: A systematic review. *Clinical Child and Family Psychology Review, 19*(3), 216–235. https://doi.org/10.1007/s10567-016-0208-z

Collard, J., & O'Kelly, M. (2011). Rational emotive behaviour therapy: A positive perspective. *Journal of Rational-Emotive & Cognitive-Behavior Therapy, 29*(4), 248–256. https://doi.org/10.1007/s10942-011-0146-0

Cook, R. (2005). *It's about that time: Miles Davis on and off record.* Atlantic Books.

Csikszentmihalyi, M. (1997). *Finding flow: The psychology of engagement with everyday life.* HarperCollins.

Cuijpers, P., Reijnders, M., & Huibers, M. J. H. (2019). The role of common factors in psychotherapy outcomes. *Annual Review of Clinical Psychology, 15*(1), 207–231. https://doi.org/10.1146/annurev-clinpsy-050718-095424

Daley, D., van der Oord, S., Ferrin, M., Danckaerts, M., Doepfner, M., Cortese, S., Sonuga-Barke, E. J., & the European ADHD Guidelines Group. (2014). Behavioral interventions in attention-deficit/hyperactivity disorder: A meta-analysis of randomized controlled trials across multiple outcome domains. *Journal of the American Academy of Child & Adolescent Psychiatry, 53*(8), 835–847, 847.e1–847.e5. https://doi.org/10.1016/j.jaac.2014.05.013

Danko, C. M., Brown, T., Van Schoick, L., & Budd, K. S. (2016, June). Predictors and correlates of homework completion and treatment outcomes in parent–child interaction therapy. Springer. *Child and Youth Care Forum, 45*(3), 467–485. https://doi.org/10.1007/s10566-015-9339-5

Davis, D. E., DeBlaere, C., Owen, J., Hook, J. N., Rivera, D. P., Choe, E., Van Tongeren, D. R., Worthington, E. L., & Placeres, V. (2018). The multicultural orientation framework: A narrative review. *Psychotherapy: Theory, Research, & Practice, 55*(1), 89–100. https://doi.org/10.1037/pst0000160

Elliott, R., Bohart, A. C., Watson, J. C., & Greenberg, L. S. (2011). Empathy. In J. Norcross (Ed.), *Psychotherapy relationships that work* (2nd ed., pp. 132–152). Oxford University Press. https://doi.org/10.1093/acprof:oso/9780199737208.003.0006

Ellis, M. V., Berger, L., Hanus, A. E., Ayala, E. E., Swords, B. A., & Siembor, M. (2014). Inadequate and harmful clinical supervision: Testing a revised framework and assessing occurrence. *The Counseling Psychologist, 42*(4), 434–472. https://doi.org/10.1177/0011000013508656

Ericsson, K. A. (2003). Development of elite performance and deliberate practice: An update from the perspective of the expert performance approach. In J. L. Starkes & K. A. Ericsson (Eds.), *Expert performance in sports: Advances in research on sport expertise* (pp. 49–83). Human Kinetics.

Ericsson, K. A. (2004). Deliberate practice and the acquisition and maintenance of expert performance in medicine and related domains: Invited address. *Academic Medicine, 79*(Suppl. 10), S70–S81. https://doi.org/10.1097/00001888-200410001-00022

Ericsson, K. A. (2006). The influence of experience and deliberate practice on the development of superior expert performance. In K. A. Ericsson, N. Charness, P. J. Feltovich, & R. R. Hoffman (Eds.), *The Cambridge handbook of expertise and expert performance* (pp. 683–704). Cambridge University Press. https://doi.org/10.1017/CBO9780511816796.038

Ericsson, K. A., Hoffman, R. R., Kozbelt, A., & Williams, A. M. (Eds.). (2018). *The Cambridge handbook of expertise and expert performance* (2nd ed.). Cambridge University Press. https://doi.org/10.1017/9781316480748

Ericsson, K. A., Krampe, R. T., & Tesch-Römer, C. (1993). The role of deliberate practice in the acquisition of expert performance. *Psychological Review, 100*(3), 363–406. https://doi.org/10.1037/0033-295X.100.3.363

Ericsson, K. A., & Pool, R. (2016). *Peak: Secrets from the new science of expertise.* Houghton Mifflin Harcourt.

Evans, S. W., Owens, J. S., & Bunford, N. (2014). Evidence-based psychosocial treatments for children and adolescents with attention-deficit/hyperactivity disorder. *Journal of Clinical Child and Adolescent Psychology, 43*(4), 527–551. https://doi.org/10.1080/15374416.2013.850700

Eyberg, S. M., Nelson, M. M., & Boggs, S. R. (2008). Evidence-based psychosocial treatments for children and adolescents with disruptive behavior. *Journal of Clinical Child and Adolescent Psychology, 37*(1), 215–237. https://doi.org/10.1080/15374410701820117

Fettig, A., & Barton, E. E. (2014). Parent implementation of function-based intervention to reduce children's challenging behavior: A literature review. *Topics in Early Childhood Special Education, 34*(1), 49–61. https://doi.org/10.1177/0271121413513037

Fisher, R. P., & Craik, F. I. M. (1977). Interaction between encoding and retrieval operations in cued recall. *Journal of Experimental Psychology: Human Learning and Memory, 3*(6), 701–711. https://doi.org/10.1037/0278-7393.3.6.701

Forehand, R., Lafko, N., Parent, J., & Burt, K. B. (2014). Is parenting the mediator of change in behavioral parent training for externalizing problems of youth? *Clinical Psychology Review, 34*(8), 608–619. https://doi.org/10.1016/j.cpr.2014.10.001

Gardner, F., Burton, J., & Klimes, I. (2006). Randomised controlled trial of a parenting intervention in the voluntary sector for reducing child conduct problems: Outcomes and mechanisms of change. *Journal of Child Psychology and Psychiatry, 47*(11), 1123–1132. https://doi.org/10.1111/j.1469-7610.2006.01668.x

Ghandour, R. M., Sherman, L. J., Vladutiu, C. J., Ali, M. M., Lynch, S. E., Bitsko, R. H., & Blumberg, S. J. (2019). Prevalence and treatment of depression, anxiety, and conduct problems in US children. *The Journal of Pediatrics, 206*, 256–267.e3. https://doi.org/10.1016/j.jpeds.2018.09.021

Gladwell, M. (2008). *Outliers: The story of success.* Little, Brown & Company.

Goldberg, S. B., Babins-Wagner, R., Rousmaniere, T., Berzins, S., Hoyt, W. T., Whipple, J. L., Miller, S. D., & Wampold, B. E. (2016). Creating a climate for therapist improvement: A case study of an agency focused on outcomes and deliberate practice. *Psychotherapy: Theory, Research, & Practice, 53*(3), 367–375. https://doi.org/10.1037/pst0000060

Goodyear, R. K. (2015). Using accountability mechanisms more intentionally: A framework and its implications for training professional psychologists. *American Psychologist, 70*(8), 736–743. https://doi.org/10.1037/a0039828

Goodyear, R. K., & Nelson, M. L. (1997). The major formats of psychotherapy supervision. In C. E. Watkins, Jr. (Ed.), *Handbook of psychotherapy supervision* (pp. 328–334). John Wiley & Sons.

Graf, F. A., Grumm, M., Hein, S., & Fingerle, M. (2014). Improving parental competencies: Subjectively perceived usefulness of a parent training matters. *Journal of Child and Family Studies, 23*(1), 20–28. https://doi.org/10.1007/s10826-012-9682-1

Greenberg, L. S., & Goldman, R. L. (1988). Training in experiential therapy. *Journal of Consulting and Clinical Psychology, 56*(5), 696–702. https://doi.org/10.1037/0022-006X.56.5.696

Greene, R. W., & Ablon, J. S. (2006). *Treating explosive kids: The collaborative problem-solving approach.* The Guilford Press.

Haggerty, G., & Hilsenroth, M. J. (2011). The use of video in psychotherapy supervision. *British Journal of Psychotherapy, 27*(2), 193–210. https://doi.org/10.1111/j.1752-0118.2011.01232.x

Hajal, N. J., & Paley, B. (2020). Parental emotion and emotion regulation: A critical target of study for research and intervention to promote child emotion socialization. *Developmental Psychology, 56*(3), 403–417. https://doi.org/10.1037/dev0000864

Harris, J., Jin, J., Hoffman, S., Phan, S., Prout, T. A., Rousmaniere, T., & Vaz, A. (2024). *Deliberate practice in multicultural therapy.* American Psychological Association. https://doi.org/10.1037/0000357-000

Hatcher, R. L. (2015). Interpersonal competencies: Responsiveness, technique, and training in psychotherapy. *American Psychologist, 70*(8), 747–757. https://doi.org/10.1037/a0039803

Hawes, M. T., Carlson, G. A., Finsaas, M. C., Olino, T. M., Seely, J. R., & Klein, D. N. (2020). Dimensions of irritability in adolescents: Longitudinal associations with psychopathology in adulthood. *Psychological Medicine, 50*(16), 2759–2767. https://doi.org/10.1017/S0033291719002903

Henry, W. P., Strupp, H. H., Butler, S. F., Schacht, T. E., & Binder, J. L. (1993). Effects of training in time-limited dynamic psychotherapy: Changes in therapist behavior. *Journal of Consulting and Clinical Psychology, 61*(3), 434–440. https://doi.org/10.1037/0022-006X.61.3.434

Hill, C. E., Kivlighan, D. M. I. I. I., Rousmaniere, T., Kivlighan, D. M., Jr., Gerstenblith, J., & Hillman, J. (2020). Deliberate practice for the skill of immediacy: A multiple case study of doctoral student therapists and clients. *Psychotherapy: Theory, Research, & Practice, 57*(4), 587–597.

Hill, C. E., & Knox, S. (2013). Training and supervision in psychotherapy: Evidence for effective practice. In M. J. Lambert (Ed.), *Handbook of psychotherapy and behavior change* (6th ed., pp. 775–811). John Wiley & Sons.

Hook, J. N., Davis, D. D., Owen, J., & DeBlaere, C. (2017). *Cultural humility: Engaging diverse identities in therapy.* American Psychological Association. https://doi.org/10.1037/0000037-000

Horvath, A. O., Del Re, A. C., Flückiger, C., & Symonds, D. (2011). Alliance in individual psychotherapy. *Psychotherapy: Theory, Research, & Practice, 48*(1), 9–16. https://doi.org/10.1037/a0022186

Howard, A. L., Kennedy, T. M., Mitchell, J. T., Sibley, M. H., Hinshaw, S. P., Arnold, L. E., Roy, A., Stehli, A., Swanson, J. M., & Molina, B. S. G. (2020). Early substance use in the pathway from childhood attention-deficit/hyperactivity disorder (ADHD) to young adult substance use: Evidence of statistical mediation and substance specificity. *Psychology of Addictive Behaviors, 34*(2), 281–292. https://doi.org/10.1037/adb0000542

Johnson, A. M., Hawes, D. J., Eisenberg, N., Kohlhoff, J., & Dudeney, J. (2017). Emotion socialization and child conduct problems: A comprehensive review and meta-analysis. *Clinical Psychology Review, 54*, 65–80. https://doi.org/10.1016/j.cpr.2017.04.001

Johnston, C., & Chronis-Tuscano, A. (2015). Families and ADHD. In R. A. Barkley (Ed.), *Attention-deficit/hyperactivity disorder: A handbook for diagnosis and treatment* (4th ed., pp. 191–209). The Guilford Press.

Jungbluth, N. J., & Shirk, S. R. (2013). Promoting homework adherence in cognitive-behavioral therapy for adolescent depression. *Journal of Clinical Child and Adolescent Psychology, 42*(4), 545–553. https://doi.org/10.1080/15374416.2012.743105

Kaehler, L. A., Jacobs, M., & Jones, D. J. (2016). Distilling common history and practice elements to inform dissemination: Hanf-model BPT programs as an example. *Clinical Child and Family Psychology Review, 19*(3), 236–258. https://doi.org/10.1007/s10567-016-0210-5

Kaminski, J. W., & Claussen, A. H. (2017). Evidence base update for psychosocial treatments for disruptive behaviors in children. *Journal of Clinical Child and Adolescent Psychology, 46*(4), 477–499. https://doi.org/10.1080/15374416.2017.1310044

Kaminski, J. W., Valle, L. A., Filene, J. H., & Boyle, C. L. (2008). A meta-analytic review of components associated with parent training program effectiveness. *Journal of Abnormal Child Psychology, 36*(4), 567–589. https://doi.org/10.1007/s10802-007-9201-9

Kazantzis, N., Whittington, C., & Dattilio, F. (2010). Meta-analysis of homework effects in cognitive and behavioral therapy: A replication and extension. *Clinical Psychology, 17*(2), 144–156. https://doi.org/10.1111/j.1468-2850.2010.01204.x

Kazdin, A. E. (2000). Perceived barriers to treatment participation and treatment acceptability among antisocial children and their families. *Journal of Child and Family Studies, 9*(2), 157–174. https://doi.org/10.1023/A:1009414904228

Kazdin, A. E. (2005). *Parent management training: Treatment for oppositional, aggressive, and antisocial behavior in children and adolescents.* Oxford University Press.

Kazdin, A. E. (2008). *The Kazdin method for parenting the defiant child.* Houghton Mifflin.

Kazdin, A. E. (2017). Parent management training and problem-solving skills training for child and adolescent conduct problems. In J. R. Weisz & A. E. Kazdin (Eds.), *Evidence-based psychotherapies for children and adolescents* (3rd ed., pp. 142–158). The Guilford Press.

Kazdin, A. E., Holland, L., & Crowley, M. (1997). Family experience of barriers to treatment and premature termination from child therapy. *Journal of Consulting and Clinical Psychology, 65*(3), 453–463. https://doi.org/10.1037/0022-006X.65.3.453

Kendall, P. C., & Beidas, R. S. (2007). Smoothing the trail for dissemination of evidence-based practices for youth: Flexibility within fidelity. *Professional Psychology: Research and Practice, 38*(1), 13–20. https://doi.org/10.1037/0735-7028.38.1.13

Kendall, P. C., & Frank, H. E. (2018). Implementing evidence-based treatment protocols: Flexibility within fidelity. *Clinical Psychology: Science and Practice, 25*(4), eArticle 12271. https://doi.org/10.1111/cpsp.12271

Koziol, L. F., & Budding, D. E. (2012). Procedural learning. In N. M. Seel (Ed.), *Encyclopedia of the sciences of learning* (pp. 2694–2696). Springer. https://doi.org/10.1007/978-1-4419-1428-6_670

Lambert, M. J. (2010). Yes, it is time for clinicians to monitor treatment outcome. In B. L. Duncan, S. C. Miller, B. E. Wampold, & M. A. Hubble (Eds.), *Heart and soul of change: Delivering what works in therapy* (2nd ed., pp. 239–266). American Psychological Association. https://doi.org/10.1037/12075-008

Lambert, M. J., & Shimokawa, K. (2011). Collecting client feedback. *Psychotherapy: Theory, Research, & Practice, 48*(1), 72–79. https://doi.org/10.1037/a0022238

Leahy, R. L. (2017). *Cognitive therapy techniques: A practitioner's guide.* The Guilford Press.

Lebowitz, E. R., Omer, H., Hermes, H., & Scahill, L. (2014). Parent training for childhood anxiety disorders: The SPACE program. *Cognitive and Behavioral Practice, 21*(4), 456–469. https://doi.org/10.1016/j.cbpra.2013.10.004

Lieneman, C. C., & McNeil, C. B. (2023). *Time-out in child behavior management.* Hogrefe Publishing Corp. https://doi.org/10.1027/00509-000

Liu, C. Y., Huang, W. L., Kao, W. C., & Gau, S. S. F. (2017). Influence of disruptive behavior disorders on academic performance and school functions of youths with attention-deficit/hyperactivity disorder. *Child Psychiatry and Human Development, 48*(6), 870–880. https://doi.org/10.1007/s10578-017-0710-7

Lunkenheimer, E., Sturge-Apple, M. L., & Kelm, M. R. (2023). The importance of parent self-regulation and parent–child coregulation in research on parental discipline. *Child Development Perspectives, 17*(1), 25–31. https://doi.org/10.1111/cdep.12470

Mackler, J. S., Kelleher, R. T., Shanahan, L., Calkins, S. D., Keane, S. P., & O'Brien, M. (2015). Parenting stress, parental reactions, and externalizing behavior from ages 4 to 10. *Journal of Marriage and Family, 77*(2), 388–406. https://doi.org/10.1111/jomf.12163

Markman, K. D., & Tetlock, P. E. (2000). Accountability and close-call counterfactuals: The loser who nearly won and the winner who nearly lost. *Personality and Social Psychology Bulletin, 26*(10), 1213–1224. https://doi.org/10.1177/0146167200262004

Martin, G., & Pear, J. J. (2019). *Behavior modification: What it is and how to do it*. Routledge. https://doi.org/10.4324/9780429020599

Mausbach, B. T., Moore, R., Roesch, S., Cardenas, V., & Patterson, T. L. (2010). The relationship between homework compliance and therapy outcomes: An updated meta-analysis. *Cognitive Therapy and Research, 34*(5), 429–438. https://doi.org/10.1007/s10608-010-9297-z

McCart, M. R., Priester, P. E., Davies, W. H., & Azen, R. (2006). Differential effectiveness of behavioral parent-training and cognitive-behavioral therapy for antisocial youth: A meta-analysis. *Journal of Abnormal Child Psychology, 34*(4), 527–543. https://doi.org/10.1007/s10802-006-9031-1

McGaghie, W. C., Issenberg, S. B., Barsuk, J. H., & Wayne, D. B. (2014). A critical review of simulation-based mastery learning with translational outcomes. *Medical Education, 48*(4), 375–385. https://doi.org/10.1111/medu.12391

McLeod, J. (2017). Qualitative methods for routine outcome measurement. In T. G. Rousmaniere, R. Goodyear, D. D. Miller, & B. E. Wampold (Eds.), *The cycle of excellence: Using deliberate practice to improve supervision and training* (pp. 99–122). Wiley Blackwell. https://doi.org/10.1002/9781119165590.ch5

McMahon, R. J., & Forehand, R. L. (2005). *Helping the noncompliant child: Family-based treatment for oppositional behavior* (2nd ed.). The Guilford Press.

McMahon, R. J., & Forehand, R. L. (2019). *Helping the noncompliant child*. Springer International Publishing. https://doi.org/10.1007/978-3-319-49425-8_382

McNeil, C. B., & Hembree-Kigin, T. L. (2010). *Parent–child interaction therapy* (2nd ed.). Springer Science + Business Media. https://doi.org/10.1007/978-0-387-88639-8

Michelson, D., Davenport, C., Dretzke, J., Barlow, J., & Day, C. (2013). Do evidence-based interventions work when tested in the "real world?" A systematic review and meta-analysis of parent management training for the treatment of child disruptive behavior. *Clinical Child and Family Psychology Review, 16*(1), 18–34. https://doi.org/10.1007/s10567-013-0128-0

Miller, F. G., & Lee, D. L. (2013). Do functional behavioral assessments improve intervention effectiveness for students diagnosed with ADHD? A single-subject meta-analysis. *Journal of Behavioral Education, 22*(3), 253–282. https://doi.org/10.1007/s10864-013-9174-4

Montoya, A., Colom, F., & Ferrin, M. (2011). Is psychoeducation for parents and teachers of children and adolescents with ADHD efficacious? A systematic literature review. *European Psychiatry, 26*(3), 166–175. https://doi.org/10.1016/j.eurpsy.2010.10.005

Morris, A. S., Criss, M. M., Silk, J. S., & Houltberg, B. J. (2017). The impact of parenting on emotion regulation during childhood and adolescence. *Child Development Perspectives, 11*(4), 233–238. https://doi.org/10.1111/cdep.12238

Nock, M. K., & Kazdin, A. E. (2005). Randomized controlled trial of a brief intervention for increasing participation in parent management training. *Journal of Consulting and Clinical Psychology, 73*(5), 872–879. https://doi.org/10.1037/0022-006X.73.5.872

Norcross, J. C., & Guy, J. D. (2005). The prevalence and parameters of personal therapy in the United States. In J. D. Geller, J. C. Norcross, & D. E. Orlinsky (Eds.), *The psychotherapist's own psychotherapy: Patient and clinician perspectives* (pp. 165–176). Oxford University Press.

Norcross, J. C., Lambert, M. J., & Wampold, B. E. (2019). *Psychotherapy relationships that work* (3rd ed.). Oxford University Press.

Orlinsky, D. E., & Ronnestad, M. H. (2005). *How psychotherapists develop*. American Psychological Association.

Owen, J., & Hilsenroth, M. J. (2014). Treatment adherence: The importance of therapist flexibility in relation to therapy outcomes. *Journal of Counseling Psychology, 61*(2), 280–288. https://doi.org/10.1037/a0035753

Patterson, G. R. (1982). *Coercive family process*. Castalia Publishing Company.

Prescott, D. S., Maeschalck, C. L., & Miller, S. D. (Eds.). (2017). *Feedback-informed treatment in clinical practice: Reaching for excellence*. American Psychological Association. https://doi.org/10.1037/0000039-000

Rathus, J. H., & Miller, A. L. (2015). *DBT skills manual for adolescents*. The Guilford Press.

Reitman, D., & McMahon, R. J. (2013). Constance "Connie" Hanf (1917–2002): The mentor and the model. *Cognitive and Behavioral Practice, 20*(1), 106–116. https://doi.org/10.1016/j.cbpra.2012.02.005

Retz, W., Ginsberg, Y., Turner, D., Barra, S., Retz-Junginger, P., Larsson, H., & Asherson, P. (2021). Attention-deficit/hyperactivity disorder (ADHD), antisociality and delinquent behavior over the lifespan. *Neuroscience and Biobehavioral Reviews, 120*, 236–248. https://doi.org/10.1016/j.neubiorev.2020.11.025

Ros, R., Graziano, P. A., & Hart, K. C. (2017). Parental homework completion and treatment knowledge during group parent–child interaction therapy. *Journal of Early Intervention, 39*(4), 299–320. https://doi.org/10.1177/1053815117718491

Rousmaniere, T. G. (2016). *Deliberate practice for psychotherapists: A guide to improving clinical effectiveness.* Routledge Press/Taylor & Francis. https://doi.org/10.4324/9781315472256

Rousmaniere, T. G. (2019). *Mastering the inner skills of psychotherapy: A deliberate practice handbook.* Gold Lantern Press.

Rousmaniere, T. G., Goodyear, R., Miller, S. D., & Wampold, B. E. (Eds.). (2017). *The cycle of excellence: Using deliberate practice to improve supervision and training.* John Wiley & Sons. https://doi.org/10.1002/9781119165590

Rueger, S. Y., Katz, R. L., Risser, H. J., & Lovejoy, M. C. (2011). Relations between parental affect and parenting behaviors: A meta-analytic review. *Parenting: Science and Practice, 11*(1), 1–33. https://doi.org/10.1080/15295192.2011.539503

Sanders, M. R., Bor, W., & Morawska, A. (2007). Maintenance of treatment gains: A comparison of enhanced, standard, and self-directed Triple P-Positive Parenting Program. *Journal of Abnormal Child Psychology, 35*(6), 983–998. https://doi.org/10.1007/s10802-007-9148-x

Sanders, M. R., Kirby, J. N., Tellegen, C. L., & Day, J. J. (2014). The Triple P-Positive Parenting Program: A systematic review and meta-analysis of a multi-level system of parenting support [erratum at https://doi.org/10.1016/j.cpr.2014.09.001]. *Clinical Psychology Review, 34*(4), 337–357. https://doi.org/10.1016/j.cpr.2014.04.003

Squire, L. R. (2004). Memory systems of the brain: A brief history and current perspective. *Neurobiology of Learning and Memory, 82*(3), 171–177. https://doi.org/10.1016/j.nlm.2004.06.005

Stiles, W. B., Honos-Webb, L., & Surko, M. (1998). Responsiveness in psychotherapy. *Clinical Psychology: Science and Practice, 5*(4), 439–458. https://doi.org/10.1111/j.1468-2850.1998.tb00166.x

Stiles, W. B., & Horvath, A. O. (2017). Appropriate responsiveness as a contribution to therapist effects. In L. G. Castonguay & C. E. Hill (Eds.), *How and why are some therapists better than others? Understanding therapist effects* (pp. 71–84). American Psychological Association. https://doi.org/10.1037/0000034-005

Taylor, J. M., & Neimeyer, G. J. (2017). Lifelong professional improvement: The evolution of continuing education. In T. G. Rousmaniere, R. Goodyear, S. D. Miller, & B. Wampold (Eds.), *The cycle of excellence: Using deliberate practice to improve supervision and training* (pp. 219–248). Wiley Blackwell.

Thomas, R., Abell, B., Webb, H. J., Avdagic, E., & Zimmer-Gembeck, M. J. (2017). Parent–child interaction therapy: A meta-analysis. *Pediatrics, 140*(3), Article e20170352. https://doi.org/10.1542/peds.2017-0352

Tracey, T. J. G., Wampold, B. E., Goodyear, R. K., & Lichtenberg, J. W. (2015). Improving expertise in psychotherapy. *Psychotherapy Bulletin, 50*(1), 7–13.

Tracey, T. J. G., Wampold, B. E., Lichtenberg, J. W., & Goodyear, R. K. (2014). Expertise in psychotherapy: An elusive goal? *American Psychologist, 69*(3), 218–229. https://doi.org/10.1037/a0035099

Wampold, B. E. (2015). How important are the common factors in psychotherapy? An update. *World Psychiatry, 14*(3), 270–277. https://doi.org/10.1002/wps.20238

Wass, R., & Golding, C. (2014). Sharpening a tool for teaching: The zone of proximal development. *Teaching in Higher Education, 19*(6), 671–684. https://doi.org/10.1080/13562517.2014.901958

Webster-Stratton, C. (1998). Preventing conduct problems in Head Start children: Strengthening parenting competencies. *Journal of Consulting and Clinical Psychology, 66*(5), 715–730. https://doi.org/10.1037/0022-006X.66.5.715

Webster-Stratton, C. (2012). *Collaborating with parents to reduce children's behavior problems: A book for therapists using the Incredible Years*. Incredible Years.

Wierson, M., & Forehand, R. (1994). Parent behavioral training for child noncompliance: Rationale, concepts, and effectiveness. *Current Directions in Psychological Science, 3*(5), 146–150. https://doi.org/10.1111/1467-8721.ep10770643

Wojciechowski, T. W. (2021). The role of ADHD in predicting the development of violent behavior among juvenile offenders: Participation versus frequency. *Journal of Interpersonal Violence, 36*(1–2), NP625–NP642. https://doi.org/10.1177/0886260517734225

Zalewski, M., Lewis, J. K., & Martin, C. G. (2018). Identifying novel applications of dialectical behavior therapy: Considering emotion regulation and parenting. *Current Opinion in Psychology, 21*, 122–126. https://doi.org/10.1016/j.copsyc.2018.02.013

Zalewski, M., Maliken, A. C., Lengua, L. J., Martin, C. G., Roos, L. E., & Everett, Y. (2023). Integrating dialectical behavior therapy with child and parent training interventions: A narrative and theoretical review. *Clinical Psychology: Science and Practice, 30*(4), 365–376. https://doi.org/10.1111/cpsp.12363

Zaretskii, V. (2009). The zone of proximal development: What Vygotsky did not have time to write. *Journal of Russian & East European Psychology, 47*(6), 70–93. https://doi.org/10.2753/RPO1061-0405470604

Zimmer-Gembeck, M. J., Rudolph, J., Kerin, J., & Bohadana-Brown, G. (2022). Parent emotional regulation: A meta-analytic review of its association with parenting and child adjustment. *International Journal of Behavioral Development, 46*(1), 63–82. https://doi.org/10.1177/01650254211051086

Zitzmann, J., Rombold-George, L., Rosenbach, C., & Renneberg, B. (2024). Emotion regulation, parenting, and psychopathology: A systematic review. *Clinical Child and Family Psychology Review, 27*(1), 1–22. https://doi.org/10.1007/s10567-023-00452-5

Index

About the Authors

Mark D. Terjesen, PhD, is a licensed psychologist and professor in the Department of Psychology at St. John's University in Queens, New York. Dr. Terjesen serves as the director of clinical training (DCT) and program director of the school psychology PsyD program and has trained and supervised doctoral students throughout his tenure, having mentored more than 100 doctoral dissertation research projects. Dr. Terjesen has studied, published, and presented at a number of national and international conferences on topics related to assessment and clinical work with children, adolescents, and families. Dr. Terjesen is the coeditor with Tamara Del Vecchio of the *Handbook of Behavioral Parent Training.* He has trained many professionals internationally in the use of behavioral parent training (BPT), rational emotive behavior therapy (REBT), and cognitive and behavioral practices. Dr. Terjesen has served as both president of the School Division and Cognitive-Behavioral Therapy Division of the New York State Psychological Association and is past president of the Trainers of School Psychologists and Division 52 (International Psychology) of the American Psychological Association, of which he is also a fellow. Dr. Terjesen is a fellow of the Albert Ellis Institute and an approved supervisor. He serves as the clinical director at North Coast Psychological Services in Syosset, New York. Dr. Terjesen and his wife, Dr. Carolyn Waldecker, are the proud parents of Amelia Grace, who has allowed them to apply (not always successfully) the principles of BPT in their roles as parents.

Hilary B. Vidair, PhD, is an associate professor of psychology and former director of the clinical psychology doctoral program at LIU Post in Long Island, New York. She earned her PhD in combined clinical and school psychology from Hofstra University and completed a 3-year National Institute of Mental Health research fellowship in child and adolescent psychiatry at Columbia University and the New York State Psychiatric Institute. For more than 15 years, she has trained and supervised doctoral students in cognitive behavioral therapy and behavioral parent training. She has also served on more than 85 doctoral dissertation committees. Dr. Vidair has published and presented in the areas of evidence-based treatments for children and adolescents, behavioral parent training, and methods for training students in clinical work and research. She is the first author of the book *Navigating Research in an Applied Graduate Program: A Guide for Students in Psychology, Mental Health, and Education*. She is also a licensed psychologist and serves as the director of program development at Cognitive Behavioral Associates in Great Neck, New York, where she supervises trainees and specializes in behavioral parent training as well as cognitive behavior therapy and dialectical behavior therapy for children, adolescents, young adults, and parents. Dr. Vidair and her husband, John Giuffo, have the honor of deliberately practicing their parenting skills with their two amazing children, Elliot and Leia.

Phyllis S. Ohr, PhD, is a licensed psychologist and associate professor of psychology in the Department of Psychology at Hofstra University in Long Island, New York. Dr. Ohr serves as the assistant director of clinical training of the clinical psychology PhD program. She is also the clinical director of the Hofstra University–affiliated Child and Parent Psychological Services clinic, a skills training and research program devoted to the study and treatment of children, adolescents, and their families. Throughout her long tenure at Hofstra, Dr. Ohr has mentored countless doctoral students clinically, scientifically, and academically. She is a certified trainer of parent–child interaction therapy (PCIT) and, through her coaching and supervision, has enabled her many students to attain their own PCIT credentialing. Together, Dr. Ohr and her mentees have published and presented yearly at professional conferences on topics related to parent–child relationships, selective mutism and social anxiety, and treatment of disordered eating in young children using PCIT and BPT. In 2010, she was awarded the student-nominated Raymond D. Fowler Award for Outstanding Contribution to the Professional Development of Graduate Students by the American Psychological Association. Dr. Ohr and her endearing and long-enduring architect/husband Eric, would have liked to have known more about the principles of BPT and PCIT when they parented their now adult children, Nicole and Megan, who somehow, to their parent's surprise and immense pride, turned out to be fairly well-adjusted and actually quite wonderful.

Olivia A. Walsh, PsyD, earned her doctorate in school psychology from St. John's University. She is a certified school psychologist and postdoctoral fellow at North Coast Psychological Services. Dr. Walsh provides therapy and psychological assessments for children, adolescents, and young adults in both private practice and school settings. She has received clinical training at institutions such as Northwell Health–Zucker Hillside Hospital and St. John's University. Dr. Walsh's research focuses on deliberate practice in behavioral parent training (BPT). Her dissertation, *Deliberate Practice in Behavioral Parent Training*, received grant funding to support a pilot study exploring its impact. She has presented original research at national conferences on cognitive behavior therapy, behavioral parent training, and deliberate practice. In addition to her clinical and research work, Dr. Walsh has served as an adjunct instructor at St. John's University, teaching undergraduate psychology courses. In recognition of her contributions to the field, she was awarded the Ted Bernstein Award by the New York Association of School Psychologists in 2022.

Tony Rousmaniere, PsyD, is cofounder and program director of Sentio University and the Sentio Counseling Center. He provides workshops, webinars, and advanced clinical training and supervision to clinicians around the world. Dr. Rousmaniere is the author/coeditor of many books on deliberate practice and psychotherapy training. In 2017, he published the widely cited article in *The Atlantic*, "What Your Therapist Doesn't Know." Dr. Rousmaniere supports the open-data movement and publishes his aggregated clinical outcome data, in deidentified form, on his website at https://drtonyr.com. Dr. Rousmaniere is past president of Division 29 of the American Psychological Association (Society for the Advancement of Psychotherapy).

Alexandre Vaz, PhD, is cofounder and chief academic officer of Sentio University and the Sentio Counseling Center. He provides workshops, webinars, and advanced clinical training and supervision to clinicians around the world. Dr. Vaz is the author/coeditor of more than a dozen books on deliberate practice and psychotherapy training. He has held multiple committee roles for the Society for the Exploration of Psychotherapy Integration (SEPI) and the Society for Psychotherapy Research (SPR). Dr. Vaz is founder and host of *Psychotherapy Expert Talks*, an acclaimed interview series with distinguished psychotherapists and therapy researchers.